RESEARCH METHODS AND GLOBAL ONLINE COMMUNITIES

Research Methods and Global Online Communities

A Case Study

ALEXIA MADDOX
Deakin University, Australia

Routledge
Taylor & Francis Group
LONDON AND NEW YORK

First published 2015 by Ashgate Publishing

2 Park Square, Milton Park, Abingdon, Oxfordshire OX14 4RN
52 Vanderbilt Avenue, New York, NY 10017

Routledge is an imprint of the Taylor & Francis Group, an informa business

First issued in paperback 2020

British Library Cataloguing in Publication Data
A catalogue record for this book is available from the British Library

Library of Congress Cataloging-in-Publication Data
Maddox, Alexia.
Research methods and global online communities : a case study / by Alexia Maddox.
pages cm
Includes bibliographical references and index.
ISBN 978–1–4724–3457–9 (hardback : alk. paper)
1. Online social networks. 2. Social sciences – Research. 3. Communities. 4. Globalization.
I. Title.
HM742.M325 2015
302.30285–dc23 2015008097

ISBN 978-1-4724-3457-9 (hbk)
ISBN 978-0-367-59802-0 (pbk)

Contents

List of Figures and Tables

Figures

Tables

Acknowledgements

The journey from immersive fieldwork to writing a research methods book has transformed me, both as a person and as a research practitioner. In particular, I acknowledge the contribution made by the people who participated in the herper community research presented in these pages. I am grateful that you took the time to share your experiences and passions with me and opened my world to the beautiful and unique nature of amphibians and reptiles. This is my contribution to you in return. Thank you.

It was a pleasure to work with Dr Kevin Brown, Dr Vince Marotta and Dr Brad Warren as the supervisors of my doctoral research, which forms the foundation of learning held in this book. You provided me with much that has been instrumental in my growth and capacity as a researcher and held the space for me to complete this research. Thank you. I also acknowledge with gratitude the intellectual contributions to this work of Professor Roger Burrows, Professor Gustavo Mesch, Associate Professor Karen Farquharson and Associate Professor Malcolm Alexander.

During the travelling lifestyle that is at the core of this research, and my exposure to the range of research methods available, I had many inspiring conversations with academics around the world. In particular I would like to acknowledge Professor Richard Rogers, Professor Bruno Latour, Professor Barry Wellman, Dr Robert Ackland, Professor Garry Robins, and Professor Deborah Lupton for the directions and possibilities that you introduced me to.

Throughout the transformation of this research, I received personal and professional support from Harry Nazikian, Dr Sophie Vasiliadis, Dr Monica Barratt, Dr Esther Chan, Dr Jolynna Sinanan, Peter Benda, Associate Professor Bryan Fry, Tina Lavelle, Dr Janette Norman and Dianna Tarr. Thank you for helping me to make it through this journey with limbs, heart, soul and data intact. To Catherine, Carolyn and Cec Maddox, I am grateful for the life-lessons and support you have provided over the years.

I am also grateful to the people who gave technical assistance along the way: My thanks and appreciation go to Ralph Lavelle and the Kilbot Factory for assistance in digitising a custom survey, to Kingsnake.com for hosting the survey and to David Semetsky, Dr Erin O'Dwyer and Stu Hatton for editing the work and mentoring me in the art of writing.

An earlier version of Chapters 2 and 3 have been published elsewhere, as a conference publication for the Australian Sociological Association in an article titled *Reassessing the theorisation of community experience with the digitally mediated, global context* (Maddox and Warren, 2011).

Finally, for inspiring conversations and helpful comments, I would like to thank Meredith Lewis, Romaine Logere, Dr Chris Marmo, Dr Ken Winkel, Dr Kim Roelants, Dr Christofer Clemente, Dr Karen Lane, and the many people through whom I have gained ideas and inspiration, both big and small, that have led to the accumulated insights presented here.

Foreword

The aim of this book is to rethink how to identify the characteristics of community in the information age. In doing so, the book uses the case study of the herper community as a way to introduce scholars into a contemporary approach to the study of communities. The study of communities has a long tradition within the social sciences. In practice, this established field of research supports the ability of the community researcher to build upon resilient conceptual and methodological toolkits that facilitate scholarly practice and research rigour. For the researcher, a community is often the site from which we collect data to generate sociological insight because of its clearly defined parameters and implied social coherence. These parameters exist in the capacity of a community to be observed and in the presence of internal social, organisational and institutional connections that indicate a cohesion and commonality of social experience. In this way, community becomes regarded as a microcosm of the wider society that it is contextual to.

In choosing to study a community, the researcher must balance their choice to study collective social patterns and experiences with the burgeoning research trend towards 'big data' analysis to produce social insights. While big data is able to provide environmental information for community studies, it presents a scale of challenges through its conceptual underdevelopment, lack of direction by a research question and developing methodologies. Despite the sophistication of these techniques and approaches, the question of consistency and congruency of the parameters through which big data is formed remains one of the main challenges for data mining and interpretation. Consequently, research into communities is one of the key processes that social scientists use to make sense of the patterns of social life we see around us, particularly those patterns that suggest a capacity for collective action, social support and individual well-being within societies.

While community may be proclaimed to be the safety net of society (Bauman, 2001), it is also the safety net of social researchers. However, this book argues that it is time for community scholars to examine the foundations of our assumptions on the community construct and consider whether these are stifling the relevance, impact and applicability of social insights we can produce from studying contemporary community formats. The reason for this being the premise of the safety-net, that community occurs within a time and place. For digital community, these notions are augmented to argue that community occurs across decentralised, open social structures that emerge both through and beyond the constraints of a single place or time and flourish in an evolving space of technological enablement.

As will be argued in this book, this understanding transforms the notion of social boundaries as externally porous, internally differentiating and enacted across the digital and physical environment. From a methods perspective what this means is that social boundaries cannot be defined by a single location. It also requires a concert of data collection and observation techniques (or approaches) that can be deployed within the offline (IRL) and online community spaces, in addition to having the capacity to integrate information from multiple locations. Consequently, this incorporation of an open social structure and mediated sociability as the backbone of community form and function affects the methodology and methods choices through which researchers characterise and collect data.

In generating this approach, from the green abundance of community studies to the cyborg constructions within the sociology of technology, my understanding of community has been disfigured, reconfigured and digitised. In releasing the ties of community from a place in time, a quandary arose that my research practice needed to resolve; without defining how to locate and observe a community, there is a reduced evidence base from which to connect theoretical developments with observable social trends. In response to this, I have developed an argument that we can locate communities to study by taking an environmental approach that positions the community within a social ecology, which can also be thought of as a niche habitat. The location of the community can be reconstructed through examining its technological layer, consisting of the technologies, place and the built environment. The patterns of organisation that characterise the coherence of the community can be articulated through a study of its social layer, such as organisational influence, social networks and structuring forces. The heart of the community, however, can be witnessed through the discursive and experiential layer articulated within its mediating culture. This approach allows for a methodical analysis of the classical attributes of a community, such as its place, composition, boundaries and cohesion, as it is enacted within a digitised context.

From the outset, my research was intended to be a sociological study of a contemporary community that is globally distributed and mediated by the Internet and ICTs. I refer to this as the study of digital community and view the Internet as the central nervous system through which community experience is generated and mediated. I found, that while helpful from the perspective of social theory, this understanding has far reaching consequences for research practice and the generation of a robust research methodology. Through the presentation of the herper community case study, this book aims to increase the confidence and capacity of researchers to engage with community research as it reconfigures across the contemporary digital environment. I offer pathways through what I have learnt from conducting the case study as a knowledge bridge for others to tread further into the unknown frontiers of digital social behaviour.

Chapter 1
Introduction

This chapter aims to provide context for the study of digital community, introducing the major themes that are subsequently addressed in this book.

Section 1.1 provides an introduction to the key ideas evident in the literature that may assist the researcher in identifying the signature of digital community within research practice. It also introduces a series of definitional discussions of these key ideas in order to situate and anchor the reader through some of the more technical language used to describe the conceptualisation of individual agency and structural influences within a digital community. Section 1.2 provides an overview of the book structure, beginning with a discussion of the conceptual understandings of community reviewed in Part I and introducing how the case study of the herper community will be utilised to provide the research practitioner with practical directions and examples of these concepts in action within research practice in Part II. Section 1.3 briefly introduces the community case study and starts the personal narrative of my research experience and how I employed these ideas to a real world community that defied the cosy glow that ideas of solidarity and support usually evoke.

From the outset, a key understanding that directs the discussion of community within these pages is that, theoretically, it is both a social and spatial concept; with the definitional discussion of this idea splitting community concepts into a discussion of place or different modes of sociability. Notwithstanding, this understanding of how to present a community study is often unrelated to our intentions to characterise and investigate a community. As researchers, we may be looking for evidence of collective engagement and activism that leads to social change. On the other hand, we may be looking at community as a stable social form that provides a sense of connectedness, support, security, identity and meaning, all facilitating wellbeing for the individual. Either way, these perspectives into the mechanisms of social change or stability and security speak to our understanding of community as a foundation of social organisation. It is the mediating link between the individual and society and is consequently the engine room of social theory and research practice.

1.1 Searching the Research Literature for Signatures of Digital Community

In the exploration of scholarly perspectives into the imbrication of community structures and process with the Internet, I was prompted to the questions of whether people are able to connect in with each other and whether they could generate a shared identity within and across the online-offline social contexts. This question stemmed from the key concern of community studies, mechanisms of social cohesion and the intellectual concern for increased social alienation and disconnection wrought by the digital environment. As a researcher, I wondered exactly how trust and reciprocity plays out across the technologically augmented and spatially distributed community context, in which some people knew each other before connecting online and others did not. I also had to consider whether, when looking at a community whose membership was choice-driven and much social interaction was technologically mediated, I was going to be able to find instances of exchange in social support, access to desired opportunities and locations and information sharing. These elements, essential components of social cohesion and continuity, were drawn out and operationalised in the literature discussing social capital. This positioned social capital indicators as effective indicators of a community and suggested that I needed to find evidence for them in order to argue that I was actually looking at cohesive community experience. These concerns for and of social connection online did not exist within traditional approaches to community studies because, by default, strangers were not a part of the community and trust and reciprocity was often built within the context of co-location, a lack of choice in membership and in the face of strong social repercussions and limited social mobility (socially, spatially and economically). In response to this knowledge vacuum and the race of technological innovation, a nascent body of literature considering the social impact of the Internet sprung up in the 1990s and matured over the course of 20 years. For me, in reconciling community studies with the bodies of Internet research that had galloped rampantly from the gate with few moments of reflection and integration, I had many questions for how to enact and investigate these insights within a real life community.

An overarching concern amongst scholars and public intellectuals in the domain of Internet research was whether connecting with people online led to, or indicated, disconnection with people in real life (IRL). The dimensions and influence of this discussion can be found within the research literature through a preoccupation with the easy disconnect inherent to online membership, the development of trust online and the weakening of reciprocity within communities and society more generally. This concern manifested its greatest polarities in perspective through the approach of observing social action within the online and offline domains as distinct, both spatially and socially. The early debates about the social implications of the Internet (DiMaggio et al., 2001) resonated with Georg Simmel's despair for increasing industrialisation (and its correlate of an urbanised society) as enhancing social alienation. Through the theoretical polarisation of the digital and physical interaction, this argument was seeded into the technological infrastructure of the Network Society (Manuel Castells, 1996). While much about this approach is self-evident, there are differences in how we interact online versus in-person, the implications for polarising social experience through digital behaviours and place-based interactions amplified the debate around whether mediated sociability facilitated in-person social alienation (Nie, Hillygus, & Erbring, 2002) or increased wider social connection (Rheingold, 2000). This concern about infrastructural changes 'causing' social dysfunction or its mirror, increasing cohesion, is a long held preoccupation of studies of society and is evident in contemporary discussions of disruptive technologies.

Given the complexity of these debates, I would like to pause and take time to clarify my choices in selecting from the different discourses and their accompanying technical vocabulary, that the reader will come across in this work, that are used to describe the experience of community in its virtual and physical incarnations. Terms we have met so far include digital community, online and offline community and IRL (in real life) or physical community and virtual community. The reader of Internet studies will also come across discussions of computer-mediated communication (CMC) from the field of human-computer interactions (HCI) (Bagozzi & Dholakia, 2002; Jacobson, 1999; Morkes, Kernal, & Nass, 1999; Walther, 1995, 1996, 1997; Walther, Anderson, & Park, 1994; Walther, Loh, & Granka, 2005). This was language often used in early research exploring social interaction online and comes from a Computer Sciences perspective. Mediated sociality or mediated sociability is terminology more commonly used in contemporary works within sociological or psychological discourses. In discussing this terminology, I will focus initially on the choice of language (and discourse) for discussing technologically enabled interactions and then move on to clarifying the language used for a community that incorporates this. The use of communications technologies as the media through which non-placed based social interaction occurs characterised interaction through presence and absence of people rather than through spatial proximity. This approach of viewing interaction as 24/7 access and 'always on' technologies has further evolved through scholarly understandings in the HCI field of the mobility of personal computing devices and the increasing ubiquity of passive computing through which real-time behavioural, indirect or sensory interactions can occur. In this research, I will refer to these ideas through the notion of mediated sociability, following the work of scholars connecting ideas of online interactions with relational forms of analysis (Anderson & Jack, 2002; Comunello, 2012; Foth & Hearn, 2007; Hampton, 1998; Hardey, 2002; Hardey,

2007; Matzat, 2010; G. S. Mesch & Talmud, 2010; Nie, 2001; Wellman & Gulia, 1995; Wellman & Haythornthwaite, 2002; Wellman, Quan Haase, Witte, & Hampton, 2001). This approach prioritises the perspective of person-to-person (or avatar-to-avatar) interactions or social behaviour rather than that of interacting with (and through) the device.

The communal correlate of capturing mediated sociability within the boundaries and culture of a social form, can be found in discussions of digital, virtual and online communities. The caveat is that these ideas do not represent one and the same construct. Just as with the language for mediate sociability takes us down slightly different conceptual pathways, so do the difference conceptualisations of community in cyberspace. Virtual community and physical community are paired as oppositional constructs within the literature. Physical community is best understood through the traditional community studies of the Chicago School in which a neighbourhood or ethnically homogeneous immigrant community is studied. This is a particularly located and embodied understanding of community. On the other hand, a virtual community is often represented as a social simulation because it is not embodied and occurs in a specific location online. An example of this would be 'Second Life', even the name of which implies that engagement with others online is not your real (IRL) or 'first' life. Consequently, a virtual community occurs solely online, within a specific software environment and is characterised by its mediation of social connection through the Internet. Virtual community studies proliferated from the early 90s onwards. They are an example of the first flush of researching life online and, I would argue, can be seen as a novelty stream of research springing out of a reaction to the physical located-ness and geography of social life and community practice that preceded this.

In contrast to this, offline community was developed conceptually at a later period as a consort to the idea of an online community. This differs from the virtual-physical pairing, as the idea of an 'offline' community does not pre-exist the idea of an 'online' community. Again, these represent community in physical space and community in virtual or cyber-space, but speak more specifically to ideas of the co-location of embodied social interaction (in-person) in opposition to the presence-absence dynamic of co-presence in the online environment (disembodied). While the online community is seen as disembodied, it has theoretically been used to discuss the nature of mediated sociability and co-presence rather than to present the location of community as polarised between the cyber and physical geographies. A digital community, a consequent idea stemming from the argument of this book, is a notion through which community can be characterised by both its virtual and physical attributes.

These definitions, and their differences, have implications for research methodology. The clarity surrounding their use will be key for the reader in following the evolution of ideas and their methodological implications presented in this book. This connects to the aim of this book to rethink how to identify the characteristics of a community both methodologically and theoretically and act as a bridge to introduce scholars into the contemporary study of communities. Consequently, the intention of the ideas presented here are to contribute to the discourse surrounding the nature of online communities. A central tenant of this book is that the Internet is now embedded across and interlaces most domains of contemporary social experience. However the issues of social life being a combination of online and offline actions, and the premise that contemporary social systems are not defined by a single time and place, seems to bely the possibility that these elements can be leveraged to identify a community for study.

1.2 Navigating the Structure of the Book

The book is structured in two parts, with Part I (Chapters 2 through 6) positioning the conceptualisation of community through an environmental approach and Part II (Chapters 7 through 10) presenting examples from the herper community case study on how these ideas are enacted as a research methodology, from design and data collection to data analysis and research reporting. To this end, each chapter presented in Part I replaces our understandings of the conceptual and methodological approaches available to the community researcher. Chapter 2, presents a discussion of the connections evident in the research literature between community studies and research into the social adoption and appropriation of communication technologies. The connections between research into place-based community and mediated sociability presented in this discussion leads the reader through debates surrounding the characterisation and construction of place within the community context and the social composition of groups online. Through this discussion, we come to a particular focus upon the impacts of the Internet upon patterns of social organisation, of which community is a primary form.

Chapter 3 introduces the theoretical foundations for the methodological approach I followed in my own community study. Consideration of the literature on mediated sociability led to the understanding that community depicted either through its physical or virtual aspects, diminished my capacity to present the full story of community experience in a digital age. Why did I have to take one view or the other, I wondered, when these elements were plainly integrated into the everyday life experience of my participants? Consequently, I take the reader through consecutive questions, 'How did online community studies develop?' and 'Who is doing what in the field right now?' This approach brings the literature reviewing online sociability and CMC, that emerged almost as a separate stream of research, in dialogue with the pre-occupations of community studies; these being in characterising place, composition, boundaries and mechanisms of cohesion within a group. In Chapter 3, I discuss research and approaches that reconcile this divergence through investigating a stream of research literature into ecological forms, such as media ecologies, the information ecology of a library and the communicative ecology of an apartment complex, that led to the conceptual development of a social ecology to describe a community structure that is globally distributed and technologically mediated. This conceptual toolkit leads into a discussion of a research methodology that has the capacity to collect data and integrate insight across the online and offline environments of a community (Chapter 4). With this scene set, and the tools for research practice on the table, Chapters 5 and 6 takes the reader into the world of people with reptile and amphibian interests and discusses the sensitisation of the methodology to a community under study. These chapters discuss how these tools were refined for application within a heaving and evolving community space that through its function and process dispensed with a dualistic explanation of social action and community experience.

In Part II of the book, Chapters 7 through to 10, I use the methods and findings of the herper community case study to illustrate for the reader how community place, composition, boundaries and cohesion were identified through this research practice. To do this, I review the techniques and research findings that articulate the technological and social layers of the community with its mediating culture. The second half of the book is consequently the meeting and merging of two paradigms; with the four elements of community characterisation of place, composition, boundaries and cohesion presented in each consecutive chapter. Within each of these consecutive chapters, I present the community domain through its dialogue with the three elements used to identify the social ecology of the community, the technical and social layers and the mediating culture. This approach speaks to the emergent and dynamic nature of community that constructs itself across a digital context, rather than being anchored to a single location, such as a neighbourhood, or identifiable through social homogeneity, such as the early immigrant communities of the United States. In segmenting the presentation of the research findings and methods used across the technological layer, social layer and mediating culture of the community, we can see how the environmental imprint of a community can be generated through the lived experiences of its members. This approach reflects a desire not to define these elements through researcher definition and theoretical proxies prior to the conduct of a study, as has traditionally been the methodological practice within community studies. In the case of the open social structures of digital community, place, composition, boundaries and mechanisms of cohesion may not be known prior to the conduct of the research. As I sometimes joke, I had to complete my research in order to start it.

1.3 The Community Case Study

At this point, I hear you wondering about what kind of community would lend itself to this research approach? I had had exposure to the community of people with reptile and amphibian interests through a personal connection and knew that they were busily occupying the new and evolving social spaces online, while having a long tradition through conventional societies and the natural history movement. How this particular case study came about is, as with all moments of life serendipity, a long story that landed me in unusual circumstances. I went to a party themed 'If looks could kill' dressed as Medusa and ended up next day with my introduction to a personal collection of snakes and an extended relationship with an active figure in the herpetological community. From this exposure and the early budding of my sociological lens, I could see that what was special about this group was not that they were different or a 'subculture' but that they are no different from you or me, the group was socially diverse and cohered through overlapping rather than shared values. Their community structure may be more conventionally considered through an amateur-professional lens. This is a common approach for communities within Science and Technology Studies (STS) that investigate communities forming around scientific endeavour, knowledge generation and technology. Or they could be considered through their animal focus and connection with the pet trade, characterised by legislative and market dynamics. However aspect this often expressed itself alongside their common concern with environmental conservation that could have classified this group as a social movement. For me, these existing approaches, which required me to choose one perspective or another within my population, limited me in interpreting what I was seeing. Essentially, existing paradigms through which to study this community asked me to ignore the apparent connectedness and interweaving of people, objects and knowledge across these points of view. I felt I would lose access to what the community was really about if I couldn't find another way to conceptually frame and methodological approach research in it.

During the 'getting to know you' phase, I had experienced the veil between theory and social practice torn away. I was exposed to sticky, elongated social networks that could not be described by conventional community theory, but that did have resonance with theories of the impacts of globalisation and communication technology upon social organisation. In those early moments of fear and shock, I experienced a gap between theories about the social world and while I was in the social world. I had stepped into this research with a limited set of parameters to guide my point of enquiry and interpret what I was experiencing, and the only way to create them was to do the research. When asking what community means as an idea and in reality, I was confronted with a non-ideal, and yet very real, community. I saw that this community was marginalised in many ways through its shared focus of activity, reptiles and amphibians. Socially, people generally had polarised reactions to these animals; from phobic (fear-based) to philic (fascination for) responses and very little in between. Symbolically, reptiles are diversely associated with rebirth and evil, and are often phallic in their representation. These symbols invoke fear, temptation, desire, creation and instinctual or base behaviours, ideas that are often socially repressed. The polarised social reaction and repressive symbolic positioning of these animals has often been associated with the people interested in them.

As I commonly observe now, but did not realise at the time, I could not meet even the basic methodological requirements of a community study, to define my population of study in place, time and composition. The herper network is characterised by the unique group of people that numbers in the millions of animal lovers, adventure tourists, scientists, photographers, zoo and government employees, museum curators, entrepreneurs, school and university students, medical professionals, veterinarians, smugglers, organisations, businesses and families that affiliate themselves with reptiles and amphibians. What is unique about these people is that a love of reptiles and amphibians is not an interest that can usually be pursued through mainstream culture in any society. This is a social world where the basic unit of exchange is the 'herptile', a shorthand term used to refer to reptiles and amphibians. The animal is objectified as a symbol or value that is traded, bred, related to, documented, displayed, legislated, digitised, dissected and recombined, loved and loathed.

As has been observed to me at different points, how could a group with so many social distinctions be considered a community? It exists within a spatially distributed social system that is characterised by a unique market system, the production and consumption of knowledge, a distinct vocabulary, squabbles and rivalry, cultures of consumption, a virtual landscape of websites, forums and other digital resources, a physical landscape of deeply regulated spaces, transnational flows and a black-market underbelly, and dominated by personalities, informal social networks and societies and other organisations. The question of how to conceptualise the emergent form of this group, its boundaries, its membership patterns, its spaces of social cohesion, continuity and change and its co-ordinates in time and place ended up being the challenges of the research.

1.4 Conclusion

In retrospect, I am now able to see that the unique contribution of this research has been tracing a theoretical lineage of community studies into the contemporary Internet environment and the integration of disparate fields discussing the social phenomenon of the online environment. The research design employed a mixed-method approach of semi-structured interviews conducted during participant observation and a quantitative online survey. I triangulated results collected from the online environment with results collected from the physical environment (offline), which facilitated an integrated interpretation of offline and online social experience and the digital footprint of the community. Triangulation of methods is not new, however the comparison of data collected online and offline provided a novel contextual analysis that revealed the relationship between statistical patterns and social experience in a mobile, online/offline and open social formation. I constructed a theoretical approach or model to assist me in doing this, which I have given the handle of social ecology. For me, this acknowledges the connection in this environmental approach to describing digital community with current theorisation of media ecologies and communicative ecologies, but also acknowledges its debt to the Chicago school scholars who advanced the discipline of Human Ecology.

When I talk about this research now, I realise that its main contribution was not the knowledge it generated about this community, or the theoretical contribution it made to the literature on community studies. I see the main contribution of this research as providing a methodological approach that does not require a priori definitions of a community in time and place before the research has begun. I believe that we are now working with emergent social forms that exist beyond any single place and extend into the virtual domains of everyday life – these are what I classify as open social structures, where boundaries are internally generated and externally porous. This point of view towards describing the edges of a community form contradicts traditional approaches in which the boundaries of a community (both spatially and socially) are distinct enough to define them as a site of study. This difference in what I was observing in my population and reading in the technology focused research literature led to the unwelcome realisation that I needed to tinker with foundational concepts of how community is constituted in order to conduct viable research.

I have seen the Internet referred to as the Large Hadron Collider of the social sciences and I would argue that it has reconfigured the format of community to make it almost unrecognisable when using traditional research methods. For me, trying to wrangle with a community for which the Internet was both its spine and central nervous system left few choices. I was forced a return to the basics of how to characterise a community and connect these to contemporary understandings of Internet culture. In this book, I draw on concepts from urban informatics, social network analysis, Internet research, interaction design, systems theories and community studies. These are the most significant contributing areas, but there are more. I pursued this pathway, linking and bridging all the way, as a means to articulate a conceptual toolkit that can be used to research contemporary community formats. Like a compass recalibrating its coordinates, the approach of viewing a community as existing within a niche habitat, or social ecology proposed within these pages, is intended to take us out of the current bind of community research and set new directions in research practice and conceptual development. In the rebuild, we will look at both the spatial and social understandings of the community construct. Through this we can interrogate how they reconfigure into a unified research toolkit that incorporates current understandings of online sociability, the new frontier for the social sciences.

PART I
The Study of Global Online Communities

Chapter 2
Community and Technology

2.1 Introduction

Chapter 2 traces the journey of neighbourhood community studies in the tradition of the Chicago School to the utopian/dystopian polarity of virtual community studies, and in so doing draw attention to both their disjunctures and their similarities. Section 2.2 focuses on earlier approaches to constructing community as a site of research, in which scholars sought to understand the capacity of groups, networks, communities and societies for collective action and the promotion of personal wellbeing and identity projects through socialisation. Section 2.3 introduces an alternative approach to studying communities founded through the Chicago School scholars, the environmental approach of Human Ecology. This section points to intellectual foundations of the research methodology discussed within this book. Section 2.4 draws the line from these classical perspectives to consider how and whether the community concepts discussed have continuity with the augmentation of community through the online environment. Section 2.5 focuses specifically on the conceptualisation and research conducted into virtual communities, with Section 2.6 suggesting the possible limitations of this approach for researchers interested in pursuing non dualistic understanding of community as it is expressed across the online and offline contexts. These ideas are presented to assist the research practitioner in conceptually positioning a community study within the contemporary sociocultural milieu.

2.2 Early Approaches to Constructing Community as a Site of Study

This section discusses the early insights towards characterising community that community research has generated. While this research was done at a time when the Internet had not pervaded social life, there are key insights that these scholars contribute to our understanding of the formation of communities within societies. In particular I turn the light on the contribution that Chicago School scholars made to providing a way forward through this seemingly intractable dichotomy between the locational and relational understanding of the experience of community. The following discussion will focus on the contribution of Robert Park, Ernest Burgess and Roderick D. McKenzie to the connections made between community experience and its environment in the conceptualisation of Human Ecology. A further detailed discussion of this approach can be found in the works of other key theorists of the Chicago School (cf. Abbott, 1999; Bulmer, 1984; Hawley, 1944, 1950; Platt, 1996). The final element of this discussion moves into the separation of community experience into place-based and virtual community, which I refer to here as the online-offline dualism.

Classical sociological studies of community reviewed here are those conducted within the early Chicago School tradition by Frederic Thrasher's *The Gang* (1927), William Whyte's *Street Corner Society* (1943) and Herbert Gans' *The Urban Villagers* (1962). The work of Thrasher, Whyte and Gans are definitive studies of community that provide us with insight into both its relational aspects and its intrinsic and extrinsic agents of formation. However, are they all really Chicago School? In terms of the development of a distinctive Chicago approach to 'community studies' and 'urban ecology' research into this area conducted by the following authors are, at least, as important but will not be reviewed: Nels Anderson, Edward Franklin Frazier, Everett Hughes, George Herbert Mead, Walter C. Reckless, Edwin Sutherland, W. I. Thomas, Louis Wirth and Florian Znaniecki. In particular this school of thought developed articulations of place and social bonds within community formats that provide foundational insight and direction for researchers into digital community. The following discussion will focus on their insight into community formation through environmental influence, emergent form, social ties and gender dynamics. These themes come up again in the case study of the Herpers and contribute to the development of the social ecology approach to investigate open social structures.

The first point we must start at is the simple observation that remains relevant to contemporary research into community: there is no consistent conceptualisation of community expressed in these studies. The common elements exist in the focus upon lower socio-economic neighbourhoods in Boston and Chicago 'slum' areas, and two of the studies focused in particular on a single ethnic migrant group. These common elements reinforce foundational notions behind community formation of shared identity, group socialisation processes, shared values and the social homogeneity of members. Whyte's and Thrasher's focus upon gang structure, distribution and formation demonstrates an attempt to uncover the basic principles behind the formation and continuity of social groups. To this end, Thrasher (1927) conducted an ecological survey of 1,313 gangs in Chicago. He argued that the informal structure of the gang, once formed, engages with the context of a feudal system called 'Gangland' that exists within three domains of Chicago, each of which in turn breaks up into smaller kingdoms. Thrasher argued that 'they are natural areas, differentiated in the process of human interaction, and having their own characteristic place in the mosaic of city life' (Thrasher, 1927, p. 6). In this way, Thrasher saw the social patterns of the gang as tied to a specific spatial location in the city that was, both in terms of place and deviant behaviour, socially interstitial.

Thrasher's approach was an example of Robert Park's Human Ecology perspective on how the spatial relationships of human populations adapted to their environment. Park, an influential theorist of the Chicago School, argued that there were forces at work within the limits of the urban community that tended to bring about an orderly and typical grouping of its population and institutions (Park, Burgess, & McKenzie, 1925, p. 1). He went on to argue that transportation and communication technologies, as the media that brought about the mobility and concentration of urban populations, were primary factors in the ecological organisation of the city. Park's colleague McKenzie, in his own contribution to this idea, argued that Human Ecology was the study of 'the spatial and temporal relations of human beings as affected by the selective, distributive, and accommodative forces of the environment' (McKenzie, 1967, p. 63). I will use this development of the 'man and environment relationship' to develop the construct of a social ecology. Unlike these studies, I build this relationship through a discussion of contemporary literature on networked individualism, communicative ecologies and digital formations in the following chapter. This discussion of virtual community and networked sociability will demonstrate how our connection to place has changed to our connection to space and the mediating environment. It will also raise the influence of mobility in people, ICTs and the global connectivity of virtual space on our understandings of group environments. For Park and McKenzie, the Internet did not exist as an influential force in social organisation. However they both highlight the contextuality of groups of people to space, time, transportation and communication technologies.

However, I would now like to return to the two other community studies mentioned, William Whyte's (1943) *Street Corner Society* and Herbert Gans' (1962) *Urban Villagers*. Whyte's study of community looked at two ethnic gangs in an Italian-American slum he called 'Cornerville' in Boston's North End. He demonstrates a clear contrast between the intrinsic social ties within an informally organised gang and the extrinsic social ties of a formally organised one. The two case studies of a place-based gang represent a socially static connection to the community through the maintenance of strong ties in the informally organised gang, and social mobility through disconnection from the community and the accumulation of weak social ties in the formally organised gang. This indicates the different actions of strong ties as holding people within a specific group and being more personally supportive and weak ties as being easier to disconnect from and socially advantageous. I return to these themes in a discussion of the literature on networked sociability.

Herbert Gans' (1962) *Urban Villagers* study focused upon a lower socio-economic Italian-American immigrant community in Boston's West End. The study was initiated to investigate the impact upon neighbourhood residents of having their apartments torn down due to urban renewal programs. Gans' observations were that there was minimal collective action amongst residents to stop the development and to retain their homes, despite not having the economic capacity to choose where else to go. What he did find, however, is that the people in this neighbourhood were bonded in a closed community and that this was defined by their relationships to each other (characterised by gendered divisions) rather than their relationship to the place. Importantly, this was an Italian migrant settlement and participants were connected to each other through this shared cultural background, family relationships and their gender-specific peer groups. He developed the notion of the Peer Group Society to describe the fundamental nature of social ties amongst peers, rather than the neighbourhood place or family units, in creating the cohesion and continuity of community experience (support and socialisation). This notion of the community experience introduces the idea of peer support and sociability being independent of physical location and engendered by the culture of the community.

Each of these early studies employed differing perspectives on the relationship between place, social relations and community experience due to the non-standardised theoretical frameworks within the Chicago School ethnography. The lack of a shared theoretical conception of community is evident in these works and this trend has been argued to be the case for the wider body of community studies literature (Bell & Newby, 1972). The common elements in these three works are the detailed ethnography that went towards describing group dynamics through social relations within their environmental context. The result of this bias towards observation over theoretical and methodological consistency can be seen in Gans' extrapolation of the observed social relations as a reflection of the internal processes of the individual, which was then reflected into the external world of the group. The internal psychology of the individual was seen as embedded in a reciprocal process that reinforced the group structure, values and boundary production of the community as a whole.

The Chicago School researchers concluded independently that an individual's social immersion within the group resulted in the group determining their identity and the individuals' sense-making of the world. The result of this collective identity was that they were largely incapable, as individuals and as a community, of relating to people socially outside of this structure. Gans viewed this as a class subculture cut off from the larger society due to the lack of shared values. What is particularly clear from these early community studies is that closed social relations and group patterns kept people within their social position rather than assisting in their social mobility. The end result of this static social situation was made particularly clear in the work of Gans by his demonstration of the incapacity of the immigrant community for collective action due to their highly individualised identities within their peer group and the inability of community members to connect with heterogeneous others.

2.3 An Alternative to Community Conceptualisation: The Ecological Perspective

The first mention of a possible alternative approach within community research can be found in the ecological perspectives of Chicago School scholars. These were the early ethnographers, statisticians and surveyors of community who took an environmental perspective that incorporated concepts beyond place to understand the construction of community. They developed the discipline of Human Ecology out of the University of Chicago and took a functionalist approach to characterising the relationship between place, organisations and the structural form of communities. Most significantly, they also included the impact of infrastructure such as roads and telecommunications in shaping communities. This perspective was set in the context of early observations on the impact of industrialisation and institutionalisation upon social organisation. From this point of view, community was argued to be a product of institutions that were both physical buildings and structuring forces. Because of the geographical relationship observed between social structures and community formation, proponents of Human Ecology such as Park (1915; Park & Burgess, 1921; Park et al., 1925), McKenzie (1967) and Hawley (1944) argued that institutions and communities could be investigated through mapping population distributions. This methodological approach towards mapping the environments of communities led to numerous studies on the spatial distribution of human populations, with a particular emphasis on urban areas (Lawrence, 2003, pp. 31–2). This observation of the influence of the environment upon the formation of community remains just as relevant today, however environments are now augmented by the social use of ICTs. In light of this augmentation, contemporary scholars have found a renewed interest in environmental influence upon group formations through the use of GIS (Batty et al., 2010), geographies of social relationships (Bunnell et al., 2001) and data visualisation tools (Bruns, 2007; Bruns et al., 2011; Rogers, 2009b, 2012). These techniques and tools extend how social groups can be spatially constructed by researchers through the research process rather than through prior definitions.

In contrast to the social trends observed by the Chicago School scholars, the current prevailing trend is towards individualisation rather than institutionalisation (Beck, 1992; Beck & Beck-Gernsheim, 1996, 2002; Woodman, 2011). This fundamental difference suggests the misfit of Human Ecology theory to providing analytical insight into current trends in community formation. Regardless of this, the continued interest in mapping the geography of social relations demonstrates the potential relevance of an ecological approach to describing the space of a community. Network theory, a relational approach, has incorporated this and yet is configured around the concept of individualisation and the augmentation of social relations through ICTs (Boase, 2008; Burt, 2000; Carl, 2006; Castells, 1996,

2002, 2010; Comunello, 2012; Foth & Hearn, 2007; Freeman & Audia, 2006; Fuchs, 2005; Lin, 1999; Mesch & Talmud, 2010; Rainie & Wellman, 2012; Rogers & Kincaid, 1981; Sih, Hanser, & McHugh, 2009; Swyngedouw, 2004; van Dijk, 2006; Watts, 2004; Wellman, Boase, & Chen, 2002; Wittel, 2001). Unlike Human Ecology, the formation and cohesion of community in the information age is argued to occur around foci of activity (Feld, 1981), also referred to as portfolios of sociability (Foth & Hearn, 2007), and the unit of observation is the social tie (Foth & Hearn, 2007; Granovetter, 1973; Wellman, 1979; Wellman et al., 2003). This contrasts to the Human Ecology approach where McKenzie (1968, p. 115) argued that the institution was the fundamental unit in modern society and that the trend was away from individual enterprise.

In the scholarly debate surrounding the decline of Human Ecology, it was critiqued as focusing on habitat to the neglect of humans, where consideration of physical circumstances 'crowded out' consideration of the social and cultural. In addition to this, critics argued that Human Ecology neglected the social-psychological aspects of community and subscribed to a form of biological determinism (MacDonald, 2011, pp. 266–7). These limitations to the Human Ecology approach highlight the key strengths of the social ecology approach, which integrates analysis of the cultural, environmental and social-psychological aspects of community experience. The critique of environmental determinism is especially relevant to the use of the ecological concept. This critique resonates with the careful distinction to be made between the study of a group interested in biology rather than the application of biological metaphors to explain community formation. I would argue that while I am interested in the adaptive nature of community, this work does not subscribe to a form of Darwinism or attempt to speak to evolutionary theory. An additional critique that viewing community as digitally augmented adds to the critique of Human Ecology is drawn from theoretical and technical developments surrounding the notion of the semantic web, also referred to as Web 3.0. I would argue that the Human Ecology approach lacks a sense of the environment 'looking back' (Haraway, 2008). This critique draws upon research into the semantic web by which our environments react 'intelligently' according to how we interact with them (Angeletou, 2008; Breslin, Passant, & Decker, 2009; Garcia-Castro et al., 2010; Mika, 2004). From this discussion, we can see how pivotal the nature of communication technologies are to evolving the understandings of community that these researchers founded.

2.4 The Construction of Online Communities as a Site of Study

So how have scholars viewed the social implications of mediated interactions in online communities? One of the early and striking impressions was that community online was seen as disconnected or exceptional to daily social life because of the perceived ephemerality of virtual interactions (Castells, 2001, p. 130). I would argue that this was generated through the perceived disconnection from physical place that the online environment carried in this early research, often characterised through references to cyberspace as a discrete place (Marshall, 2001). This disconnection between physical and virtual social space most likely developed in dialogue with the early literature on identity exploration online that worried people would become fragmented through the pursuit of multiple identities that form across parallel lives in cyberspace (Turkle, 1997b, 1999). This lack of identity cohesion was attributed to the effects of anonymity online and exposure to heterogeneous others and was translated to a lack of social cohesion in communities online. These connections occurred in the early and heady days of researching new and evolving online spaces that were slowly attracting people. The main and lasting contention that these scholars introduced was the separation of physical life from virtual experience – thereby introducing an online-offline dichotomy to community experience that has persisted within research to this day.

This perception of the ephemerality of online interactions is most recently reiterated in the work of Andrew Keen (2007) who argues that the unsubstantial nature of peer-production, through a caste of 'amateurs', is destroying culture, economy and values. This point of view implies the conclusion that digitally mediated interactions cannot be experienced as truly emotionally supportive, cohesive or continuous because they lack substance. In critiquing Keen's position, Frenkel-Faran (2008) argues that this approach dismisses that there is an amalgamation of community and collaboration on an unprecedented scale. He argues that this scale 'lives on in the thriving blogosphere, the compendium of knowledge Wikipedia, the people's network YouTube, editor-free news-aggregation sites such as Digg and the online metropolises of Facebook and MySpace' (Frenkel-Faran, 2008, p. 675). This critique and value that Frenkel-Faran argues to be assigned to peer collaboration online suggests that what is happening in mediated social space is also viewed by contemporary Internet researchers as substantial and socially valued. In particular his contention highlights the negative perception of an unregulated and user-produced online space that Keen propagates through his thesis.

In the field of community theory, Zygmunt Bauman (2001) weighed into this debate early on to decry these social trends away from community as place-bound by arguing that this trend has resulted in the loss of community rather than simply its reconfiguration. His perspective feeds into the idea that because we do not see community in the places we used to through observing densities of in-person relationships, that must mean we have 'lost' it. This approach of imaging loss through absence is also reflected in Robert Putnam's (2000; 1995) proposition of the decline of social capital (another measure of community cohesion and collectivity in society). These contentions reflect an 'ideology of lament' coined by Robert Nisbet in 1953, and is argued by Sampson (2002, p. 215) to have been as wrong 100 years ago as it remains today. I would argue that, with the overwhelming volume of research that identifies social value and community maintenance in the online environment, community has not been lost and we are not experiencing a decline in social capital. I believe these theorists indicate that it is time to evolve our methods and concepts to identify community that may have shifted location, become more mobile and be in different formats from traditional understandings.

As highlighted in the discussion above, this perception of easy connect and disconnect and the ephemerality or lack of substance to interaction in the online environment is based upon the idea that technology use is not a part of our everyday lives. A range of literature has focused upon the immersion of ICT-mediated social relations into everyday life, including Bakardjieva and Smith (2001), Katz and Rice (2002), Wellman and Haythornthwaite (2002) and Wellman et al. (2002). Wellman argues that in accepting the everyday use of ICTs as embedded in our relationships, we can understand the notion of community through networks of interpersonal ties.

> Given the movement from the local and densely knit to the far flung and the sparsely knit, it is not useful to think about community as group-like neighborhoods and villages. It is more useful to define community as networks of interpersonal ties that provide sociability, support, information, a sense of belonging and social identity.
>
> (Wellman et al., 2002, p. 153)

As we saw in the discussion of an early community study by Herbert Gans (1962), the physical environment of in-person interaction, whilst providing the opportunity for exposure, is less influential on group cohesion than the social bonds that people create with each other. This supports the efficacy of Wellman's transition from understanding community as placed-based to a relational construct to speak to the imbrication of community and technology within everyday life. In the discussion of the literature to this point, we can already see a reflexive gap emerging, one that asks what our assumptions are about community online and what we already know about our contemporary social environment that may challenge these assumptions. To lead us through this, the next section considers contemporary research into Virtual Community and reviews whether research conducted through this lens has the capacity to move us through the relational-place based conundrum. From this, I argue that unlike traditional community studies, online community studies are not space-bound but expand into several utopian and dystopian directions. While the ecological approach of the Chicago School scholars may assist us in resolving the good with the bad, they have nothing to say about the online-offline dualism that arises through our understanding of cyberspace as a parallel and self-referential social location.

2.5 Virtual Community

Within the research literature, the notion of Virtual community is dichotomously represented by theorists as a social utopia or dystopia (Fisher & Wright, 2001; Hampton, 2001). The key implications of the utopia/dystopia debate on virtual community lies in the capacity of the Internet to facilitate or impede collective action and individual wellbeing and promote a sense of community. This discourse has long surrounded the notion of community as an elixir for social disconnection, which Sampson (2002, p. 214) argues is antediluvian and dilutes the power of this construct to provide analytical insight.

> If community has come to mean everything good, as a concept it loses its analytical bite and therefore means nothing. Despite widespread interest across multiple disciplines, the nature, sources, and consequences of community in modern society remain ambiguous and largely unscathed by serious social scientific inquiry.
>
> (Sampson, 2002, p. 215)

This observation remains relevant to scholarly use of the notion of virtual community as a social dystopia or utopia. Boase and Wellman (2006, p. 3) argue that dystopian theorists find life online is problematic because online relationships would never measure up to the face-to-face relationships of real life. Wellman (1997, p. 445) develops our understanding of this dystopian perspective by adding that dystopian thinkers believe cyberspace represents social disconnection from a sense of place, reality and community. In addition, dystopians claim that democracy crumbles because the social fabric of society becomes fragmented when people become more isolated from one another when online (Fisher & Wright, 2001). However, as Keith Hampton outlines, the utopians saw the social effects of online communities to be the exact opposite. In this environment, Hampton argued that the utopian perspective emphasised not only social activism but 'the ability of computer networks to connect people in strong, supportive relationships that blindly extend beyond characteristics of ethnicity, religion or national origins' (2001, p. 2). As the quintessential utopian theorist of virtual community, Harold Rheingold (2000) argued for the potential of computer-mediated communication (CMC) to create the civic space that is lacking in industrial society (Plotkin, 1995, p. 284). Others have argued that the utopian approach to virtual community operates in the context of a dystopian reality (Fox & Roberts, 1999, p. 667).

The utopian perspective also finds expression in the work conducted on online political activism. The potential to become more autonomous human beings is applied to online social life when theorists argue that we are moving into new forms of social organisation that liberate us from authoritarian governments. This perspective is particularly represented in literature surrounding the blogosphere and activist movements under oppressed regimes such as Egypt, Iran and China (Zuckerman, 2008) and the recent 'Occupy' movements (Land, 2012; Skinner, 2011). This perspective often focuses on how the slow build-up of collective blogging online is like the collective unconscious, building for years, which 'spontaneously uprises' (Ensler 2011, cited in Land, 2012). The utopian position can also be found in the approach known as techno-realism (Fisher & Wright, 2001) which looks specifically at how people use the Internet to connect with others and can be seen as a 'front-end', user-focused perspective. This approach is particularly employed in discussions of online sociability and anonymity as providing a less socially judgemental environment in which people connect more honestly with diverse others through avatars (Bente, Rüggenberg, Krämer, & Eschenburg, 2008). However, the concern of dystopians with the ephemerality of anonymity online also resonates with early arguments about the elusive and ambiguous constructions of individual and collective identities mediated by these technologies (Wilson & Peterson, 2002). The review will return to this body of literature in the discussion of networked individualism where the focus turns to online sociability with known others.

This debate between utopians and dystopians on the social effect and existence of virtual communities situates itself in arguments about whether online interaction connects (Boase, Horrigan, Wellman, & Raine, 2006; Hampton & Wellman, 2001; Rheingold, 2000; Wellman, 2001a) or disconnects people from each other and place (Nie & Erbring, 2002; Nie et al., 2002; Nie, 2001; Nie & Hillygus, 2002; Turkle, 1997a, 2003, 2007a, 2007b, 2011). These perspectives demonstrate that there is indeed a broad-scale theoretical disconnect occurring (Kolb, 2008). However, such disconnections may also provide the conceptual space to articulate an alternative analytical framework to virtual community in which we are able to rethink social collectivity and the experience of community.

Fisher and Wright (2001) propose that the conflicting views within this debate are a result of the focus on the effects of the Internet on society (utopian perspective) versus understanding the phenomenon of the user's experience (generally perceived as inherently negative – the dystopian perspective). The dualism of this outlook indicates that the Internet is affecting people at both the macro and the micro level (social structure and social agency) and that these effects may at times be contradictory. This contradiction, whilst inherent to social behaviour, also lies in the lack of connection between these two outlooks. As Frenkel-Faran (2008) comments, the disciplinary controversy that sprung up around the vitriolic outlook of Keen led to a questioning of the uncritical acceptance that the architecture of the Internet is also its social affect. This questioning asks us to understand that whilst the Internet is decentralised, with no one central control mechanism, its technical features do not necessarily reflect the entire range of social behaviours online. What we do know now is that the social occupation of this many-to-many communication architecture (Poster, 1999), based upon user-generated content, matches our ideals of an egalitarian body politic, but has turned out to be much more complex. Boase and Wellman (2006) argue that the simple dualism of utopian and dystopian writers occurred because of their failure to place social behaviour online in a broader pattern of common social tendencies.

> Both have assumed that the Internet actually *does* have the power to pull people away from their everyday lives and immerse them in a world that is radically different from the one in which they previously lived. Their technologically deterministic assumptions have attributed a large amount of causal power to the technology itself, ignoring the complex array of social factors that affect how the Internet is actually used by the general population.
>
> (Boase & Wellman, 2006, p. 4)

This acknowledgement of the complex array of social factors that affect how the Internet is used is reflected in the case study of the herpetological community. This research will demonstrate how the online environment contains a unique array of social factors that influence the way it is experienced by the participants. In a similar vein, Fisher and Wright (2001) have argued that the Internet has the capacity to change how individuals interact with others as well as increase access to information. This debate demonstrates that the key aspects of the Internet - decentralisation of information and mediated social connection – affect and change how collective action happens (Fuchs, 2006; Johnston & Laxer, 2003; Lai-Yee, 2007; Mesch & Levanon, 2006; Tilly, 2004) and how people generate emotional and social connections and wellbeing in this environment (Boase & Wellman, 2006; Burrows, Nettleton, Pleace, Loader, & Muncer, 2000; Eysenbach et al., 2004; Fox et al, 2002; Im et al., 2007; Josefsson, 2005; Klemm & Hardie, 2002; Valkenburg & Peter, 2009). I situate this research in the middle of these perspectives and draw from this debate around virtual community in which the electronic environment has the capacity to connect people globally, for better or worse. I am also sympathetic to the position of dystopians, that the user may experience disconnection through anonymity in this environment as much as they may experience connection and support. From those who see virtual community as holding the capacity for social liberation, I draw on the idea that online dialogue is a large-scale conversation through which people figure out who is likely to be active around certain issues and what the key figures and most effective channels for activism are. I also incorporate the perspective that these networks take time to establish online and social action that emerges from these large-scale conversations is not immediately observable.

2.6 Possible Limitations to the Virtual Community Construct

The early community studies literature and the work on virtual communities both employed place-based boundaries in their conceptions of community. The only difference being that such 'boundedness' now referred to the relatively fixed spaces of a website address and a website's software environment. The link between community studies and virtual community was made by the transfer of thinking about community as place-bound, for example to a neighbourhood, to understanding it as bound to a particular website online, such as to Facebook. Hence, consistency was found in the notion of community being a group of people in a particular space. This reflects a tendency of researchers to treat these two bodies of work as 'before' and 'after' the social adoption of the Internet. This approach fits into the historical trajectory of the elongation of social structures through the time-space distantiation of technological innovation argued by Anthony Giddens (1984). From this perspective, community was place-based and social interactions were face-to-face and in real time. Reciprocity, self-regulation and collective monitoring were enforced through geographic proximity. Community in this context also represented a lack of social choice as the geographic position of a person defined their community by default. Further along this time-space distantiation timeline is where virtual community is commonly positioned. In this context, virtual community occurs at a single virtual location but members are in different places and time zones. In this electronic environment, the time of interaction can be synchronous or asynchronous. Interactions are disembodied and mediated and geography has limited impact on co-presence. The technological affordance of the online environment is easy to connect to and disconnect from, creating the possibility for social interaction to be choice-driven, non-reciprocal and unregulated. As the literature on networked sociability will discuss, research into mediated social interaction does not reflect this dichotomy. However, these perspectives are derived from what is made possible by the Internet environment rather than what people actually do in these environments. It is this architectural affordance that tends to drive the utopian/dystopian debate.

Within the historical context, proponents of the utopian/dystopian debate were prolific around the turn of the century. This represented a time when theoretical ideas were developing alongside technological innovations and changing social configurations, but the pace of evidence-based research lagged. In this gap between theory development and evidence-based research, it appears that theorists extrapolated the affordances of the technological architecture of the Internet to be the likely articulation of how people would then use this technology. In an associated identification of this trend, Jensen (2011, p. 43) points out that this divide between online and offline practices in the early years of Internet studies may have been a necessary step for theory development. An example of the fruit of this labour is the early contribution to discussions on identity construction in this environment by Sherry Turkle, who has been influential on how we now view the multiplicity of identity. Ten years on, however, there remains an artifactual focus upon virtual community as a discrete online phenomenon in the research literature. This phenomenon is attributable to persistent interest in engaging people in online environments and the development of research techniques to investigate groups online.

Virtual ethnography has perpetuated the concept of virtual community from a research basis (Paccagnella, 1997). The goal of ethnography is to produce thick descriptions of particular settings, groups or organisations (Hammersley, 1990). This has translated into research that positions the online environment as a site for community (Carter, 2005; Hine, 2008, p. 257), new cultural practices in identity development (Rybas, 2007) and Internet-generated community experiences such as Second Life (Bardzell & Odom, 2008; Guitton, 2012). Whilst there are ethnographic works that point to the online-offline or 'multi-sited' environment of community (Beneito-Montagut, 2011; Sade-Beck, 2008), analysis of the online social environment appears to be a primary focus of methodological development in this field (Murthy, 2008). Virtual ethnographers have raised insightful questions about (Gatson & Zweerink, 2004) and techniques for investigating groups online (Carter, 2005; Crichton & Kinash, 2003; Domínguez et al., 2007; Garcia et al., 2009; Goodsell & Williamson, 2008; Greschke, 2007; Hine, 2000; Mann & Stewart, 2000). This scholarly engagement has substantially contributed to the methodological and theoretical literature and positioned virtual ethnography as the 'go-to' discipline for techniques to observe and study groups online. Much of the research in this field is now being referred to as digital ethnography (Murthy, 2008). In an interdisciplinary application, these questions and techniques are drawn upon within the field of interaction design (Bardzell & Odom, 2008; Preece, Nonnecke, & Andrews, 2004). By its very nature, the use of these research techniques for interaction design reinforces the application of the virtual community construct to describe groups of people in online spaces. I would argue that this preoccupation with thick descriptions of groups online and the interdisciplinary use of these techniques has propagated the concept of virtual community within the research literature rather than normalising multimodal forms of interaction and the blurring of online and offline environments.

Another reason that virtual community has remained in focus is the research agenda to understand how social engagement in these environments can be viably retained over time (Rothaermel & Sugiyama, 2001), often tying motivations such as commercial, educational, entertainment and social networking into one platform. Examples of this include online learning management systems and online education (Dougiamas & Taylor, 2003; Kemp & Livingstone, 2006; Yang, 2006; Yang, Chen, & Shao, 2004), online shopping (Cyr et al., 2007; Hsiu-Fen, 2008; Jepsen, 2006; Miller, 2009; Mutz, 2009; Xie, 2008), online gaming (Ege & Koullapis, 2009; Isabella, 2007; Postigo, 2007; Yee, 2006), social bookmarking and multimedia platforms such as deviantART and YouTube (Lange, 2007; Pronovost, 2009; Santos et al., 2007; Zontea, 2010), online support platforms for disability, disease and emotional disorders (Eun-Ok et al., 2007; Fox & Roberts, 1999; Gavrin, 2005; Høybye, Johansen, & Tjørnhøj-Thomsen, 2005; Sharp, 2000) and Web 2.0 platforms such as Facebook and Myspace (Beer & Burrows, 2007; boyd, 2006, 2007a, 2007b, 2008; boyd & Ellison, 2008; Ellison, Steinfield, & Lampe, 2007; Goodings, Locke, & Brown, 2007; Hardey, 2007; Pasek, More, & Romer, 2009; Steinfield, Ellison, & Lampe, 2008). Whilst these platform environments present unique ecosystems from which notions such as online trust (in strangers and the online environment itself), prosumption (Beer & Burrows, 2010; Ritzer & Jurgenson, 2010) (the production and consumption of content by the user), user engagement and online support can be explored, they generally do not relate their findings back to the core concerns of community studies. Nor do they necessarily draw connections back from online worlds to offline ones. This is in line with the discussion above on the gap between theory development and evidence-based research that has reinforced this conceptual division of online and offline behaviours. Another reason for this lack of connection is the research has been generated for specific agendas such as usability and gaming design, marketing, student retention, media studies and health modelling.

This contemporary literature on virtual communities that are bounded by their software environment and single website address has disconnected from the sociological agenda of community studies and yet has perpetuated its assumption that community is spatially bound. A key insight from this debate that will shape the discussion in this book is that these are the spaces where people do go online and that there are issues of trust, anonymous interaction and unrestrained social behaviours such as trolling (Herring et al., 2002; Shin, 2008) and flaming (Eysenbach et al., 2004; Turnage, 2007) in these environments. I also acknowledge that this environment is easy to disconnect from and connect to, however there is no imperative to follow the assumptions that online membership and participation must belong to a single platform or that users are able to behave online in an unregulated manner without repercussions (see discussions of collective shaming and community self-regulation in Skoric et al., 2010; Williams, 2007). Other useful concepts include the idea of prosumption and precarious labour in which users voluntarily contribute their time and knowledge to online projects such as Wikipedia.

2.7 Conclusion

This chapter has argued that community is classically defined by the attributes of membership, cohesion, continuity and the solidarity achieved through a collective identity. In research practice this has been considered to translate to definitions of group place, composition, boundaries and mechanisms of social cohesion as the parameters of a site of study. The conceptual mechanics for discussing and defining social groups have been considered in this chapter as either spatially bound (proximity) or situated within a network of social ties based upon a common interest (foci of activity). Classic examples of this were presented from the neighbourhood studies within urban sociology and studies of subcultures that focus on gangs. From this, the chapter then considered the conceptual shifts that have been associated with community due to the advent of the Internet and social life moving online. When aspects of community experience are mediated by digital technology, they are commonly understood to be about virtual community. This concept has arisen to deal with the integration of information communication technologies (ICTs) as the media that enable social interaction across local and non-local (dispersed) contexts and through many-to-many communication. As Section 2.5 highlighted however, to this day the idea that community is associated with a geographical space persists in the social sciences. This articulation of community through its place and social networks has been argued to point to a defining dichotomy within the conceptualisation and definition of a community as a site of study. This gulf has been widened through the impact of communities becoming digital, effectively separating the relationship between place and common interest. This dichotomy of community as defined by both geographic terms and relational patterns has been argued to have led to an unreconciled divergence in community research, leaving the methods practitioner with an uncomfortable either/ or scenario that may limit the capacity of their research to provide holistic insight into the contemporary experience of community.

The following chapter will consider how this divergence can best be reconciled through a third more loose-knit position, while retaining the insights and understandings of the Chicago School scholars and their development of the ecological approach to the study of community. This approach firstly enables a focus upon community structures based on social ties within a digitally mediated environment, but also does not ignore conceptions of community that are contextual to place. Despite the complexities and apparent contradictions, these two dimensions of community – as the study of the herpetological community will demonstrate – are not mutually exclusive.

Chapter 3
Transcending the Dualism

3.1 Introduction

The aim of this chapter is to chart a path for the research practitioner from the dualism of virtual community to characterising social interaction online through the relational ideas of 'mediated sociability'. Section 3.2 introduces the concept and language of mediated sociability that flags a divergence of perspective towards social behaviour online away from group behaviours and focusing on computer-mediated, interactional behaviour. Section 3.3 then characterises networked notions of social capital that overlay the framework of relational interaction proposed by mediated sociability. Section 3.4 then takes us to a discussion of the networked individual, who is argued to be a relational actor through which mediated sociability and networked social capital are enacted. Section 3.5 then connects the relational actions of the networked individual into a cohesive environment through which digital community occurs. These discussions assist the research practitioner in navigating their way forward to conceptualising and then operationalising the layers of activity and exchange that constitute the form of digital community.

The notion of mediated sociability positions interactive experiences online through a user-hardware/software-user perspective (Rice & Love, 1987; Simpson, 2002; Walther, 1995, 1996). In positioning the group participant as a computer or mobile device user, this body of research was disconnected from the initial concerns raised in the virtual community literature over the capacity for civic engagement and collective action online, but retained a focus upon individual wellbeing. While the notion of mediated sociability was not designed as a conceptual tool designed to drill down into the social imaginary of collective spaces online, it allowed researchers to focus upon technical questions of social engagement in the online environment. Meaning we were asking less about the 'why' and more about the 'how'. The key contribution of this area of research to digital community studies, ironically, was the connection it made between online behaviours and physical engagement with hardware and software. Consequently, the effect of this connection between disembodied interactions online and embodied behaviours such as 'computer use' inherent to the idea of mediated sociability anchored discussions of online engagement with the physical world.

From this user-centric approach, a relational understanding of online engagement began to develop that acknowledged both the physical and virtual dimensions of online interaction. From this, the capacity for scholars to connect online and offline 'worlds' (Xie, 2007, 2008) and introduce multimodal forms of social interaction (Schroeder, 2010) broadened the parameters of community experience beyond virtual community in a single space and on a single medium. Consequently, the literature drawing on the idea of mediated sociability is now populated by case studies of online environments that, rather than treating cyberspace as a new venue for bounded community, explore the thorough integration of Internet use into everyday life (see Wellman & Haythornthwaite, 2002 for several discussions of this trend). The effect of this connection was to dilute the anticipated impacts of digital ephemerality and unregulated online behaviours across multiple identities with the mundane and socially integrated behaviours of everyday life. The Internet was no longer our subconscious writ large, but the way we paid our bills and kept in contact with loved ones and extended friendship networks.

Alongside these conceptual developments also strode technological innovation; this was reflected in the changing nature of the mediated environment from web 1.0 forms of interaction to a web 2.0 focus upon social networks. However even that has been superseded by future focused technology research, with web 3.0 formats heralded through research into the Internet of Things (Kortuem et al., 2010; Tuters & Varnelis, 2006) and the smartification of everyday life (Crang & Graham, 2007). Underpinning this trend is the increasing focus upon artificial intelligence in notions of the sentient web, in which the technology gains agency and the capacity to observe, connect, predict and react to us. From these transitions, we can see the development from viewing the Internet as a way to augment our reality to it becoming our omniscient and collective brain, knowing us before we know ourselves: no longer a passive mirror, but a shaping force within our everyday lives. Within this paradigm, we see the emergence of the quantified self-movement and a social landscape of self-monitoring and digital reflexivity (Lupton, 2014). We are now operating in an online landscape that watches us; pre-emptively responding to what we consume, how we manage our privacy and our browsing behaviours. These developments effectively augment and shape the purpose, potentials and practices of online engagement and its application to everyday life.

In this context, Comunello (2012) sees that the notion of virtual community as misleading if it is understood as the main pattern of sociability found online. I would argue that it is also somewhat naïve to assume that this constitutes the greater majority of behaviours online. Drawing on the work of Parks (2011) and Baym (2010), Comunello describes communities as arising through specific patterns both online and offline, but that they cannot be understood as the dominant form of sociability. This argument is a key example of how the notion of mediated sociability has enabled scholars to think beyond the scope of previous conceptualisations of the online environment. Comunello leverages this argument from the work of Barry Wellman to posit that most of the time, and in most contexts, people are immersed in sparsely knit, self-centred networks. Here we can see the impact of the user perspective derived from Information Systems thinking overlaying the infrastructural nature of the Internet as a system of decentralised networks consisting of computers and routers rather than centralised and organised systems. The World Wide Web, being a layer over the top of this infrastructure providing the social surface through which most mediated sociability occurs. The overlaying of these two systems with the social network perspective of Barry Wellman facilitates and grounds Comunello's broader framework in describing patterns of social engagement in the online environment. However she does not give up entirely on the idea of the digitised collective, arguing that while the online environment is less characterised by immersion in densely knit communities, these sparse networks can also include densely knit groups. However it is from other bodies of literature that we may follow the circuitous route back to understanding how to describe, and the methods of research that provide access to, the contemporary nature and experience of community in this environment.

3.2 Networked Sociability

Even in the age of online community research, the Chicago School scholars show their continued influence upon community studies through author acknowledgements, mentorships and academic sleights of hand. For example, there can be little doubt that Keith Hampton's influential study of community in a wired neighbourhood, 'Netville' (2001), is a direct allusion and homage to Whyte's earlier 'Cornerville' study. In this study, Hampton explores the form and parameters of digitised communities within an offline neighbourhood and the ensuing interpersonal/intergroup relations and social ties. This consequently links notions of mediated sociability with strong and weak social ties (the relational aspect) and leverages the discussion of community cohesion through the use of the notion of social capital. Key arguments resulting from Hampton's work include: the intermingling by residents of mediated and face-to-face connections for support (or the mixing of online/offline sociability); that high-speed Internet access supports neighbouring rather than weakening it (Wellman et al., 2003); and the connection between relational notions of digitised community experience and networked social capital. This research approach demonstrates the application of exploring multimodal forms of interaction and the connection of online activities with offline environments in a strengthening, rather than weakening, relationship. This strengthening of community is demonstrated through the increasing interconnectivity of local social ties and the presence of social capital enhanced by digital engagements.

This link, provided by Hampton, will take us on a consideration of the literature on social capital and how it relates back to the methodological and conceptual development of digital community. Within community studies literature, social capital is linked with notions of social cohesion (Chan, To, & Chan, 2006; Dayton-Johnson, 2003; Forrest & Kearns, 2001; Friedkin, 2004; Lupi & Musterd, 2006; Moody & White, 2003; Portes & Vickstrom, 2011). There is an increasing focus on how social capital relates to measuring the capacity for collective action, social support and group cohesion through the network structure of online and online/offline strong and weak social ties, which in short is referred to as networked social capital (Anderson & Jack, 2002; Ellison et al., 2007; Ferlander & Timms, 2007; Franzen, 2003; Keith Hampton & Wellman, 2003; Kobayashi, 2010; Kobayashi, Ikeda, & Miyata, 2006; Mesch & Levanon, 2006; Pasek et al., 2009; Quan-Haase et al., 2008; Uslaner & Conley, 2003; Valenzuela, Park, & Kee, 2009; Wellman et al., 2001; Williams, 2006, 2007). This idea of social cohesion being identifiable through notions of networked social capital has been extrapolated in the literature on social capital (Lin, 2001; Snijders, 1999; Van Der Gaag & Snijders, 2005) and transferred into discussions of mediated sociability (Franzen, 2003; J. E. Katz & Rice, 2002). In following through on this scholarly discussion, we begin the task of conceptualising social capital within the contemporary community environment that incorporates multimodal interaction within a multi-site community.

3.3 Networked Social Capital

Networked social capital is a cornerstone concept to digital community, not only because it speaks to cohesion within communities, but also because the interest group under study functions through networks of mediated strong and weak social ties that challenge our understanding of the role of trust within social exchange. The network profile of patterns of social organisation begins with a language and spidering visual of the actions of nodes and hubs in brokering innovation and information, sharing knowledge, resources and access (elements of social capital). These cliques and connections are defined by the dark matter of structural holes; one way of thinking about structural holes being as social voids spanned by weak ties that intersperse and connect social cliques (Burt, 1992, 1997a, 1997b, 2000, 2004). These structural holes are one way of talking about the defining impact of 'othering' and general levels of trust have upon social engagement and the function and dispersion of social capital across a network. As Mark Granovetter (1985, pp. 487–92) describes, the role and diverse enactment types of trust within social relationships is more complex than the dynamic between 'trust' and reciprocity assumed in ideas of social capital more generally.

Social exchange of information and support across ICTs and the Internet has magnified this complexity by affording an increase in anonymous interactions (Parks & Floyd, 1996), de-personified exchanges and the reconceptualisation of the production and consumption of content, a social good that is exchanged. Consequently, theorists have developed ways of conceptualising the person and what they do online that are derived from the decentralised and user-produced nature of the environment. A person who produces content online is referred to as a prosumer or produser (Bird, 2011; Ritzer & Jurgenson, 2010; Skågeby, 2011) as they both produce and consume content at the same time. They voluntarily produce social resources such as gaming mods as a form of play online (Kuecklich, 2005). Precarious playbour becomes a one-to-many voluntary act of content production that translates as a resource available to a community. The 'exchange' that this constitutes is an element of social capital, but is specific to the digital domain. This augmentation of social behaviour and information consumption is also accompanied by an augmentation of scamming, surveillance and deception practices within digital social transactions. In response to this sense of digital deception and detection, the online environment is characterised by low levels of trust both in the new technologies and software and challenges to personal privacy and security from the environment. A feeling of 'surveillant anxiety' (Crawford, 2014) or 'anxieties of control' (Leszczynski, forthcoming) and identity risk to operating in the digital environment may be increased through the disruptive presence of digital counter-cultures such as hacktivists (Coleman & Golub, 2008; Coleman, 2012; Hollinger, 1991; Jordan & Taylor, 1998) and malign individual actors such trolls (Buckels, Trapnell, & Paulhus, 2014).

From the above, we can see that there is likely to be a need to extend upon the notions of trust and exchange when social capital is connected with the concept of mediated sociability. However even deciding on what social capital is probably a more fundamental concern for its research and methods application. This next section will spend some time considering this discussion in order to connect it back into the digital domain. Social capital is a term that operates with the split identity of being defined as either the potential for collective action or the access to and exchange of social resources, these ideas not being mutually exclusive. Forrest and Kearns (2001) begin their discussion of social capital as a set of social conditions rather than as the exchange of social resources by drawing on Putnam's 'well rehearsed' definition:

> … social capital refers to features of social organisation such as networks, norms and trust that facilitate co-ordination and co-operation for mutual benefit. Social capital enhances the benefits of investment in physical and human capital.
>
> (Putnam, 1993, p. 35)

Building upon this definition of social capital as the conditions which enhance investment in physical and human capital, Borgida et al. (2002) argue that social capital reflects the norms and social relations embedded in the social structure of societies that enable people to coordinate community action to achieve desired goals. From this perspective, social capital can be measured through the levels of trust and reciprocity that exist within the network. However, these notions do not adapt well to the mediated environment as they do not take into account online anonymity, crowdsourcing (Wang, Zeng, & Hendler, 2010), precarious labour (Kuecklich, 2005) or prosumption (Beer & Burrows, 2010) as a social resource. These online phenomena are not necessarily based upon trust-relationships, broader social norms or exchange with known others, but they are an exchange network that constitutes the social 'wealth' of a digital community. These social trends challenge our assumptions of how to conceptualise and identify social capital within contemporary community environment that incorporate multimodal interaction.

The body of literature on mediated sociability differentiates between types of social capital according to the strength (close) or 'weakness' (not close) of social ties. Hampton (2001, pp. 17–18) argued (in line with Putnam, 1995, 2000) that network social capital (or bridging capital) recognises that access to diverse social ties of different strengths provides access to a broad range of supportive resources. Bonding social capital, on the other hand, facilitates increased norms of trust and measures the capacity for collective action and group cohesion. This introduction of the relationship between different types of social capital across mediated weak and strong social ties (bridging and bonding social capital) builds upon early network theory work on the strength of weak social ties in getting jobs observed by Granovetter (1973). In taking this approach, the notions of networked social capital challenges group-based social organisation by including open networks that reach beyond the norms of trust, reciprocity and mutuality within an environment. For example, ICT mediation of these processes facilitates the reach of weak ties across a global context rather than a local one.

As discussed above, the concept of social capital is based upon the idea that general trust amongst people facilitates the exchange of social resources. Networked social capital sees this as occurring across strong and weak social ties and turns a pragmatic focus towards access of social resources. Consequently, high levels of social capital would exist within the context of social networks that consist of both strong and weak ties that interlock local and global spaces. This is relevant for the multi-sited, as well as multimodal, nature of digital community. These social ties would be characterised by the practice of ICT-mediated exchange and reciprocity (which speaks to the notion of mediated sociability) and enhanced by the presence of trust-based relationships and organisational engagement. Access, rather than outcomes, would consequently be an indication of high levels of social capital. On the other hand, low social capital would be characterised by low levels of exchange across weak social ties (reducing levels of bridging social capital). In addition to this, low levels of general trust and organisational participation imply poor access to social resources. Under these conditions, one may expect limited social exchange of support, information and access (low levels of social capital) across mediated networks. The operationalisation of these understandings of networked social capital will be further developed in the research methodology (Chapter 4) and the relationship between the mediated environment, trust as a facilitator of social exchange and social capital as access rather than outcome will be discussed throughout this book. This discussion reflects the social ecology approach as viewing social cohesion, operationalised by the measurement of networked social capital, through configurations of space, organisation and interaction of the network.

The experience of community is derived from a group-based social environment in which a sense of support, socialisation and shared identity can be experienced. Characteristically, a community is a rich site of social exchange and engagement, with differing levels of commitment and membership. Contemporary community is experienced as a portfolio of relationships, and the individual is likely to engage with more than one. A network of relationships can be included in a community, but social networks do not, by default, provide the experience of community. There is something more to community experience; it includes how the interconnectedness of these relationships provides a sense of continuity, stability and enables members. These ideas are referred to as social cohesion and social mobility. The social cohesion of a community is examined through an investigation of social capital and the influence of the group environment upon patterns of social organisation (the ecological approach). In this case, the environment is both physical and virtual. Social capital is viewed as the affordances of social connections and can be exchanged through in-person and mediated interactions (ICTs). The exchange of social capital in the form of information, access and support is facilitated by trust and the mobility of reputation amongst group members. Levels of social capital within a community are enhanced by trust in the environment (the way things work and where they occur) and organisational engagement (both physical and virtual). The social ecology that results from these intersections of common interests, place, technology, social relationships, reciprocity and organisational participation is the contemporary niche of community.

3.4 Networked Individualism

These ideas slithering around my head have led to the focus upon ego-centred individualism that operates as a site of differentiation, multiplicity and connection in a group. Within the literature this idea is captured in the concept of networked individualism (Rainie & Wellman, 2012; Wellman, 2001b; Wellman et al., 2003). Networked individualism is derived from the personalisation of communication devices and platforms, it is also about the customisation of self-image over the cultivation of group identity.

In a related set of ideas on networked sociability and configurations of strong and weak social ties, Wellman has argued for the transition of community networks into personalised ones based upon a concept called 'networked individualism' (Wellman, 2001b; Wellman et al., 2003). He argues that there is a convergence in thinking about the transformation of community from solidary groups to individualised networks (2001, p. 228). Wellman's idea of individualism is not strongly tied to a theoretical lineage, however he briefly situates it in the work of Beck (1996), Giddens (1984) and Parsons (1943) as the condition of modern society. It is worth spending time exploring the background to this discussion of where Wellman's notion of individualism is derived from because it will help to clarify its later use in this book. Ulrich Beck, in a follow up discussion of his theory of the Risk Society (Ulrich Beck, 1992), outlines a social trend in which life has become an individual project.

> The normal biography thus becomes the 'elective biography', the 'do-it-yourself biography'. This does not necessarily happen by choice, neither does it necessarily succeed. The do-it-yourself biography is always a 'risk biography', indeed a 'tightrope biography', a state of permanent (partly overt, partly concealed) endangerment.
>
> (Beck & Beck-Gernsheim, 1996, p. 25)

Beck's notion of structural individualisation is argued by Woodman (2011, p. 5) to refer to the idea that people are left to resolve structural contradictions themselves, reflecting a structural shift of responsibility from the institution to the individual. This reflects the move from a solidary community as providing support and buffering to personal networks as providing support and a higher level of exposure through a more open structural framework proposed by Wellman. The second aspect of Beck's structural individualisation being that the exact set of rules and guidelines that a person is exposed to and the exact set of contradictions is less likely to overlap with others. This trend overlaps indirectly with Wellman's notion of portfolios of sociability that will be discussed in the following paragraph. Whilst Wellman has vaguely situated the concept of networked individualism within this paradigm of structural individualisation, this theoretical affiliation does not reflect the likely origins of his use of an individual agent being characterised within networks of strong and weak social ties. In his theoretical discussion, Wellman does not overtly acknowledge his methodological affiliation with the field of social network analysis from which this concept is mostly likely derived. However, an investigation of his collected body of works reveals that he actively employs this methodological technique in the analysis of social ties and the mediated environment and particularly in the ways that he and his collaborators and students employ this notion of networked individualism. In the above discussion of Keith Hampton's 'Netville' research, which was one of the research bases from which networked individualism was launched, he employs the technique of social network analysis, and Barry Wellman was his Ph.D. supervisor for this project. In an entry in the *Blackwell Encyclopedia of Sociology Online* (2007), Wellman locates the origin of this perspective in the field of anthropology. Anthropologists use this idea to describe complex sets of relationships between members of social systems at all scales, from interpersonal to international. Wellman explains how the application of social network analysis introduces the idea that social relations cut across group classifications:

> Yet not until the 1950s did they start using the term systematically and self-consciously to denote patterns of ties that cut across the concepts traditionally used by social scientists: bounded groups (e.g., tribes, families) and social categories (e.g., gender, ethnicity). Social network analysis has now moved from being a suggestive metaphor to an analytic approach to a paradigm, with its own theoretical statements, methods, and research findings.
>
> (Wellman, 2007)

In demonstrating this cross-pollination of ideas from social network analysis, we can understand how Wellman has proposed that networked individualism transcends the solidarity of traditional notions of community. However, it seems likely that the egocentric focus of this concept is derived from a personal networks tool employed in the field of social psychology, which developed the methods of social network analysis to investigate nets of social relationships (Wasserman & Faust, 1992). To describe this particular aspect, Wellman writes:

> Some network analysts study egocentric (or personal) networks, defined from the standpoints of egos (or focal individuals). Analysts typically use survey research to gather information about the networks' composition, […] structure, […] and contents. This is useful for studying far-flung communities, the provision of social support, and the mobilization of social capital.
>
> (Wellman, 2007)

We can see from this that the 'ego', when used in this sense, refers to the individual as a node in a network, but cannot be extrapolated to ideas of individualistic or selfish behaviours that the term egocentric usually connotes. These behaviours would theoretically lead directly to the discussion of social isolation.

However as Comunello (2012) articulates, the idea that the disconnection of the individual from traditional community formats and the egocentric focus of personal networks that characterise networked individualism do not lead to isolation, but instead are argued to give rise to new patterns of sociability. Thus the networked individual is not necessarily self-focused; however their way of experiencing community is derived from the individual pursuit of choice-based social relations in a mediated environment.

Wellman's discussion of networked individualism highlights that whilst personal community networks predated cyberspace, recent developments in ICTs have afforded their emergence as the dominant form of social organisation (Wellman, 2001b, p. 228). Comunello (2012) synthesises Wellman's viewpoint as situated in the transition of place-to-place networks to person-to-person and role-to-role connectivity in which the person becomes the portal (Wellman, 2001b). Contextually, this shift in the nature of social relationships has been facilitated by both mass transit and telecommunication systems. Within this technological and social shift, people connect in multiple, self-directed social networks rather than in communal groups (Wellman, 2001b), and in so doing move beyond the physical boundedness of community addressed in the early parts of this chapter. Further to this, Wellman and Boase (Wellman et al., 2003) argued that these fragmented, partial, heavily communicating social networks are based upon digitally mediated personalised ones. In their turn, Foth and Hearn (2007) argue that Wellman's notion of networked individualism describes the ambivalent nature inherent in any given person's egocentric yet still well-connected social interactions:

> Individuals take control of their personal portfolio of sociability and add, grow, connect, disconnect, merge and split with other nodes and social clusters as they see fit. The behaviour that governs these social relationships is driven by the individuals themselves and their personal needs and preferences. This constitutes a shift from the traditional sense of community as collective group behaviour.
>
> (Foth & Hearn, 2007, p. 750)

The networked individual shows that the boundaries of networked societies are permeable; Wellman describes the permeability that occurs through these interactions as 'with diverse others, connections switch between multiple networks, and hierarchies can be flatter and recursive' (Wellman et al., 2001, p. 227). This trend of personal portfolios of sociability goes hand in hand with the trend towards customisation and personalisation of the web experience. The implications for identity formation, meaning creation and social intimacy in this environment are that they can either be understood through the reconfiguration of emotional (dis)connection created by technological mediation or that re-theorisation of these experiences will demonstrate an alternative space in which communal formats do occur. This latter approach is the position of the book and reflects its agenda for developing the notion of community experiences as occurring within a social ecology discussed in the last section of this review.

From Wellman's perspective, the communal experience of identity construction, socialisation, exchange and support occurs within a technologically mediated ecosystem of partially attended or 'portfolio' relationships. In a succinct list, Comunello (2012) highlights the key features of these relationships as developed by Wellman (2001b) and later extrapolated by Wellman and Boase (2006):

1. Relationships are both local and long-distance;
2. Personal networks are sparsely knit but include densely knit groups;
3. Relationships are more easily formed and abandoned;
4. While homophily still exists, many relationships are with people from different social backgrounds;
5. Some social ties are strong, but many more are weak.

For the book, the implications of this framework for community experience are that both the local and the global context are embedded in an open social structure that also incorporates clusters of closed networks. This reflects the local-global intermingling identified in the literature on globalisation (Gille & Riain, 2002), and the associated concept of glocalisation (Robertson, 1995). Hampton (2001) integrates this trend in his discussion of the 'Netville' study by arguing that as computer-mediated communication moves into the home, there will be an increase in both local and global relations that brings about a 'glocalisation' of society. This connection in the literature between local-global relationships and the networked individual demonstrates that social connectivity is also related to the permeability of social boundaries and place that challenge traditional notions of community boundaries. In addition to this we see the theme of easy connect and disconnect that has been highlighted in virtual community theory as a characteristic of networked individualism. However the conclusion of social isolation which preoccupied researchers for a period of time (DiMaggio et al., 2001; Franzen, 2000), is not carried over in Wellman's idea due to the focus on the connective behaviours of the individual. In addition to this, these mediated and extended social ties also introduce the idea that the social composition of relationships is heterogeneous. This is the direct opposite of the community studies of the Chicago School in which community populations were socially homogeneous with shared values. It also is the opposite to literature on social structures organised by foci of activity, which argued that the resulting social composition of groups formed through a common interest was homophily (Feld, 1981, 1982, 1984). This transition of social composition from homogeneity to heterogeneity was first articulated in the early globalisation literature and attributed to the impact of ICTs (see Featherstone, Lash, & Robertson, 1995, p. 61 for a succinct discussion of this trend). This fluidity of boundaries created by ICTs and the transition from social homogeneity in a common interest group to social heterogeneity will be highlighted in the examination of the herpetological community. In this environment, the social portfolios of the networked individual are likely to be with diverse others who partially share values. This is also represented in the higher levels of latent social ties and weak social ties (acquaintances) of the networked individual. In the research literature on the impact of Internet-based, many-to-many communication platforms we see this profile of the building of latent social ties and weak social ties (Haythornthwaite, 2002, 2005; Williams & Copes, 2005).

Specific literature on mediated sociability is a separate yet related body of work that supports our understanding of the impact of ICTs on the ways social networks actually interact. A key concept from this field is the effect of modern, connect-from-anywhere computing, also referred to as pervasive or ubiquitous computing (Greenfield, 2006; Vetere, Howard, & Gibbs, 2005), on the mobility and accessibility of our social relations. This type of connectivity creates a situation whereby we are 'always on' (Hampton 2001, p. 29), that is a 24/7 access period characterised by constant social presence, or presence-in-absence (Green, 2002; Howard et al., 2006). Given the convergence (Schroeder, 2010; van Dijk, 2006) and multimedia interactivity of video, sound and textual communication channels within social relations (Heyer & Brereton, 2006), the public/private space of relationships is demonstrably changing (boyd, 2007a, 2008; Donath & boyd, 2004; Lange, 2007). The capacity for anonymity online and its resultant social effects were feared by dystopian theorists. However the discussion of online anonymity has moved beyond a fear-based reaction and into a deeper understanding of the benefits as well as the negative effects that online anonymity creates (see Barratt, 2011 for a contemporary perspective on online anonymity).

Given the function of the Internet in generating strong and weak social ties, and the embeddedness of ICTs in everyday social relations, Internet accessibility is of key importance and is discussed in the body of work on the impact of the digital divide proposed by Manuel Castells (2001). The presence of mediated sociability in everyday lives highlights the capacity for all people in a network to have access to ICTs. The United Nations has declared that Internet access is a human right (United Nations & Rue, 2011) however Castells (2001, p. 265) describes the digital divide as existing in the uneven development of Internet accessibility at the local, national and global level. Benitez (2006, p. 193) argues that different dimensions of the digital divide, such as knowledge and gender, can be influenced by the accessibility and quality of technological connectivity alongside the social appropriation of the Internet and ICTs. Further to this, digital literacy is proposed to be an important variable of access (Hargittai, 2005,

2007; Hargittai & Hinnant, 2006; Scardamalia, 2003). All of these factors stratify and alter the potential for people to engage with their social networks via ICTs and may exclude them from contemporary forms of community experience. The implication for this in the case study of the herpetological community is to understand whether differential access has the capacity to exclude members from the social capital of the network. The case study of the herpetological network will establish the access profile of participants to establish their capacity to engage in the social capital of the network and it will also look to the social appropriation of this ICT environment to see whether participants who are not fully engaged in the media ecology are excluded from the network.

Lastly, the network theory literature highlights the notion of the serendipity effect of 'known' strong- and weak-tie relations and the intermingling with anonymous others online. The non-linearity of social ties and network configurations in this social environment results in the potential for the form and frequency of flows between two points to have reverberations in unexpected paths far removed from those intended (Hargittai & Centeno, 2001). This relates to the classic notion of the 'six degrees of separation' that has its empirical basis in research on the small-world phenomenon which demonstrates that:

> the structure of a network can have dramatic implications for the collective dynamics of a system, whose connectivity the network represents. In particular, … large changes in dynamical behavior could be driven by even subtle modifications to the network structure – modifications that may be imperceptible to actors with only local knowledge of the network.
>
> (Watts, 2004, p. 246)

Kleinberg (2000a, 2000b) refined this idea of an all-connected network effect by arguing that social networks were not only searchable but also made 'small' (read 'more easily accessed', in the same sense that the world is becoming 'smaller' as a result of improving information technologies) through their links. He demonstrated that network structure is important not only locally, where an individual's neighbourhood provides them with information and resources, but also globally in that it enables them to navigate when searching for information or resources outside of their immediate locality (discussed in Watts 2004, p. 248).

3.5 Taking an Environmental Approach to the Study of Digital Community

To this point, we have seen that there is a diversity of approaches towards understanding community experience in the contemporary ICT environment, from virtual community to networked individualism. The limitations of virtual community were discussed in Chapter 2, Section 2.6 as applying the boundedness of place in traditional community studies to social spaces in the digital environment. As we have seen in the work of Comunello (2012), the patterns of social organisation in the digital environment are characterised more by social networks than community formats. Wellman's networked individualism points to the permeability of group structures by strong and weak social ties through portfolios of sociability. This problematises the use of place to define community experience and introduces the importance of interest groups in generating community experience in this environment. What we can understand from this is that community experience occurs within a local-global spatial context that incorporates both group clusters and online/offline networks of strong and weak social ties. Boundaries become permeable in this context but the experience of community continues to exist in the development of identity, the sharing of partial values and the gaining of support and social capital by the networked individual. In drawing on the notion of human ecology proposed by Robert Park, it is possible to move beyond the context of a single place and a single group to explore community as located in an environment that constitutes places, ICTs and flows of people. This section will discuss how the concept of a social ecology has been developed from the scholarly discourse on ICT environments to incorporate this in a contextual approach to social relations.

It is clear from the above discussion that networked sociability occurs in a mediating environment or media ecology (Pew, 2011) of online and offline social ties. The notion of virtual community has been demonstrated to be insufficient, at least on its own, to describe this environment and the idea of networked sociability has been added to the theoretical mix, as it were, to describe the types of interactions that do occur and the impact that ICTs have upon this interaction. This idea of discussing social relations as contained by an ecology of *mobile* social relations mediated by equally mobile technology is reminiscent of Park's ecological approach to offline neighbourhoods described above. In what can be interpreted as a relatively linear development, Nardi and O'Day (1999) focus on the information ecology inherent in a local environment, such as a library, which does not include the distance relations that Hampton's 'Netville' study pointed out as being a critical aspect of social action in our contemporary techno-milieu. The power of their idea is their use of 'ecology' as a metaphor/organising principle to describe a social form in continual change. As Foth and Hearn (2007, p. 756) argue, an ecology operates as a 'web of life' and a web is a network. This therefore ties the ecological approach firmly to the network approach. Foth and Hearn argued that a communicative ecology integrates the three dimensions of 'online and offline', 'global and local' and 'collective and networked' (2007, p. 751). Their definition of a communicative ecology operationalises the layers of infrastructure, people and content that circulate within the environment. Their three dimensions or layers are further defined thus:

> [1] A technological layer which consists of the devices and connecting media that enable communication and interaction. [2] A social layer which consists of people and social modes of organizing those people – which might include, for example, everything from informal social networks to more formal community associations, as well as commercial or legal entities .... [and 3] a discursive layer which is the content, that is, the ideas or themes that constitute the conversations and narratives of the ecology.
>
> (Foth and Hearn, 2007, p. 756)

These layers of a communicative ecology remain locally based or place-based entities that then focus upon the reach of the network outwards to the global while being geographically connected inwards. Whilst Foth and Hearn (2007) draw upon Wellman's personalised portfolios of sociability, the communicative ecology that they describe is the social networks of residents in three inner-city apartment buildings rather than an ecology based around the intersection of a range of socially linked portfolios that represent a non-place-based networked community. What they do achieve, however, is to provide the initial parameters of how to conceptualise a 'place' in which networked social interactions occur that combine online and offline interactions, people, organisations and content-oriented clusters.

Latham and Sassen (2005) propose a conception of the digital formation that enhances the notion of a communicative ecology and builds towards the idea of a social ecology. The distinction of the digital formation is that it is not tied to local place (online or off-) but retains a unique ecology. They propose that communication and information structures are human 'habitats' or ecologies with mediating cultures that are anchored in the social relations associated with public spheres, networks, organisations, and markets (2005, p. 8), but not tied firmly to them. The fluidity of a social form across space represented in this discussion decentralises the use of place as a defining boundary for group coherence. The key contribution of this concept to the social ecology construct is in its contrast to the pivotal use of place in the conceptualisation of an information ecology and a communicative ecology. In a digital formation, the coherence of the form is to be identified by the *configurations* of space, organisation and interaction (2005, p. 10). That is, this definition of form creates a social space that is technologically and socially tied, but not as situated. The scale of the digital formation is a defining key variable in this instance as it allows such forms to consist of non-state actors, cross-border processes and associated changes in the scope, exclusivity and competence of state authority over its territory (2005, p. 34). This idea matches the notions of scalability in network theory (Barabasi & Albert, 1999) and theories of globalisation (Sassen, 2008; Swyngedouw, 2004). Latham and Sassen argue that digital networks strengthen the multi-scalar character of many social processes, particularly processes that do not fit into nested hierarchies (2005, p. 23). Their 'digital formations' fit comfortably with Wellman's 'networked individualism' and 'portfolios of sociability' which he argues are flattened and recursive social structures. This demonstrates that Wellman's ideas do not constitute hierarchically nested concepts either. In terms of how digital formations relate to the notion of community, Latham and Sassen argue that:

> Community, especially as thought about in electronic terms, is a complicated matter, but we take it to mean that configurations of space, organization, and interaction sustain a common identity around shared goals and reciprocal relations among participants, and that such identity, goals, and reciprocity are an important and substantive aspect each of participant's life, professional or personal.
>
> (Latham and Sassen, 2005, p. 13)

In this way, we can see that it is the multi-scalar nature of mediated reciprocity that underlies the community experience of identity and values as established by the Chicago School theorists. These ecological approaches to defining social form point to the changing environment in which community experience occurs and the requirement for the re-theorisation of community experience within the digitally mediated, global context.

The line from the earliest, place-based theorisations of community attributable to the Chicago School, through to the range of endeavours seeking to explain today's on- and offline techno-cultural environments, is discontinuous. Nonetheless, drawing on 'ecology' as a connecting thread or recurrent theme, as above, such a line can be drawn.

Understandings of contemporary community are enhanced not through abandoning one theory in favour of the next, but through the consideration of related bodies of work in light of one another. This approach incorporates enduring aspects of preceding theories into current formulations. The idea of a communicative ecology developed by Foth and Hearn extends the ecological approach of the Chicago School into the digital environment. This extension highlights the blurring of the boundary between online and offline life, and suggests not the disappearance of community but its reinvention.

3.6 Conclusion

It is the argument of this book is that the herper community is best understood through an ecological perspective, in which the community occupies a socio-technical niche that can be characterised through its environmental imprint. In particular, this chapter has demonstrated the relevance of investigating digital community through multimodal forms of social interaction that blurs the distinction between the online and offline worlds. The review of the literature in this chapter has suggested that key components of contemporary community experiences include an understanding of the social impact and use of an ICT environment through an investigation of mediated sociability. In terms of research methodology, this can be articulated through the ICT use patterns of the networked individual within the interest network, in association with their capacity to access this environment through digital literacy skills and Internet connectivity (see Chapter 7 for the presentation of this approach within the case study). In terms of identifying the cohesive aspects of digital community through research methods, constructs of networked social capital, organisational participation, participants' networks of strong and weak social ties and the associated local and global reach of these ties will be investigated through the case study approach (see Chapter 10). Drawing from the trends of social diversity online and the social heterogeneity of populations identified in the globalisation literature, the social composition of the herper community will be explored in Chapter 8 to integrate the discussion of how social diversity can be related to notions of social cohesion through a real world example. This trend in particular contradicts traditional notions of community experience that argue for shared values and social homogeneity as binding forces. The discussion of boundaries to describe the form of digital community is problematised by the downgrading of place as a key identifier of social space articulated in the literature. The notion of social ecology will draw upon the idea of an open social structure articulated in Wellman's development of the networked individual concept and explore group boundary construction through the mediating culture and discursive content of the herpetological network as proposed by Foth and Hearn (2007) and Latham and Sassen (2005). See Chapter 9 for how the discussion of community boundaries, as they are conceptualised here, is achieved within a real world data set. The ideas presented in this chapter will be unpacked and operationalised in the following Chapter (Chapter 4) to demonstrate for the research practitioner how a conceptual discussion of digital community is translated into a research methodology.

Chapter 4
A Methodological Approach for Researching Digital Community

4.1 Introduction

In this chapter I explore how the idea of a social ecology can be operationalised into a resilient research methodology and constellation of methods for data collection and analysis. In Section 4.2, I begin with a discussion of the metaphors of social form, as a way to situate the methodological approach that will be taken in this book. Section 4.3 presents the argument for taking an ecological approach and outlines how this transforms the methodological assumptions of community research into research questions. Essentially, this section argues that positioning these elements as the end product, rather than the starting point of research, provides a pragmatic foundation for researching open social structures. Flipping the traditional input knowledge of community studies to output knowledge also allows us to collapse the dualisms identified in Chapter 2 that have emerged within the conceptual approaches and their associated methods. Section 4.4 makes the connection between the conceptual approach behind the research methodology to the types of data that were collected within the herper community case study.

When seeking the chimera of community, particularly digital community, one would be forgiven for thinking of it as a mirage that disappears upon close inspection. Consequently, seeking an assemblage of methods that can capture it appears counterintuitive to the nature of open social structures that episodically coalesce rather than consistently 'exist', waiting for the researcher's gaze. This mirage effect is a reoccurring narrative for explorers of new frontiers, setting their compasses only to find that their intended destination has disappeared. I think the metaphor is apt in the case of social research. I often talk about designing methodology in the way that explorers of times past would prepare for adventuring into unknown oceans. I think of it as preparing a ship, with each element contributing to a water tight and resilient vessel that has the capacity to sail the research into the unknown *and* make it back … with intelligible data. This entails a contextual approach that combines knowledge of the social environment with observable patterns of social action (also referred to as social practices), a hallmark approach of the Chicago School tradition (Abbott, 1997, p. 1161). The network motifs threading though the sociology of technology can also be employed to locate a theoretical and methodologically connective space through which to investigate community experience. Consequently, this approach blends the findings of contemporary Internet research and user-based studies with the theoretical body of community studies, albeit with the contemporary modification in which the social ecology is constituted through open social structures and mediated sociability.

4.2 Metaphors of Social Form

This section presents a potted discussion of influential understandings of social structure and agency available within the cannon of sociological thinking. The intention behind this plain language approach is to assist the research practitioner in situating and deciding which ideas and data collection techniques are most likely to work at a conceptual level, as well as at a practical level, as effective tools through which to collect data across the open social structures of a digital community. The discussion of existing metaphors of social form here is unlikely to be comprehensive. What it will provide is a range of thought tools and directions, while identifying some of system thinking's well-charted potholes and loopholes. As has been argued through the review of the literature, the most effective approach towards identifying and defining community in the digital age is to seek its imprint or environmental niche within a socio-technical landscape that is dynamic and fluid. Contrarily, the metaphor for social form that this discussion will lead to is somewhat amorphous. Because of this, our lens will put structure-agency considerations out of focus and bring into focus the environmental imprint of a community. Through the change of focus, the research practitioner can disengage with some of the philosophical knots behind structure-agency thinking.

When considering the structural mechanics of social order and its associated patterns of social organisation, a lasting metaphor has been society as an organism (cf. Spencer, 1876). Conceptually, the social organism is constituted through the sum of its parts, with all parts having a specific role to play (Parsons, 1951). In structural functionalism thinking, which this is, the individual actor has little social mobility and is conceptualised through roles and social norms. Within this model, the social system is ordered and rationalised to such a degree that it cannot possibly hope to reflect the messiness of social reality. This way of thinking does not overlay into the digital environment well, particularly when considering online user-generated cultures.

Another way of considering social order was to consider it as stratified through class structures and social status, with power accumulated amongst a small set of elites at the top. A variety of thinkers, including Marx and Weber, looked at social stratification and class structures as the divisive lines of social order; both imagining the individual actor with little social mobility and a system in which social structures reinforced themselves through a trickle down hierarchy of decreasing social access to wealth, status, power and the means of production (ownership). In considering Bourdieu's (1992) ideas of habitus, power and fields or Giddens' (1984) structuration theory as an explanation of social order, Fligstein & McAdam (2011) argue that there is limited conceptualisation of adaptive structures, social change and collective action in these models. This critique also applies to concepts of social order that over emphasise social structures and attribute very little in terms of the power dynamics to social agency through collective action.

The exception for social change in these reproducing or static systems thinking being through revolution, as seen in the writing of Marx, and the destruction of the existing power structures and institutional formats. The 'destruction' hypothesis being evident through the dystopian literature on the social impact of the Internet discussed in the literature review. A common connection made is the idea being that social order is related to social stability and achieved through the enactment of social norms. Disorder, a proxy for change, is related to social instability and involves the breaking of social norms. This invokes the need for social regulation and the practice of forms of social ostracism and isolation, such as incarceration. The relationship between system order and disorder is often conceptualised through notions of balance or equilibrium (cf. Durkheim, 1966). Given the dynamic nature of the online environment and the perforation of nation-states by globalisation and the Internet, thinking in flows and local-global dynamics that characterise these contemporary trends does not overlay natively these metaphors of social form. I would argue that these ideas do not contain the digital in their DNA and may limit the scope through which the researcher can imagine the form and environment of digital community.

Within these macro ideas of social structure, mid-level influences upon patterns of social organisation are usually thought of in terms of hierarchies of power expressed through organisations and institutions. The nation-state is usually considered a key social structure that is geographic, regulatory and political, with individuals considered citizens, voters and community members. Other collective actors within the nation-state through which power and influence is pooled include organisations, institutions for education and health and commercial ventures that are local, regional and transnational. Within the community context, there is the imagined community of the nation-state, the neighbourhood and subcultures that are likely to be socially marginal and culturally specific. Within these metaphors of social form, the individual actor is defined through their community affiliation, geography, social status, aspirations and consumption profile. As a community member they are considered through grouping units such as family, as a fan, engaged through a topic-of-interest, or divided into amateurs and professionals. For social movements, which are not as cohesive and continuous as communities, the individual actor is thought of as an activist and has the capacity to be both a local and global actor. This metaphor of social form is situated both within and beyond the nation-state, with historical roots in the union movements. In the commercial and consumption context, the individual is conceptualised through a role basis such as an employer or employee or as a consumer/prosumer or entrepreneur. While these types of social form and role attribution are proposed to enhance a sense of security and stability, reduce risks and provide collective identity, there remains little agency, mobility and choice for the individual actor. Using these thought tools tends to feed into digital dualism at a conceptual and methodological level and may reduce the impact of qualitative data, the provision of voice to a community, in the analysis.

While systems thinking went out of vogue in the onslaught of postmodernist critique, contemporary ideas on how a social system is constituted persist through a renewed interest in the digital. The reconfiguration of social organisation and emerging tools for the analysis of digital trace data have prompted renewed thinking into collective behaviour, as this book is witness to. The field of science and technology studies (STS) has recently proliferated with ideas of assemblages, particularly using this idea to imagine data assemblages from social media (Gerlitz & Lury, 2014), assemblages of health (Duff, 2014) or surveillance assemblages (Haggerty & Ericson, 2000). The core-periphery concept is commonly used as a metaphor of form in this context, particularly through data visualisation practices. In a commonly associated trend, Big Data analysis has strong resonance with the notion of assemblages in terms of how to recognise a coalescence of social form on a moment-by-moment or 'slice in time' basis. Uprichard (2012) refers to this as the plastic present, which should suggest to the community scholar that these ideas may not map well over the historical context and longitudinal nature that usually characterises community structures. Consequently, while the notion of an assemblage may map well over emergent digital structures, it may not capture more long-term patterns of social continuity when thinking about mechanisms of cohesion within digital community.

Within the view that social life as dominated by complex webs, patterns of social organisation derived from thinking about social systems as emergent can also be found within the intersection of organisational and social movement theory. Fligstein and McAdam (2011) posit social process as characterised through strategic action fields. They define these as:

> [. . .] a meso-level social order where actors (who can be individual or collective) interact with knowledge of one another under a set of common understandings about the purposes of the field, the relationships in the field (including who has power and why), and the field's rules.
>
> (Fligstein & McAdam, 2011, p. 3)

For Fligstein and McAdam, this concept speaks to the slice of social order through which collective strategic action is enacted, with a focus on the mechanism of social change. They view agency as both individual and collective, with each strategic action field (SAF) being constituted by and constituting SAFs, like a series of Russian dolls. While resonant with Bourdieu's concepts of habitus, capital and fields as an explanation of social order, they argue that the idea of SAFs is that they focus upon emergence, stability and transformation, rather than the replication of existing social structures.

Nascent research using Big Data and social media analysis has begun drawing on field theory (Fligstein & McAdam, 2012) as a way to imagine collective action recognisable within the analysis and visualisation of digital trace data (Ackland, O'Neil, & Pérez, 2014). With all fields viewed as embedded in other fields, the self-replication inherent to this idea feels rather 'flat' and should make the reader wonder about the container or macro theory through which this occurs. As Martin (2003, p. 12) highlights, field theory never makes explanation reach *outside* the field and insight stops at the constitution of the field. For this reason, Martin argues that field analysis does not develop a fully constituted metaphor of social form. He argues that while field theory may stress the self-organisation of the system, it does not require that the system be understood in contradistinction to an environment. In this case, if the 'container' of fields is considered to be the globe of the earth, then it evokes an image of shifting sands that underplay, rather than allow for, the stickiness of the environment to hold and articulate power and social structure through social action. These ideas have begun to be addressed from within the field of social network analysis, which has historically struggled to articulate the influence of social structure. Research using the idea of social-ecological systems (Anderies et al., 2012) provides for the influence of the environment upon social actors. This computational and algorithmic enactment of these ideas through SNA analytical tools suggests that field theory may develop further discussions and ideas in this direction in the future should it continue to be used to analyse and interpret social media trends within Big Data.

In a similar, although differently derived, set of metaphors to field theory, the self-replicating or self-organising social system can also be found in ideas memetic or viral process that are captured through the use of bubbles (Francisco, 2010; D. Garcia, 2011) and rhizomes (cf. Broadfoot, Munshi, & Nelson-Marsh, 2010) as metaphors of social organisation. An alternative theoretical framework that harnesses these emergent, viral and episodic properties into a notion of contemporary social form can be found in complexity theory (cf. Tilly, 2004). Derived from disciplines such as ecology, computer science and mathematics and rooted in cybernetic thinking, this idea is native to the function and process of the digital environment. Cham and Johnson (2007) note the adoption of this concept by social scientists in their exploration of the collective behaviours of complex systems, using these ideas to define social systems specifically as adaptive. The work on the self-organising and emergent properties of cyber protests is an example of the use of complexity theory within social thinking (Fuchs, 2006). Walby (2007) provides an insightful analysis of complexity theory(ies) and how they intersect with social theory. She highlights how complexity thinking, while not unified, transcends the limitations of much traditional thinking on social systems that relied on notions of hierarchies and nested systems:

> The distinction between system and environment is disarmingly simple, but it is key to a series of revisions that enable greater flexibility in the conceptualization of systems. It enables the notion that each system takes all other systems as its environment (Bertalanffy, 1968). This makes it possible to go beyond the old notion that the parts of a system make up the whole. Instead, each social system (whether economy, polity, violence nexus, or civil society) takes all other systems as its environment. Likewise each set of social relations (e.g. gender, ethnicity, class) is a system, taking all others as its environment.
>
> This distinction between a system and its environment does not entail a presumption of hierarchy between inter-connected phenomena; rather hierarchy is a special case of differentiated systems. This makes for a more flexible conceptualization, providing the conceptual possibility to avoid rigidities such as that of 'part and whole' (Parsons, 1951) and of 'base- superstructure' (Marx, 1967), as well as the ambiguities of 'relative autonomy' (Althusser, 1971). These involve some kind of hierarchical relationship between nested sub-parts of a system.
>
> (Walby, 2007, p. 458)

As observed by Walby above, social systems are relational to their environment, rather than nested subsets. In this case, the social environment of a digital community is not 'sub' to its broader cultural context but deeply interwoven through the extension of tendrils across porous external boundaries. Social form in this context is largely driven through agency (through social networks), rather than ordered through the tidy boxes of organisations and institutions that hierarchical thinking engenders. Consequently, we can think of complexity theory as having the capacity to capture social change through reflecting dynamic mechanisms of social cohesion; without positing social revolution or systemic/ social decay. Complexity thinking is a useful thought tool, but does tend to under emphasise the power dynamics enacted by state actors and institutions. Ideas conceptualising patterns of social organisation within this context include swarms, mobs and flows, which are fundamentally episodic in nature, but are most commonly expressed through the notion of open social structures.

The environmental approach proposed within this book, seeks to identify emergent form through its structural nature as network configured and relational. This idea incorporates a sense of historical context alongside fluid transnational structures that form ecologies that incorporate the built environment (physical and virtual), the interlacing of information communication technologies to build local-global connections and the networked individual as an agent that resolves structural tensions and is characterised by choice and partial participation. The individual agent in this context has both the capacity for mobility and choice, alongside being situated in social structures that tend to be dynamic and flexible. In developing a balanced methodology that accepts both the impact of structure and agency upon a community, the environmental approach tends to allow for the strengths of each method by utilising the quantitative practice of pattern recognition alongside the qualitative practice of presenting a community voice and individual perspectives.

This section considers data collection methods compatible with an environmental understanding of community to provide a sense of 'forward compatibility' of the social ecology approach within the ever-evolving landscape of digital research methods. When considering the types of data that can be used to illustrate the social environment created through the impact of social structure, and thus providing social context for the community, there are several existing and potential data sets that can be drawn upon. Geo-demographic data provides a socio-spatial understanding of consumption patterns at the local (postcode), regional, national and increasingly at the global level. This data tends to serve as a benchmark for the consumption, behavioural and social network profiles of consumers by products, service use and companies. This type of data is complimentary to population comparisons provided by national census data and perhaps more nuanced in some ways as it is based upon digital trace data rather than survey responses. Organisational data and institutional databases are available that tend to provide information on legal/regulatory influences, health profiles and civic engagement by individuals. These formal sources of socially contextual and structured information can be counterbalanced by the passively collected, and less easily interpretable, digital footprints left by 'users' across the ICT environment and social media. This includes digital trace data analysis by software platform (i.e. twitter), teleco customer databases and use patterns, analysis of the network structure of hyperlinks, the relational information through 'friends' on social networking sites, content analytics and self-tracking practices. In addition to this, the researcher may consider stepping further into the environmental domain and consider visual and sensory scapes that illustrate social context through passive observational data collected through CCTV/spatial monitoring and social surveillance by governments and corporations. These data collection options are new and evolving and require the researcher to experimentally develop an understanding of the strengths and limitations of these data sets within research practice. The risk here in generating interpretable and theoretically founded research insight may be great, however the insights and opportunities provided by these new and evolving data sources and visualisation techniques requires practitioners to embrace and understand them.

4.3 The Relationship between the Conceptual Approach and Data Collection

As is illustrated in the previous section, the permutations of what data to collect and methods available to articulate key research concepts appear without end. However, given the connection that the literature review in Chapters 2 and 3 have established with the early Chicago School and the social ecology approach, these choices can be directed through a brief detour back into what Sampson (2002) considers to be the seven themes of the Chicago School. Sampson argues that these themes include:

> (1) A relentless focus on context (especially place); (2) a focus on properties of communities and cities as social systems; (3) a relational concern with variability in forms of social organization as opposed to population attributes (or composition); (4) continual attention to neighborhood change and spatial dynamics (time and space); (5) an eclectic style of data collection that relies on multiple methods but that always connects to some form of observation; (6) a concern for public affairs and the improvement of community life; and (7) an integrating theme of *theoretically interpretive empirical research.*
>
> (Sampson, 2002, p. 217)

These themes reinforce the approach of triangulation of research methods and the selection of socially contextual and eclectic styles of data collection. The concept of digital formations referred to in the literature review provides the sense of approaching a group as a social system, in this case an open one that is based upon a network structure. In keeping with theme three, the relational concern of the case study research is highlighted in its alignment with the definition of community proposed by Wellman and the focus upon social networks. Synchronous and asynchronous time and the embedding of virtual interactions into everyday life (the merging of physical and virtual space) are positioned in this book as the core of mediated social interaction and cohesion. This approach speaks to theme four and influences the herper community case study method choice of participant observation, which allows for immersion in these community dynamics over time. The case study research and methodology behind this approach contains no inherent agenda for the improvement of community life, however it is intended to provide contemporary knowledge on how community is experienced. This approach benchmarks the location and format of contemporary community experience for the consideration of researchers and policy makers and increases the possibility of accurate forecasting of social trends.

The research questions and modes of data collection that underpinned the case study are theoretically directed by engagement with the literature on community and ICT use. The analytical framework that directs the research design is based on the understanding of contemporary community experience occurring in a social ecology, as we have seen from the literature review. The research question and design used for the case study attempts to identify this ecology without prior assumptions of what constitutes this social space. The reason for this is that, without asking, we do not know where people go, what ICTs and media platforms they use, why they go there, who they meet and what kind of social experience this generates. Our basic understandings for defining concrete parameters do not sit well with the contemporary social patterns of mobile spaces and virtual interaction that are described as flows by John Urry (2000) and the space of flows by Manuel Castells (1996). We do not know how to define these parameters because social experience is moving into new environments. Scholars are still developing insight and conceptual tools to understand what effects this has on our use of place and our ways of seeking support and cultivating a sense of belonging and identity.

The challenge offered by Sampson (2002) is for scholars to ask ourselves what we mean when we use the terminology of community studies.

> And *so* it is that debates on social capital and civic society tend to romanticize the idea of community rather than pose hard questions subject to empirical scrutiny. What do we mean by community? Does the concept refer to geographic locales, such as neighborhoods, or to common membership in non place-based groups? Does it mean shared values and deep commitments, and if *so,* to what? What does community 'supply' that makes it *so* in demand?
>
> (Sampson, 2002, p. 215)

In the contemporary social context described in the literature review, these assumptions of community experience are repositioned as questions in order to encompass the reconfiguring of social space and organisation that the Internet has facilitated. The theoretical connection, methods and the consequent findings of this case study are both novel and derivative in how they have been combined. The key point is that this combined approach has not been employed in the context of a globally distributed and technologically mediated interest network. The reason for this being that we have lacked connections between a higher-level theory of social organisation such as Castells' (1996) 'Network Society' and Latham and Sassen's (2005) 'Digital Formations' with middle-range theories

(Merton, 1948) such as Wellman's (Rainie & Wellman, 2012; Wellman, 2001b; Wellman et al., 2003) 'Networked Individualism', all of which are abstract ideas that can be referred to as 'back-end theories'. This is in contrast to the fast and prolific development of Internet research and its particular focus upon mediated sociability and the social effects of the new media environment that were minimally tethered to these theories. This field of ideas that are more applied and practical explorations of social behaviour has been termed 'front-end' research in the review. This division of ideas into back-end and front-end pragmatically demonstrates the conceptual layers behind the construct of a social ecology from abstract to practical application. In addition to this previous lack of linking between abstract and applied concepts, methods and findings, another reason for the disconnection has been the low levels of interdisciplinary dialogue between these fields of research. For this reason, the research design and literature review constitutes for the reader an initial stage of making links and triangulating methods as a way to begin this dialogue within the research itself.

Consequently, the idea of this research started without boundaries and fairly intuitively. I began my exposure to people with interests in herpetology before I was able to articulate what it was that was unique in what I was seeing and how it could be conceptualised within a research framework. The options in the diverse body of literature for how to approach the notion of a social ecology of this population were overwhelming and the need to set parameters was clear. But which parameters were going to allow me to investigate the experience of community in a mediated, open social system without first defining who the population was, where they were located, what their boundaries were and the organisations and forms for how they cohered? I was stumped at the very beginning. Most research methods require these parameters to be set by the researcher. But of this group, I could not say what they were without having done the research. This contradiction between the practice of defining boundaries for methodological purposes and the fluid and at times invisible nature of these boundaries in everyday life made me question the assumptions upon which these sampling criteria rest.

In terms of practical concerns, setting these parameters is related to the representative nature of the findings, the relevance of these findings to the population under study and the provision of an exclusion criterion. Drawn from the literature, the terms to approach this containment were environment, technological architecture, social networks, patterns of mediated sociability, social capital and community. Whilst these conceptual tools can speak to specific and measurable behaviours, they also needed to connect with socially amorphous concepts such as 'open social framework' and 'online anonymity' in which, as described in the literature review, boundaries are permeable and individual agents invisible. This transition in sociological focus from closed to open systems is highlighted by the changing theoretical construction of social clustering ideas discussed in contemporary literature (Latour, 2005; Touraine, 2003a, 2003b). The social fluidity created by an open social system and online anonymity can be seen as a challenge to setting the boundaries for research methods, but it can also be seen as an asset.

To define a community by its physical place or homogeneous population is to miss the complexity of what is happening to our online social environments. To employ a research design and methodology that is not sensitive to this is to miss an opportunity to explore and develop conceptual tools that will link us in to new frontiers of social analysis whilst retaining the deep knowledge and insights of established theoretical frameworks and research. In light of this, the research questions that were used to direct the case study research are parsed to the assumptions of any community study – that a group of people in a single location with shared values and social homogeneity can be described as a community. In this case of the case study research, these assumptions become the overt questions that inquire about the place, population composition, boundaries and existence of cohesion amongst a cluster of people who are spatially distributed and therefore likely to be socially diverse. The foci of activity group that was used as a case study to explore these questions of place, population composition, boundaries and existence of cohesion in a social ecology is the community of people with herpetological interests. This is a network of people who share a common interest in reptiles and amphibians. At this stage of the research story, what we know about these people is that they share a few common characteristics that we can identify them by, namely their interests in reptiles and amphibians and the field of herpetology. We do not know who they are, where they are, where they go and what they get from sharing their interests with others. From my pre-existing knowledge about this population, it was clear that they are active in online spaces and physical spaces. Having this knowledge and access to key informants in this network was pivotal in the research design and selection of a research methodology.

Taking up Sampson's challenge, the research question that directed the herper community case study is: How can we locate community experience in the contemporary environment of digital mediation and global distribution of social networks? Through this question, we explore a case study of a non-ideal community that is digitally mediated and globally distributed. The research question is not primarily concerned with the benefits of community participation as such, but seeks to locate community experience in the contemporary social environment. This direction is a response to literature suggesting the loss of community. The position of this book is not about loss but about the capacity for change and resilience that the open social structures of digital community bring. It builds upon the long history of community studies and contemporary Internet research to understand and identify this reconfiguration of community experience.

The approach of social ecology positions community structures as having reconfigured in the changing social environment. It begins with the assumption that we are investigating a mobile social form rather than a fixed one. Consequently, the research questions that drive the design and methodology deployed for the case study is an approach that it seeks to locate the environment of social engagement, and thus its form, that is both emergent and dynamic. Through the review we have seen that the contemporary social environment is less visible, but no less powerful in how it draws clusters of people together and provides for them the experience of community.

In this section, I introduce the conceptual construct used to direct the research methodology as it is illustrated in Figure 4.1 below. Turning back to the work of Foth and collaborators on communicative ecologies (Foth & Hearn, 2007; Klaebe, Adkins, Foth, & Hearn, 2009) and Sassen and collaborators on digital formations (Latham & Sassen, 2005; Sassen, 2000, 2001, 2002, 2007); as a collective body of work, they present an environmental discussion of community architecture and form through three layers: these layers are the technological layer, the social layer and the mediating culture. I argue that the use of these conceptual sorting tools for organising data collection and analysis provides an imprint of the community that has the capacity to rearticulate form and respond to their contemporary format as open social structures that are dynamic, digital and mobile. Through the analysis of the case study data, I further refined the definitions of these layers from the ideas presented in Chapter 2. For the technological layer, I broadened this definition to encompass discussions of technology use, place and the built environment (Indergaard & McInerney, 1998). This approach aligns with the Chicago school's understandings of the influence of roads and communication networks upon the location of communities. From some preliminary ideas shared by Indergaard and McInerney (1998) we can understand the built environment to be digitally augmented yet strategically anchored in urban and social structure. While the technological layer encompasses architectural structures, such buildings, as the housing of social space, it also considers flows through and beyond physical space through infrastructural systems such as communication and transportation. In doing so, it extends the notion of a built space through the coded space or code/space of the Internet (cf. Dodge & Kitchin 2004, 2009 Kitchin & Dodge 2011) to argue that the virtual environment or digital space is also a built environment. While this is apparent through the use of code and algorithms to construct virtual space, it remains a connection that is important to make overt in a methods discussion of place and the environmental niche of a digital community. As presented in Figure 4.1 below, the data collection methods aligned to this layer include surveys (statistical measures and social network data), digital trace data or 'Big Data' analysis, and qualitative interviews. This data also feeds back into the four domains of community that need to be articulated through the data; that of place (the where), social composition (the who), boundaries (where it stops, starts and polarises) and social cohesion (how it sticks together). A further discussion of how this is achieved within each layer is offered in the sections below.

As indicated through the diagram, the overall idea of a community structure that directs this research is derived from Feld's concept of the foci of activity group (Feld, 1981; Feld & Carter, 1998). This conceptualisation of community translates effectively into digitally augmented social structures and is a relational notion derived from the field of social network analysis. Digital communities are often topic focused, given the indexing and database nature of the information environment (cf. Bowker & Star, 1999), making them an appropriate overlay of models. With the layer discussing technology, place and the built environment discussed above, we can now move on to the left side of the diagram and consider what data and methods constitute the social layer of a community. The social layer of the community, as argued by both Foth et al. and Sassen et al., is characterised by research methods and data used to present patterns of social organisation. As such, while I do not extend upon this definition, the research practice of the case study made clear the kinds of data that can speak to this. Data sources of patterns of social organisation can include census data for population profiling, as an example; data derived from established survey measures that indicate population patterns; and social network data that presents configurations of relationships. Because this layer connects the demographics and configurations of sociality and connection within the network, it can also draw upon wider population data and Big Data to provide the social context of the community as it compares to broader populations. This assists the researcher to articulate what is both unique and mundane to the nature of the particular community under study. It also provides the benchmarks needed to articulate an understanding of the foci of activity group as compared to other similar communities.

The mediating culture of the community can be observed most effectively through ethnographic techniques suited to bringing out the community voice and translate the context of community values that seem foreign to a wider audience. This often involves thick description in terms of field notes taken during participant observation and qualitative interviewing techniques such as unstructured interviewing or more structured approaches taken through focus groups. This aspect of research engages most deeply with the community itself and is subject to the most rigorous regulation through research ethics. This is because the impact of the research must be considered both upon the research population and the researcher. Research ethics ask the researcher to weigh up the social impacts of doing the study with its anticipated benefits for the population under study and to wider society. While this rigour may seem to impede the pace of the research process through the additional scrutiny and evaluation, it is a crucial journey for the researcher in ensuring the validity and contribution of their work.

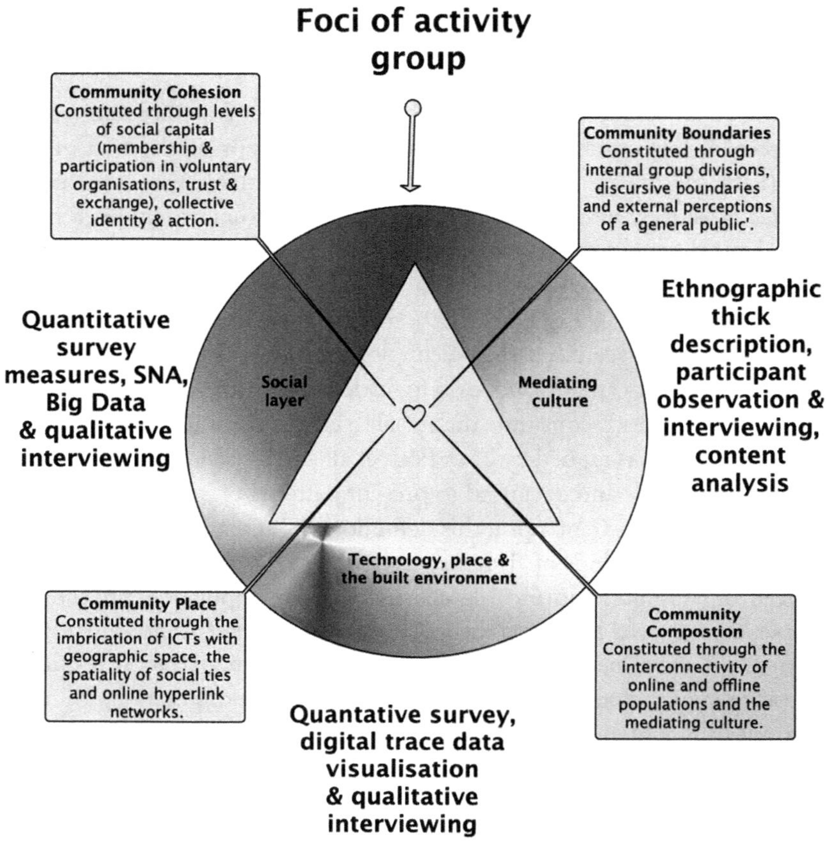

Figure 4.1 The conceptual model directing data collection

The research literature suggests that the types of information important to conceptualising an open or unbounded social form were the exploration of strong and weak social ties, social capital, trust and reciprocity, digital literacy, digital access and social personality, boundaries and online anonymity. The survey questions addressing these topics covered all the connective aspects of social behaviour in the network, with the answers providing the social form of the network. As with any social survey, these needed to be combined with socio-economic demographics in order to demonstrate the social heterogeneity and composition of the group. Contextual information on the type of community experience the person had, why they were involved, duration and their commitment levels over the time they were involved and the types of animals they were interested in was collected. What I understood from the fieldwork and the notion of portfolios of sociability was that these questions needed to be made specific to the herpetological experience. Participants were members of multiple networks, such as conservation networks and academic networks rather than being embedded solely in the herpetological network. This social behaviour is theoretically encapsulated in the idea of portfolios of sociability which argues that we merge and split with other social clusters as we see fit (Foth & Hearn, 2007, p. 750) rather than being entirely immersed in any one network. The following sections develop our understanding of the concepts, methods and the types of data collected used within the case study and makes overt the links between the data collected and the logic used to illustrate the four domains of community characterisation.

4.3.1 Community Place

This question of the place of a community seeks to locate the social space of the community by understanding that place is a multimodal social space that is configured through networks of social relations, physical infrastructure and technological mediation. In this way we begin again with the assumption that the space of the community is somewhat mobile, and blurs the distinction between the online and offline environments. Consequently, the 'place' of a network emerges from social interactions and the environment of technological interconnection. This is where the intersection of place with the social layer and a technological layer within a community occurs. What this question does not do is to assume that any one location, physical or virtual, is the place of this community. It is the interconnections between locations (both physical and virtual) that provides us with the 'place' or locations of social interaction and exchange that forms the bedrock of community experience.

Within the case study, community place is articulated by the technological layer, addressing technology, place and the built environment, through the following types of data collection and analysis. Quantitative data on ICT use patterns were collected to illustrate the communication channels through which community members intersected. This includes data collected about skill levels, access points, mode and regularity of interaction with others within the community through in person interaction and mediated interaction over telephone, email and by internet mediated connections that included VoIp through Skype, instant messaging and forum engagement. A hyperlink map of websites that survey respondents submitted provides a sense of the space of the community in the online environment. The social layer was articulated the geographic spatiality of the social networks survey respondents had. This was determined through the numbers of community members survey respondents engaged with as viewed through distance, in terms of travel time, and location, in terms of local, regional, national, international or online, that a participants social network was reached. The mediating culture and its relationship to community place was articulated through the ethnographic data, particularly in participants' descriptions of the influence of physical and virtual locations upon their activities, the spatiality of their networks and the impact of the online environment upon their patterns of community engagement.

4.3.2 Community Composition

In asking about the population composition of the network, this question allows for the possibility that social heterogeneity may be the key characteristic here. As observed in the review, traditionally community populations were assumed to be socially homogeneous through their shared values, life experiences and location within a neighbourhood. As discussed in the literature review, scholarly research on the social effect of Internet use has shown an increase in the social diversity of digitally-mediated groups. This finding is also evident in globalisation research that identifies the increase of social heterogeneity and the permeability of social boundaries through international networks, global markets, international data flows and mass communication through the Internet and other media.

Essentially, a discussion of community composition within the case study draws upon existing quantitative information characterising online and offline populations, and thick, qualitative description of the population composition drawn from comparative communities. Data collected in these areas speaks to the social layer of the community, including survey data collection of respondent demographics, cross-sectioned by their technology use profile. This indicates the imbrication of data collected and insights that occurs between the layers. The mediating culture draws upon ethnographic data collected by participant observation and interviewing to present a sense of how social diversity, rather than homogeneity characterises the herper community experience. Articulations within technology, place and the built environment inform upon population composition through a qualitative description of the networked individual and how they enact their portfolio of participation, illustrated through the quantitative survey data. The social profile of community members as networked individuals articulates in endogenous understanding of community composition. The second half of this book presents the data collected from the case study population according to its articulations of community place (Chapter 6), social composition (Chapter 7), community boundaries (Chapter 8) and mechanisms of community cohesion (Chapter 9). Within each chapter, the data collection approach directed by the methodology will demonstrate how the layers provide insight into the community form and function for each of the four domains.

4.3.3 Community Boundaries

In asking about the boundaries of this network, this question allows for the possibility that community boundaries are permeable and set within the context of networked individualism. To investigate this question, we will need to understand how social form emerges within open social structures that are based upon social networks. Seemingly, these social networks have no actual edges; however group behaviour may have dealt with this openness through its own forms of closure and clustering. With the increasing permeability of external group boundaries, it appears necessary to look at other boundary dynamics to identify groups of people.

A key idea to the identification of a social ecology, which is by default externally permeable through its open social structure, is the pivotal nature of internal group boundaries. Abbott (1995) refers to internal group boundaries as proto-boundaries. He argues that these internal divisions give rise to the form of the group. Because of this, a community, which is in effect an invisible social assemblage, can be identified through its internal divisions. According to Abbott:

> … we should start with boundaries and investigate how people create entities by linking those boundaries into units. We should not look for boundaries of things but for things of boundaries.
>
> (Abbott, 1995, p. 857)

Abbott's notion of proto-boundaries as internal boundaries which define a group is drawn from the idea of interactional fields used by Chicago School scholars (Abbott, 1997). He describes interactional fields as community boundaries that consist of mutual constraints, such as geographic, social and economic constraints. In particular, he describes the motion of every group within such a community as dependent on that of the others. Because of this interdependency, these fields are a whole network of intertwined processes, rather than a single process (Abbott, 1997, pp. 1154–5). This idea speaks to understandings of community experience as occurring within social systems that are based upon network processes.

Abbott's description of interactional fields is reminiscent of the functionalist idea of an organic whole being the sum of interdependent parts that have specialised roles. In contrast to this, the thesis of this book does not argue for the interdependency of discrete or specialised parts within a social system. It sees each aspect of engagement within the community form as partial, as in the idea of portfolios of sociability, and each process as complex and overlapping. However, internal differences create tensions and ambiguity through which social relationships and processes may reconfigure and resolve. These internal boundaries articulate patterns of social cohesion in which differences and contradictory processes are given space to exist, creating a resilient and tolerant social structure.

This idea of internal boundaries giving rise to social form is in opposition to group cohesion created by closed external boundaries in which the 'other' is clearly defined. The proto-boundary concept proposed by Abbott sits neatly with the research design to turn a priori parameters of community into research questions. When this idea is placed in the context of networked individualism, we can draw from this that contemporary community boundaries (both internal and external) are enacted within person-to-person and role-to-role relations, in the partial sharing of knowledge and values and in the divisions that exist within the network.

Within the case study, community boundaries are articulated within the technological layer, addressing technology, place and the built environment through the qualitative data discussing the meshwork of legislations that interlock local, regional, national and international governance systems. In discussion of how the social layer articulates community boundaries, the quantitative data identifies discursive boundaries and the influence of demographics, such as gender, upon internal social divisions that is most apparent in the qualitative data. Boundaries articulated through mediating culture of the community are discussed in terms of internal polarisations, Abbott's proto-boundaries, and external boundaries or perceptions of a 'general public' evident in the qualitative data collected through interviews and participant observation.

4.3.4 Community Cohesion

There is something more to community experience; it includes how the interconnectedness of social relationships provides a sense of continuity, stability and enables members. These ideas are referred to as social cohesion and social mobility. The social cohesion of a community is examined through an investigation of social capital and the influence of the group environment upon patterns of social organisation (the ecological approach). In this case, the environment is both physical and virtual. Social capital is viewed as the affordances of social connections and can be exchanged through in-person and mediated interactions (ICTs). The exchange of social capital in the form of information, access and support is facilitated by trust and the mobility of reputation amongst group members. Levels of social capital within a community are enhanced by trust in the environment (the way things work and where they occur) and organisational engagement (both physical and virtual). The social ecology that results from these intersections of common interests, place, technology, social relationships, reciprocity and organisational participation is the contemporary niche of community.

In asking about the cohesive aspects such as the presence of social capital, continuity and stability, this question is opened to the possibility that these aspects occur in the online/offline experience, through social heterogeneity and across social networks as well as within organisational formats. Alongside this is the possibility that the contemporary form of community is both dynamic and ambiguous. These characteristics provide a challenge to the intuitive understanding that some level of structural fixity is required to create the environment for social cohesion. Beginning with the position that social cohesion can be located within configurations of space, organisation and interaction as argued by Latham and Sassen (2005) in their conceptualisation of digital formations.

Within the case study, community cohesion is articulated by the technological layer, addressing technology, place and the built environment, through a quantitative and qualitative discussion of the geography of membership and participation in voluntary organisations. Through the social layer, quantitative data illustrating social connection and social capital measures is presented, with an extension on a discussion of trust in the community illustrated through the qualitative data. Within the mediating culture, discussions of social cohesion are located through incidents of activism and experiences of continuity over time within participants' community experience.

4.4 Triangulation of Research Data

The case study of the global network of people interested in reptiles and amphibians (abbreviated as the 'herper community') provides an illustration of the application of this methodology to a real-world community. By combining insights into social relations with describing their contextual spatial environment, the methodological design becomes sensitive to the Chicago School agenda. This echoes the theoretical trajectory drawn from the early Chicago School community studies and Park's notion of Human Ecology discussed in Chapter 1. These factors have informed the use of mixed methods and triangulation of the results. For this study, data collection was conducted through an online survey and semi-structured interviews informed by participant observation. While much of the insights from this data are dated and specific to the time it was collected in 2006, much can be learnt from how it was conducted. These methods and complimentary analytical tools were employed discretely, but their results are triangulated to provide a critical perspective upon each method used and to explore how these results inform each other. As triangulation of the results across qualitative and quantitative methods is key to integrating and producing knowledge, our first port of call is a discussion of the literature that provides us with a refined understanding and practical tips for doing this. Östlund et al. (2011, p. 370) argue that triangulation is a methodological metaphor that facilitates the integration of qualitative and quantitative findings and aids the development of new theory. Similarly, Kelle (2005) argues that the use of triangulation integrates different perspectives on the investigated phenomenon. As will be discussed below, this approach is in line with the philosophy of the Chicago School that advocated the use of multiple methods that connect to some form of observation (Sampson, 2002, p. 217). Thus triangulation is seen as a way to strengthen the results of each method employed (Kiessling & Harvey, 2005, p. 30) and explore these different points of observation. This is the key strength of a mixed-method study, however triangulation has come under fire in the methods literature (Brannen, 2007; Hammersley, 2008; Kelle, 2005; Woolley, 2009) for its agenda of pitting different data sources as a way to verify a single knowable reality (Blaikie, 1991; Denzin, 2010). A second criticism of this approach is far more fundamental and is derived from the paradigm wars of the 1980s (Denzin, 2012, p. 81). This relates to the assumption that the choice of theories and methods may be emancipated from their ontological and epistemological roots (Modell, 2009, p. 209). From this perspective, the integration of qualitative and quantitative analysis is not possible due to the incompatibility of the paradigms that underlie these methods. This conclusion, whilst theoretically valid, has not impeded the consistent growth in mixed-method research since 2000 (Ivankova & Kawamura, 2010). It is likely that this debate is further fuelled by qualitative researchers being required to defend the validity of subjective findings in light of funding directives linking the empirical emphasis upon validity, reliability and objectivity with the requirements of research reporting (Denzin, 2012, p. 81; Clark, 2010). Fielding (2012) steps away from this debate and offers a deft alternative viewpoint on the integration of qualitative and quantitative methods. From the work of Maxwell (2010), he argues that the distinction is between 'understanding the world by a theory of variance featuring variables and correlations and understanding the world by a theory of process in terms of events and interactions' (Fielding, 2012, p. 126). The mixed-method approach and the use of triangulation of these results therefore integrate these two fundamental ways of thinking about social phenomena.

In this research, the notion of triangulation of results is about the dialogue between the findings of each method as a way to shed light on different aspects of the social ecology and is philosophically united through the consistent use of a network metaphor. The quantitative data collection was based upon closed questions and some string variables such as website addresses and names of societies where people are active. This approach imposed a structured pattern to the social action of the community, from which elements of the technological environment, patterns of social organisation that constitute the frameworks of the social layer and attributes of social cohesion caught within quantitative notions of social capital were articulated. When brought together, these quantitative elements provide a point-in-time insight into the constitution of the social ecology. The qualitative interviews, whilst semi-structured, reflect the specific experiences of the participant engaging in the culture of the community and provide historical context and social experience of its evolution over time. The pattern that emerges in this analytical context is interrelated themes of social behaviour and community experience that reflect the mediating culture of the network. While these are the broad brush-strokes of how each method contributes to understandings of the social ecology via its layers, the subsequent discussions in this chapter and book will consider how the data collected through the qualitative and quantitative methods inform the definition the place, social composition, mechanisms of social cohesion and boundaries across this open social structure.

The triangulation of data across the qualitative and quantitative data sets allows some discussion and generalisation of the findings, where they are replicated or congruent across both data sets, however the purpose of this research was to provide an evidenced based discussion of the social ecology approach as a way to articulate the elements that define a collective community form across open social structures. The participant populations for the quantitative and qualitative data collection methods are discrete, with some possible cross-over, providing both breadth and depth across the online and offline environments of the community. However as the population cohorts for both methods were community samples, rather than randomised ones, the findings of the quantitative analysis are specific to those who responded. Regardless, the use of both techniques across different populations is intended to provide some balance to biases that may have been introduced by the method of data collection. Following the approach of Barratt (2011), there is a great deal of insight that can be gained by introducing the idea of a crystal rather than the metaphor of the triangle to a discussion of how mixed-methods research can produce complementary perspectives into an issue. Denzin and Lincoln (2005) argue in this context, the metaphor of a crystal is more appropriate than that of a triangle. In a crystal, the many sides reflect and refract light from and through multiple perspectives. This introduces the possibility of competing representations to the research data. However, the competition of ideas only becomes polarised if there is a competing conceptual framework driving these ideas. As Kelle (2005) argues, the most crucial problem of the methodological discussions surrounding mixed-method (qualitative and quantitative) designs is that epistemological and methodological concepts are not sufficiently linked to theoretical considerations about the nature of the investigated social structures and social processes. In the context of the social ecology, the network metaphor has been introduced as the conceptual connection between levels of theory, across disciplinary boundaries and within the methodological context (see

Knox, Savage, & Harvey, 2006 for a discussion of the efficacy of the network metaphor to achieve these connections).

Neither the survey data nor the qualitative interviewing collected social network data, but they were built upon an understanding of social action as involving social networks and agency. An example of this can be found in the measurement of social capital within the survey as contextual to strong and weak social ties. Within the interviews, elements of social capital were explored through discussions with participants about associations with key figures, the development of friendship circles and experiences of exchange, support and opportunities gained through offline and online contacts within the experiences of participants. Through participant observation the development of social capital, in its guise of involvement in voluntary organisations, was observed through my attendance at society meetings and trading expositions through which Herpers gather, connect and exchange. This approach reflects Kelle's advice that:

> Looking at the challenges which are posed by modernisation processes, sociologists who do not wish to give up claims to understand and explain macrosocial phenomena are well-advised not to invest too much effort in methodological warfare but to make intensive use of the richness of differing methodological traditions.
>
> (Kelle, 2005, p. 115)

The methodology and choice of methods presented here reflects this pragmatic advice. However, Denzin (2012, p. 81) takes issue with this pursuit of pragmatism in mixed-methods research. The heart of his criticism is the perception of a methodological hierarchy, with quantitative methods at the top, relegating qualitative methods to a largely auxiliary role. This is not the case in this research, with each method discretely contributing its unique insight and specific perspective upon the research questions. In addition to ethnography and quantitative surveys, the phenomenon of social life online provides the opportunity for new methods of interpreting digital data to be incorporated into social research. This has allowed for the inclusion of a co-link analysis of herpetological websites demonstrating the issue network online. From this we are able to see who the key players mediating the online networks were. The strength of quantitative surveys and ethnography is in their ability to provide different insights into dispersed populations. As a result of the inclusion of these methods in the study, the analyses draw on a rich body of social experience that is balanced by its contextual perspectives. This approach reflects Flick's (2007) perspective that triangulation is an alternative to validation in that it adds rigour, breadth, complexity, richness and depth to any inquiry. By integrating the results of physical observation with online data collection this enables the connection of the data collected with the idea of a community that is both digital and physical.

4.4.1 Bias in Non-random Data Collection

The notion of triangulation covers both the triangulation of results and the triangulation of the methods. This section will discuss how the mixed-methods approach has informed the biases in each method used. Particular biases pointed out in the preceding methods discussion include the non-random population sampling of both methods and the comparison of virtually collected data from a disembodied population with physically collected data and face-to-face or embodied interactions. This particular aspect also relates to two further characteristics of these methods that are the reach of online surveys into Internet-specific spaces and the reach of participant observation into physical places where the Internet does not reach.

In both the quantitative and qualitative data there is educational, occupational and role based diversity in the respondent populations. For the online survey, this indicates that the online population who responded was not driven by social biases of who may or may not have access to the survey online and the skills to complete it. For the interview population, this indicates the diversity of people in terms of education, occupation and herpetological roles that the snowballing technique was able to reach. The most significant bias in the data is the gender ratio of both populations in which there were far more men than women in comparison to this split in national populations. Through the qualitative analysis and participant observation, this gender bias was expected and articulated to be the experience of the community. The quantitative analysis of participants' digital literacy demonstrated that women in the survey population were slightly more skilled than men, making it likely that it was not digital literacy that stopped women from completing the online survey. The lower visibility of women in forum engagement demonstrated in the quantitative analysis and the qualitative analysis speaks to the possibility that the survey links advertised on forums may not have reached women to the same extent that they reached men. However, this would lead one to think that the researcher was more likely to reach more women through physical engagement with the social networks. This was not the case and speaks to the generally low visibility of women in the network and the associated likelihood that there was just generally more men actively participating. The survey population had a 3:1 male to female gender ratio whilst the interview population had a 5:1 gender ratio. In light of a participant's observation that more women were involved with their interests in lizards and amphibians, these animal interest groups were more present in the survey results than they were in the access that the researcher had to physical populations. This reflected the interviewer's access to the network initially through people who were interested in snakes and venomous animals and the fact that her informants were male. Whilst women were actively sought to participate in the research to share their perspectives, it appears that the online survey had better reach to this less visible population. Whilst Internet populations are no longer argued to be male-biased, this research demonstrates how in the experience of people with interests in reptiles and amphibians, women are more likely to be represented and reached through online surveys.

4.4.2 Comparison of Online and Offline Findings

In terms of online versus physical methods for data collection, the online survey returned a population whose countries of origins were far more diverse (47 countries) than that of the interview population (14 countries). The greatest diversity of countries of origin was observed in personal website visitation statistics supplied by participants and during participant observation at expos and conferences. This demonstrates that both the online space and the physical spaces have global reach for recruitment purposes. It is not cost-effective for a researcher to travel to all countries in which people are likely to have interests in reptiles and amphibians, and this places the emphasis for global reach to be achieved through an online survey or for the recruitment of participants at places that draw international attendance. An advantage of the online quantitative survey in these terms is also the quantity of people that can respond versus the time limitations that exist for qualitative interviewing.

Whilst this volume and time dynamic makes sense for the researcher to be able to reach wider globally online and in more focused ways in physical spaces, there are also limitations to recruitment for interviews related to the culture of the network. In practical terms the culture of the network limited the efficacy of recruiting the diverse range of participants present at an international expo or conference. Access to this diversity through participant observation was limited by the snowballing technique of meeting contacts of contacts. It was also limited by the clique nature of the social networks reinforced by the low-trust environment. In order for the researcher's reputation, academic validity and likelihood not to be a journalist, undercover police or wildlife officer to be established, social recommendation was needed. For this reason, direct approaches to strangers at expos and these diverse social environments were not as efficient in obtaining interviews as seeking contacts of contacts. Interviews were also more efficiently obtained through the researcher being active through participant observation in fieldwork, being present at smaller reptile pet shops and attending society meetings with key figures.

Another feature of the collection of data both online and offline was the capturing of participants who were only web active or who did not have a presence online. In addition to this, web-specific spaces such as virtual herpetological societies were identified that may have been missed without an online data collection component. In terms of connection with participants who were not web active and did not draw actively from online environments, the qualitative interviews demonstrated how this neither meant disconnection from the network nor disconnection from online connections. This pointed to the importance of social networks and place-based hubs such as expos in connecting the entire range of activity in the network and demonstrated how online information and contacts are circulated through these networks. This, however, was not the case for access to physical places. Participant observation provided the deepest insight into how Herpers physically engaged with catching animals in the wild, sharing animal-handling techniques through demonstration, the practice of visiting collections and showing collections and the personal negotiation of laws that regulate the catching of animals in the wild and keeping of animals. These were essential elements to understand, and engage the analysis with, the culture and practices of the network. Because of the mixed-methods approach of online and offline data collection, these biases in data collection and population sampling may have less effect upon the overall analysis of the data and the findings of this research. What this methodological approach has achieved, however, is to extend the observations made across the entire environment of the network.

4.5 Conclusion

In this chapter, we have considered the logic behind developing a cohesive research methodology that is connected to a conceptual understanding of digital community through its environmental imprint. In section 4.2, a discussion of common metaphors for social form was provided to assist the research practitioner through the potholes and loopholes of existing system thinking within social science research. In section 4.3 the connection between the concepts directing the methodology, the methods selected and the data reviewed within the case study were presented. The final section considered the efficacy and considerations of triangulation of mixed methods data to produce research insight, addressing the biases of non-random data and social anchoring created through the comparison of data collected online and offline.

The exciting aspect of working with this literature is being on the edge of our understanding of the relationship between ICT innovations and the creation, adoption and appropriation of these technologies into social space. The daunting aspect is to develop the research questions that encompass this new knowledge and consider the range of possible methodologies that can be employed to develop it. This field is both applied and theoretical at the same time, asking questions that seek to identify back-end patterns of social organisation within the context of front-end and constantly evolving social behaviours. The first part of designing research into this area is to accept that the pace of technological and social change is faster than the time it takes to collect the data and understand it. The second part is to see that in these fields, the mix of research methodologies includes ethnographic research to elicit social meaning, surveys to collected structured data that articulate the layers, and working with digital trace data that harnesses Internet analytics software to reveal the architectures and affordances of social behaviours online. Chapters 5 and 6 will take us through a discussion of the particular considerations for the community under study and how this refined and focused the methods that would be effective within its social context. Subsequent to this, the second part of the book consisting of Chapters 7 through 10 will work through the case study of the herper community and demonstrate how the methodology and conceptual layers articulate its place, composition, boundaries and mechanism of cohesions.

Chapter 5
Sensitising Quantitative Methods to the Research Population

5.1 Introduction

In this chapter, I draw on the findings of the herper community case study to illustrate how quantitative methods are sensitised to the community under study. The appeal of conducting empirical research within a community study is in the identification of a discrete research population that is self-defined and real world. This provides the researcher with the ability to retain the social connection and comparative nature of research findings, and assists in the social impact of the research. Regardless of the data collection method employed, the unique attribute of community research is that the researcher engages, and becomes familiar with, the population under study. Indeed, the credibility and success of a community study relies on this sensitised connection between the researcher and the population. Through a discussion of the case study of the herper community, we begin to see the work involved in generating valid quantitative data and the balancing act that occurs to engage a community in research practice. Section 5.2 considers the characteristics of the community that leant itself to empirical methods. The community connection and need for experiential knowledge to conduct quantitative research is discussed in Section 5.3. Section 5.4 turns to the specific considerations that the community raised for the conduct of an online survey across a global population.

Despite the wealth of knowledge on the study of communities in the research literature, engaging with human experience in its breadth and depth remains a daunting and somewhat uncomfortable prospect for many researchers. As a researcher, I have been driven by what it means to experience community in the digital age and this curiosity has taken me way beyond my comfort zone. However curiosity is also research intuition and, in my experience, has been worth following (albeit with some caveats such as self-preservation and research contribution). Conducting a case study of the herper community, as an example of a real world digital community, was an appealing opportunity to engage with a community that I was already sensitised and connected to from the outset of the research. This provided me with a level of confidence to begin the research and a real-world population through which to explore ideas and build research insight. It is my hope that this chapter will contribute to the 'a-ha!' moment that will assist other researchers to make headway in their own practice.

5.2 Community Characteristics That Lend Themselves to Quantification

The characteristic of the herper community that made them an insightful group for me to study was that they were early adopters of the Internet. From the early days of public access to the Internet, circa the 1990s, people with interests in reptiles and amphibians were using the online environment to establish and maintain social connections, conduct transactional exchanges surrounding knowledge dispersion, and co-ordinate animal exchanges through the postal system and in person. This meant that the digital was deeply embedded in community exchange practices, sociality and collective memory during the period of data collection in 2006. This particular characteristic suggested that the herper community would provide a strong case study for exploring the social impact of the Internet upon community place, composition, boundaries and cohesion. It also meant that I was able to draw upon the emerging body of empirical research into this phenomenon and apply the associated methods of data collection and analysis; allowing for the possibility to benchmark and compare the research findings to other populations.

As a socially marginal community, this population was characterised by low social visibility and submerged social networks, making them hard to reach for the casual voyeur. The population also exhibited high levels of online presence, often characterised by anonymity, and technologically facilitated interactions with unknown others, particularly in terms of forum engagement. While forum engagement has become passé for researchers focused upon social media, it remains a group interaction mode-of-choice for some liminal communities due to its inherent capacity to facilitate many-to-many interactions with anonymous others (Aldridge & Décary-Hétu, 2014; Barratt, 2012; Barratt, Lenton, & Allen, 2012; Cohen, 1999; Martin, 2013, 2014; Phelps & Watt). Many of these practices could be considered a product of early Internet culture; however, they overlaid and no doubt facilitated the illicit underbelly of the community. This underbelly thrived upon the commodification of these animals, responded to market forces and proliferated within the global mosaic of regulatory approaches to the collection, trade, scientific study and public display of reptiles and amphibians (whether alive or dead). Researching a marginalised community of these dimensions raised implications for the design and conduct of the quantitative data collection. The following section considers how the quantitative data collection method used in the research, an online survey, was shaped by the community.

5.3 The Need for Community Engagement in Quantitative Methods

The need for experiential knowledge of a community applies whether quantitative or qualitative methods are deployed in research practice. The difference between quantitative and qualitative approaches lies in the timing; it is a question of *when* this sensitised knowledge is applied or generated within the research process. For quantitative methods, the researcher's knowledge of the community directs the questions and the channels through which the data gathering instruments are delivered. This knowledge is also generated in the way the community responds to the data-gathering instrument. In terms of a survey, this occurs through the feedback mechanisms provided, and uptake and completion rates, as much as through the data itself. To do quantitative research with the Herpers, I knew from past observations that a key way to reach them was through the online environment. Within the interview data gathered for the research, this observation was well supported. For example, Sam, an active community member in the Australian scene, observed that the Internet was largely responsible for the proliferation in interest in keeping reptiles in Australia. What this meant was that through the online survey, I could theoretically have global reach to Herpers who moved through the key virtual gathering points, which consisted of both global and local social networks. The static nature of an online survey allows the researcher to aggregate and compare community responses from a 'point-in-time' perspective, an approach particularly associated with developing an etic understanding of the social moment. In the case of the Herpers, it was possible to determine the extent to which people engaged with the community (i.e. their portfolio of participation), whether their online behaviours influenced the size and spatial distribution of their social networks, and the levels of exchange present within these networks.

For the researcher, there is a balancing act that needs to be done with making the survey interesting enough for participants to complete, while ensuring that it measures the concepts that are of value to the research. This is particularly important to pre-test before launching data collection as quantitative instruments should not be altered after they are launched as this impairs the internal consistency and comparability of data collected. This is why such tools require pilot testing before they are deployed across their target population. As de Vaus (2014, p. 117) notes, pilot testing a survey identifies ambiguous or controversial questions for the community and highlights issues with language or potential misunderstandings about the community. I pilot tested the survey with the Herpers I knew for usability and the interpretability of question and response sets. In addition to this we focused on the time taken to complete the survey, how engaged they felt by it and their overall impression of how it would be received by the Herpers they knew. Their feedback was invaluable and highlighted the use of language that did not make sense to them and questions that seemed vague or irrelevant. More generally, it seemed that they took pleasure in sharing their experience and animal passions, which was reassuring. This suggested that the survey held enough engagement to ensure its completion and submission by the respondent.

The final stage of the introductory process of launching the research is to be able to communicate the intention, purpose and impact of the research to the research population. In terms of promoting a quantitative survey, this is enacted both through the plain language statement written to introduce the research and demonstrate its ethical conduct, as well as through the informal and formal networks the researcher needs to navigate to promote the survey. For the research population, the intention to do a community study made sense mainly in the context of how an animal documentary is produced to present a story of the animal kingdom or the scientific study of speciation through focusing on specific animal populations. This commonly held perspective meant that I needed to be able to socially navigate the potentially contentious discussion of the relationship between the social and biological sciences. For a topic focused interest group such as the herper community, the study of human society made most sense when communicated in terms of biological metaphors. As a social scientist, however, there is a limit to which these metaphors hold accuracy in the discussion and conceptualisation of social systems. This is particularly evident in the use and misuse of the theory of evolution, developed to explain animal speciation and evolutionary attributes, to provide an essentialist explanation of gender roles and relationships. As stated in the introduction of this book while some of the metaphors used, such as the social ecology concept and its associated environmental approach, resonate with biological concepts such as 'niche' and ecology, they are not conceptually anchored in biological explanations. Much of the approach taken within this book is a social constructionist approach, in which people create their world rather than being passive actors of their biological destiny. Consequently, I do not seek to develop base-line observations of biological explanations and principles for social behaviour.

When it came to this point in the discussion with participants who were eager to pursue this understanding, it required me to work out a way to translate and think through the relationship between these disciplines. This is a delicate negotiation in which it is necessary to share the research brief and purpose with participants; however it is also helpful to engender within them a desire to participate in the research and clarity on its purpose. The narrative link I came up with at the time was characteristic of a novice researcher; I resorted to abstract ideas that paced relatively closely to the language and conceptual pool that they were most exposed to. I put forward the idea that consciousness and imagination is an inherent selective advantage to Homo sapiens and that we have developed complex social systems from these tools that enhance our chances of survival. If prompted, I dug a deeper hole and went on to argue that these systems are characterised by the collective behaviours of communities. These communities, in turn, are an expression of culture and social order and based upon norms and values that counterbalance and overlay basic animal instinctual behaviours and biological drivers. The community under study was to be an example of how the Internet has affected the development and enactment of these conscious social practices and reconfigured the norms, values and modes by which we connect with each other. At some point during these conversations, participants' eyes would usually glaze over, unsurprisingly, and I would say that it was a balanced study of Herpers, presenting their voice and perspective to the general public. At some point, the conversation would fall to silence and I had either lost them or engaged their curiosity and at least shown that I was a credible researcher, if a little out of touch. When the silence came after they asked me what I was doing, we talked about their animal interests.

5.4 Community Considerations for the Online Survey

The section considers the online survey constructed for the case study research and includes a discussion of the recruitment practices, piloting the survey and the feedback received. It also considers the limits to interpretation of the survey data collected and the little-acknowledged labour of data curation and its place within research methodology. As the discussion of the community reception of the online survey tool will illustrate, it is pivotal to conducting valid and connected research that the researcher takes the time to design, prepare for and consider the population at the outset of the research. I like to think of this stage of the research as rigging a ship out to sail on the open oceans of social life. Doing the occasional mid-journey repair and chronicling the 'things I missed and need for next time' list is par for the course as the research progresses. This assists the researcher to anticipate the ways that the population will engage with the research as it comes to life through the data collection and accommodate for a community response to its presence. In short, the message here is that if you light a beacon; expect moths alongside the other things you are hoping for.

The online survey was to be a digital window into the global networks of the herper community. Consequently, I needed to establish appropriate channels through which to reach and recruit eligible participants for the online component of the data collection. Knowing where the key herper spaces are online can be established through taking two main approaches. Online research such as keyword searching can be a starting point. However, it is much more efficient to get this knowledge from the community itself, by talking with them and allowing them the opportunity to talk about the survey amongst themselves. Through preparatory online research, you can establish the 'findability' of sites through their indexing within web search engines. In the forums that come up through these search results, membership sizes and active engagement in discussion threads are indicative of the relevance of a website to a group, usually thought of in terms of centrality. On the trace data side, you can also review usage statistics of websites and no doubt deploy a number of other analytical techniques for determining what sites are going to enhance the reach of your survey across a network, such as establishing influence and centrality. For a marginalised community with illicit and liminal spaces, these techniques will not fully reveal the spaces where people are active, and consequently appropriate places for the survey link to be available, as they may have taken an approach that reduces their public visibility.

Finding the appropriate locations for the placement and advertising of the survey within the community is the focus of a successful recruitment strategy. For many communities, key online 'spaces' are expressed episodically within interactions across the social networks that people have, with IRC chat channels being a good example of this. For each of these spaces, the researcher needs to negotiate with a gatekeeper or have a connection that can seed the survey where and when it is appropriate. In addition opening the space to the research and survey link, these key figures act as network hubs that have greater reach across the community and capability to penetrate the spaces (both digital and physical) where people are active and likely to be receptive to research. In network thinking, utilising the endorsement and networks of key figures and highly connected actors translates as reducing the number of social ties it takes to disperse the survey link across the eligible population. This speaks to both the social enactment of the small world hypothesis (Kleinberg, 2000a) and reflects the methodological concern of the depth of penetration possible in a network when engaging participants to recruit their friends and contacts. At some point in the chain of referral, there is usually decreasing investment amongst potential participants in the research agenda. This tends to result in the lower likelihood that those removed from the initial seed set of volunteers will recommend their friends to participate. In terms of data collection, this can result in a fairly shallow view of the network through the higher likelihood of homophily amongst participants (cf. McPherson, Smith-Lovin, & Cook, 2001; Gustavo Mesch & Talmud, 2007). The intention behind the recruitment approach of engaging gatekeepers and those who are hubs within the network is not to seek representativeness of the results, but to recruit a diverse enough range of participants to provide a deep view of who participates in the community and how they do it.

To distribute the survey link through the case study community, I located key figures with good reach across the community, in its localised and globalised instances, while travelling through America and Europe. I was able to do this through the roles I negotiated as social researcher and biological field assistant, and as the partner of a key figure in the network. Through acting in these roles, I gained a level of social access to and legitimacy to the case study community. I was welcomed to visit local herpetological societies, as well as museums and universities. This meant that key members, and those who were not, were able to get to know me and understand my agendas for conducting the research. I believe that this approach assisted the uptake of the survey link by key figures, particularly for their ability to vouch for who I was and what the research was likely to be about. During the participant observation, I also stopped in at pet shops I was directed to and spent time with private breeders and sellers looking at their collections and talking about their Herps. From this, I developed contacts who indicated their interest in the survey and who indicated that they would consider sharing it with the Herpers they knew. This spanned a broad spectrum of people who engaged with others over their interests in reptiles and amphibians, from university professors, pet shop owners and employees, and amateur snake keepers. As the survey was slated to go live while I was also conducting the participant observation, I was able to generate awareness for it through the practice of the qualitative research.

The credibility of a survey can be enhanced for a research population through its web address and sites of distribution. For the herper community, who generally valued the scientific establishment, a .edu address held credibility. I was able to host the survey on the university server, providing the initial scholarly credibility. For marginialised communities, it does assist the dispersion of a survey link if it is clear that it is not a police activity or associated with a regulatory body that is contentious within the community. The particular advantage of an online survey is that it is technically possible for a participant to respond anonymously from any country, particularly when the survey is not designed to collect identifying data, such as participants' names or digital trace information that can be acquired through the submission protocols such as IP addresses. Collecting such data may alienate many possible respondents to the survey, should be considered a research ethics issue, and would be likely to introduce a strong bias in the respondent population who objects to this practice more generally. If this is likely to be the case, then there is value in communicating to the research population that participant anonymity is achieved both within the questions the survey asks and does not ask and through the technical submission protocols of the survey interface.

To further assist the distribution and reach of the survey online, I networked with online forum moderators and web publishers that were recommended to me. Through this, I arranged with the moderator of kingsnake.com to have a banner advertisement promoting the survey for the entire period that the survey was live (1 August to 30 September 2006). This website was, and still is, an active digital space for people to engage with others on their herpetological interests. The effect of advertising in this location was very clear. I asked respondents to list the top 10 herpetological websites that they used and kingsnake.com was the site most frequently listed. People also recommended popular magazines for me to advertise the survey in and I consequently arranged exposure in *Reptiles Australia* through a short discussion piece about the research. The practice of writing a short blurb or piece on the research and placing this in relevant magazines or public discussion and publication spaces in the online environment more generally is an excellent technique that provides a credible, well read and accessible way to communicate the research agenda and call for participation. For the case study research, the recruitment locations and approaches discussed above drew in a diverse range of people from around the world to respond to the survey.

In addition to the finding the appropriate location to host the survey and place a call for participation, there are several actions that can support the survey uptake amongst the target population. In engaging with the case study population, it became apparent that it was necessary to create an online presence to clarify the research agenda and address concerns raised by community members. In recruiting Herpers online, I created an accessible presence on each forum where I had advertised the survey link and made my email address and website available so people could approach me through their preferred channel. This practice is about demonstrating a nurturing approach that curates and responds in a way that aligns with online community practice and demonstrates respect for the community by the researcher. This suggests that online recruitment for a survey requires a certain amount of cultivation by the researcher for a survey to take root within the community itself. By being available and engaging with the community in the online spaces that they are active, the researcher is also able to establish the reception and reaction of population to the research through discussion threads and social media engagement. This speaks to the need for research methodology to establish research positionality, ensure the validity of the survey findings and address possible bias that the survey reception can introduce to the profile of the respondent population. Taking the approach of providing an interactive presence online for the duration of data collection also avoids the 'hit-and-run' style recruitment approach of posting a survey link that is unattended by the researcher (Barratt & Lenton, 2010; Barratt et al., 2015). I would argue that an untended research link has the capacity to alienate online communities by signalling the disinterest and lack of community connection held by the researcher. One possible outcome of this could be the unintended effect of inviting trolling, with a definite outcome being low rates of engagement with the survey. Consequently this approach may result in a surface or shallow social sample of community members who are willing to participate in the survey and the possibility of increased malicious technical disruption to the survey while it is running live.

The two-month time period that the survey ran for was punctuated with points of re-advertisement and activity-raising such as forum discussions and the effect of key networkers distributing and endorsing the survey to their contacts. I formally re-advertised the survey on the forums and through email notification to my list of contacts midway through the time period and a week before closure. These methods for recruiting participants resulted in a community sample of 1,593 valid responses from 47 countries. The survey response numbers verified the recruitment approach and the response rates, as captured through submission time and date, demonstrated the episodic nature of the survey link dispersal through the online networks. Spreading the survey link across a range of technical and in person environments also assists in diffusing the artifactual influence of online demographics upon the survey response set. In addition to this, the respondent population of the survey is less likely to be a construct of algorithmic search techniques used by the researcher to find them. However it this approach may also increase the labour that the researcher needs to undertake in order to cultivate the space for the survey within the community. A balance between research presence and absence, alongside the use of passive explanatory digital objects and employing automated notifications of community responses to research posts are likely to assist the researcher in managing this process and successfully establishing and maintaining an interactive space within the online environment of the community.

5.4.1 Limits to Interpreting the Survey Data

A pivotal factor in the methodological decisions made was the key role of the Internet in the concept of a social ecology and within the case study population. At the time of research design, online surveys were beginning to be critically engaged with by Internet researchers. There was a sense of excitement around the idea that through the distribution of a single website link, it was possible to efficiently reach an anonymous and globally distributed population and to begin a survey of this population without knowing its actual size. As discussed above, an online survey link was easy to disseminate and, if it was a quantitative survey, easy to scale up to an unknown population size and still be able to analyse the data. However, there were critical flaws that were being pointed out in the literature about data collected anonymously online: you do not know who these people are, whether they are eligible or if they are lying. These concerns are true of traditional surveys that are mailed out to participants or handed out in public space, as the researcher has no control over who actually fills them in or the conditions under which surveys are completed. This disconnection in proximity and identification between the researcher and survey respondent is exacerbated in the online environment through higher levels of data mobility and replication amongst networks. As highlighted in Chapter 2, Section 2.5 there was a deep concern about anonymous social behaviours online, and this concern reached over into the methods that were employed in this environment. This type of data needed to be grounded and compared with physical observation of the population in order to address these concerns.

There are also several other limitations concerning how the results of online data collection can be interpreted. In terms of being able to extrapolate the results of the research to other networks, the first limitation the survey faced was that it was a community sample and not generalisable to a wider population. In other words, the results of the survey are specific to the people who responded and give rise to the discussion of the kinds of experiences possible within this network, but *only* within it. The second limitations the survey faced relates to who was likely to respond to this survey. The digital divide discussed in the literature review affects who has the technical access and digital competencies to fill out the survey. What this means in practical terms is that the people who responded did so because they wanted to (a self-selected voluntary sample with no completion incentives offered) and because they could access, and complete, the survey online. The limitations inherent in this include the sample being biased towards people who are motivated to participate and people who have the skills and access to complete an online survey. Because the survey was conducted online, the demographic profile of who is online will also influence the demographic profile of the respondent population. This was more so the case in 2006 when the survey was run, where Internet demographics were more biased towards white, educated males from the USA. The fact that this constituted a significant proportion of the respondent population for the survey raises a 'chicken-egg' question. Were these people more interested in reptiles and amphibians because they were active online? The alternative possibility being that this interest area tended to draw a population of young males with leisure time and affluence enough to pursue their interests, making them more likely to be heavily represented in the sample. In the final analysis of the results from the data sets collected, it seems likely that the answer is that both of these things are true.

The survey was written in English, and distributed initially through English-speaking contexts and networks, whilst being targeted at an international population. This meant that people who could not read or respond in English were not able to be a part of the respondent population. This limitation is a technical and cost limitation and one that I decided to acknowledge rather than attempt to address. I considered whether having access to these non-English-speaking populations within a qualitative context would have helped me to balance out whether the survey findings had traction beyond the English-speaking context. Another implication of the international reach of the survey population is that national population statistics cannot be used to benchmark the demographics of the survey population as a whole, such as average age, levels of education and styles of occupation. This remains an issue for surveys of globalised populations and is only likely to be resolved through the proliferation of Big Data that challenges and encounters these issues at larger scales and within quick pace and industry driven concerns of commercial contexts. For the purposes of this survey, the demographic questions were written using categories that had the widest application across international contexts and levels of English, allowing a reasonable comparison of these variables within a multinational respondent population.

The other factor that influences who the respondent population is likely to be is the inclusion criteria of the survey. Because I could not predetermine the role types or categories of people who may be eligible, such as amateur and professional, I oriented the inclusion criteria to the topic of interest: reptiles and amphibians. Topic-of-interest is a common approach to defining an online community, and an approach that aligns with the notion of the community used in this research as a foci-of activity-group discussed in Chapter 3. Participants were asked to self-select according to the following inclusion criteria:

> I am seeking people who are actively interested in reptiles and amphibians and who are prepared to fill out the web questionnaire on their reptiles and amphibians interests and related social activities. This survey is for people who are 18 years old and over. The following survey would take approximately 20 minutes of your time, and can be undertaken at your convenience.

The self-selection criteria included the diverse range of people who had reptile and/or amphibian interests rather than excluding people who did not keep reptiles and/or amphibians. The survey questions also did not employ grouping terminology prevalent in the herpetological vocabulary as these endogenous divisions were more about stereotyping in a local or specific social context; not using locally derived terminologies also helped to avoid predetermining the grouping and defining process before the data was collected. The effect of this open approach, that did not employ selection by roles or categories of participation, was reflected in the feedback where some respondents felt their forms of involvement were not the focus of the survey.

Given that the survey was to cover a broad array of involvement, questions asked may not have been relevant to a proportion of the respondent population. Sometimes this was expressed by respondents as a personal feeling of exclusion, or reflected an aversion to being associated with certain types of involvement. The direct quotes provided below are an example of the lack of relevance of some questions to respondents and the clear tensions and polarisations existing in the group.

a. 'The only thing I disliked about this was the lack of a distinction between research and hobby – as a researcher in the field working on snakes,

I have more respect for fellow researchers, and a lot less respect for those in the pet trade, and there was no way to split my vote on several questions based on this difference of feeling that I have for the two different types'.

b. 'questions seem more geared toward hobbyist than professional herpetologist, there are a lot of us out there who do research on herps! I did not answer the questions on my attitudes towards other herpers/ myself because I don't see the relevance'.

These comments reinforce more generally the importance of pilot testing a survey to reveal whether the survey questions are sensitive to the internal politics of the target population. In this case, I had made the decision not to play into these issues that I knew were extant in the community. I was interested in the conceptual point of view for how the community, but appreciated and integrated these perspectives offered by respondents into the research analysis.

5.4.2 The Pivotal Role of Gathering Feedback

Gathering the respondent feedback on the survey while it is live goes to the heart of online survey design and understanding respondent perceptions. Conducting the survey with the Herpers, and providing them with a space for feedback at the end of the survey, emphasised how real-time respondent feedback that can be received through an online survey tool is critical to the smooth running and dispersion of the survey across the population. Active monitoring of feedback during data collection allows the researcher to assess at the time of the survey response submission whether the survey is displaying in a usable format for respondents. An online survey that does not include a section where the participant can provide feedback on their experience of doing the survey is likely to lack reflexivity and research rigour.

Technical issues affecting the completion of the survey on a diversity of devices should also be a focus of the survey pilot testing. Within the case study population, for example, participants hit their own technical skill limitations when completing the survey, indicating this through feedback provided that they accidently submitted their survey twice. Anonymous survey submissions are an important approach when working with a marginalised community, and conducting the survey in this manner minimises the risks for participants. However, where there is no clear identity, and no IP address for a person's survey response to be attached to, this increases the potential for non-malicious duplication of survey submissions through user errors or technical glitches. For the Herper data set, this was addressed through the data cleaning practices, where duplicate responses were removed using SPSS's 'duplication' function and through a visual spot-checking of the survey data.

The type of feedback received from Herpers more generally on the experience of doing the survey related to whether the respondent thought the survey was worth doing. While those who completed and submitted the survey demonstrated a level of engagement with the research process, those who did not were unlikely to provide negative feedback – they just did not participate. This demonstrates the polarity that occurs naturally in voluntary samples and the general bias towards a lack of explanation for non-participation that the researcher is likely to receive within the survey submission. Other types of feedback that provided critical knowledge during the data curation and analysis stages included constructive comments about self-selection and self-completion. Because it is difficult to control who responds to your survey when the link is dispersed across the online environment and through social networks, it is essential that an exclusion criterion is clear so that the research population can self-select appropriately and reduce the weeding the researcher will need to do within the data cleaning process to remove survey responses submitted by those who do not meet the eligibility criteria. A few people who acknowledged (and there may be others who did not) that they were under the age of 18 still completed this survey, for example, despite the clear selection criterion of being 18 or over. This exclusion criterion was a requirement of taking a low-risk approach to the research conduct, due to the ethical considerations and additional steps that come into play for gaining consent from people under 18. As I was able to qualitatively reflect with participants over 18 about how they began their interests, there was limited value to the research in taking these additional steps. However, the Internet population of younger users still felt drawn to share their experiences. Respondent feedback, such as the examples below, clearly demonstrated interest and a desire to contribute their experience to the research.

a. 'Excellent questions asked, please except [*sic*] my entry even though I am under the age of 18'.
b. 'Herpers can be less than 18, you know'.
c. 'sorry i am not over 18 but i thought i would fill one out anyway. never know, it might come in handy. good questionaire by the way'.

In developing the exclusion criteria, the researcher does need to be sensitive as to how this will appear and be received by the community. In the case study research, the balance of participant risk in research participation, such as community ostracism, reducing consent obstacles and ethical considerations for engaging people under 18 were more influential considerations than attempting to add the extra consent processes involved in engaging young people in the research. In reflection however, I feel that it would have been appropriate to find an alternative format for excluded participants to contribute should they wish, as a large part of the herper community consisted of people under 18.

Two further examples of feedback that exemplify the community sensitisation process of online survey research are worth discussing here. The first example is drawn from the survey question asking participants to indicate their levels of general trust in and interpersonal trust with other Herpers in the community. The second example is the survey question that sought to establish the level of risk taking behaviours in the respondent population, seeking to establish whether they were more likely to be risk takers or risk averse. This question was intended to speak to the public perception of the case study community as being risk takers. As a learning, the community responses to these survey questions reveals something about the nature and culture of the case study community that I had not picked up during pilot testing or made the connection from my existing knowledge of the community.

At the outset while I was designing the survey, my head was deeply embedded in the technical and conceptual literature and I had not considered the contentious nature of trust-risk taking discussions within the community or how the concepts I was drawing on would provoke a response. The questions relevant to a discussion of trust where drawn from the social capital literature and sought to measure the presence of social cohesion through establishing the levels of general and interpersonal trust and reciprocity evident in the respondent population. These questions have been deployed rigorously and pervasively by researchers, as had the questions on risk-taking behaviours from the IPIP index that ask people whether they know how to get around the law and whether they are willing to try anything once in general. In my mind, I was asking questions that had the capacity to address negative perceptions of the community. I felt that these measures would allow me to talk about the presence or absence of risk takers in the community and to discuss trust as a social asset amongst Herpers.

The questions used in the case study survey were adapted to focus on the experience amongst Herpers. Although this approach risks the results being incomparable across populations where these measures are applied, the customised questions made more sense to the network of people under study. Initially survey respondents were introduced to the trust question set by being asked about their personal approach to their interests and, within this section, being asked to think about their personal approach to other Herpers. The questions on risk taking came in the following section asking how the participant saw themselves in relation to their herpetological interests. The questions for the trust measure, framed as statements, deployed in the survey were as follows: (Answers were on a three-point Likert scale from 'agree' to 'disagree'.)

How strongly do you agree or disagree with the following statements?

Q10.1 Most herpers can be trusted.
Q10.2 You can't be too careful in dealing with herpers.

Q10.3 There are types of herpers whom I do not trust.
Q11.7 When it comes to my herp interests, I know how to get around the rules.

The community, however, saw these questions on trust and risk taking as perhaps questioning the moral fabric rather than addressing public opinions associated with the group. Given the questions' slant towards trust, risk and connection between people with herpetological interests, some respondents felt that:

a. 'The tone of some of your questions implies that herpetologists are not to be trusted'.
b. 'Some questions do not clearly ask a question (e.g., ' … I know how to get around the rules'). Knowing how and doing it are two entirely different things. As constructed, this particular part of your inquiry will generate useless results'.
c. 'When it comes to my herp interests, I know how to get around the rules'. I know how, yes, but I obey the law. Not many law breakers are gonna admit it'.

This particular group of people is accustomed to being demonised through their interests in reptiles. The feedback above highlights the problems with applying generalised questions to measure trust-levels amongst a group of people for whom these topics may be unusually sensitive. While the data gained from these questions provided a fundamental insight for the research, they had a polarising, and perhaps discomforting, effect for respondents in completing them.

5.4.3 Data Duration

For the autonomous researcher, the online survey is an achievable task as the data collected is already digital and collated in a database. In addition to this, wide distribution of the online survey link can be achieved in a cost-effective manner. Ease of data management, real-time feedback from respondents (discussed above), volume distribution (whether for targeted outreach or mass exposure) and autonomous completion are conveniences that mean that the online survey is here to stay. Regardless of these conveniences and affordances of the online survey, data management and curation remain important and time-consuming aspects that are often unacknowledged.

As a data collection tool, the online survey is widely used for program evaluation, social research and opinion polling, generating large volumes of data that may or may not be processed through effective analysis. Already it is possible to argue that people experience survey fatigue through regular exposure to this method, and this must be factored into survey design. At the time of the case study research, online surveying was still new and standardised survey templates provided through SurveyMonkey, for example, had not been used en masse. Consequently, the case study population was receptive to completing the survey, as indicated above, however brought to this task the characteristics of a web savvy and digitally active population used to engaging with the web through their recreational and everyday life pursuits. The following discussion highlights how the location and culture of a community affect online survey completion and highlight the need for the researcher to anticipate and attended to data curation of the survey submissions.

In general, the online survey is an effective way to collect quantitative data from a dispersed population; however it does have certain limitations attached to its use (Wright, 2005). The literature on e-voting highlights a key concern of online surveying: that you cannot control the influence of the environment in which a person completes the survey. Filling out a survey during work time or in your own bedroom, versus in the lounge room or at a mate's place, influences the levels of distraction, detail and honesty that questions are likely to be answered with. For example, this effect was apparent in the following feedback to the case study survey:

a. 'thanks i have to go i'm at work at a level one trauma center and they just called a trauma alert sorry, bye!'
b. 'as I'm at an internet cafe, I don't have time to access the webpages I use'.
c. 'I hope to complete this extense survey in other moment. Thaks, and I seems that it is a good idea'.

It's also impossible to control the sobriety of the respondent. It was a notable element of participant observation that Internet users settled down with a beer or a joint (or both) and lost some time in the online forums, occasionally declaring their steadily deteriorating levels of sobriety in their posts. This was indeed the case for a person in the network who was found dead, strangled by his pet scrub python. His last communications in a reptile forum late at night recorded his declining sobriety and his large python on the chair next to him. Recreational use of the Internet also links to behaviours like trolling and flaming (using inflammatory language and deliberately being antagonistic to hijack the conversation) and other malicious behaviours such as spamming. The online survey is subject to such antisocial behaviours. Techniques such as data curation and internal logic checking go some way to addressing these issues, but such problems are also necessary considerations for the design and layout of an online survey.

As suggested in the discussion above, it is essential to curate data sets collected online for internal consistency and validity. The online survey developed for the case study research was a custom design, facilitating a high level of control over how questions and response sets were formatted and presented to participants. The quantitative data set from the online survey consists of responses to 31 questions that resulted in 239 possible variables per respondent submission and a total of 1,593 valid submissions (after duplication removal). Because it was custom designed, I made the 'interesting' decision to collect all responses through emailed simple text format in order to conduct detailed data vetting as it came in. This facilitated easy access to real time feedback, but did mean that compiling the database through automated processes was more tedious and required the services of a computer coder and database specialist. Consequently it was far less convenient than the automated database compilation and data compatibility produced by existing online survey tools. Because of my approach however, I was able to collect information in non-standard formats and control how data was transformed through the curation process. The curation process took a substantial amount of time to do, with the first analysis possible almost six months after the close of data collection.

Curation of the case study survey data involved checking the data from the online survey submission and making these responses accessible for quantitative analysis. It involved assigning numbers to string variables for quantitative analysis (such as country names) and the numerical coding and validation of websites submitted. It also involved the manual removal of duplicate data. Other types of data curation included coding a blank question response as appropriate (for example 'n/a' or question skips). Throughout the curation process, responses were verified as authentic through the spot application of internal logic checking. If I became suspicious that a person was making up their responses through flippant remarks and contradictory responses, the submission was considered invalid and removed. Other more intentional malicious behaviour found in the response set included spamming. One respondent submitted 60 identical responses. The event was recognised by the researcher through an ongoing monitoring of the emailed responses received and 59 of the responses were removed.

Given the global reach of the Internet and the potentially global reach of the survey, gathering demographic data was a challenging aspect for the survey, with the need for standardised question and response sets, which unfortunately could not cater to the diversity of education systems and occupation descriptions. Survey respondents were provided with qualitative response options for their country of residence, top 10 websites used, societies they were members of and their job description. The main consideration for the manual coding of this string data is that people spell things differently, use a different language, or provide different names for a country, such as the Netherlands versus Holland or Nederland. Country names were manually assigned numbers and resulted in 47 verified countries. A dropdown list of country names is the usual solution, but needs to be functional and quick for the participant to select from. My decision was to provide the participant with a single string box for text and take on the labour of manually indexing this myself. It is always a fine line in the development of a survey as to what you can expect your participant to do for you, versus what you need to do to make their experience of completing the survey as straightforward and intuitive as possible. The negotiation of this labour and expectation is a powerful undercurrent in the success and uptake of a survey. If there is too little anticipation of, and design for, what the participant needs to do, the survey will not appear legitimate and is likely not to gain the respect of the respondent. If there is too much expectation in terms of the labour the participant needs to put in, this decreases the likelihood that respondents will complete the survey or recommend it to their networks. In this way, the power-play surrounding the labour of completing a survey forms a subtle expression of the receptivity and nuanced understanding that the researcher holds towards the community.

The data curation involved in preparing the survey responses for analysis also extended to issues where a dropdown list was not possible given the limitations of the researcher's knowledge before conducting the research. For example, it was impossible for me to know the names of all the societies and websites that participants were likely to use. In this instance, I provided a string textbox for participants to provide a qualitative response. What this meant was that my labour in data curation extended to verifying the society names and websites they provided. While the use of qualitative string boxes to collect categorical data introduces a level of 'noise' into the dataset for information that I could not always interpret or validate online, it did provide pivotal data for the analysis. Society names were cross-referenced through online search for existence and correct spelling and then assigned a number. Through this method, 338 unique societies were identified in the Herper survey data set, ranging in membership sizes from over a 1,000 to five people. Website addresses provided by participants were similarly verified for existence and correct spelling and then assigned a number. Through this method, 1,123 unique herpetological websites were identified that were mainly in English, but they reflected the diversity of countries from which participants came.

Through data curation process discussed in this section, I became confident that I was working with a data set that was connected to the community and reflected how they moved through it. The survey responses generally appeared aligned with my observations in the field and the structural of interview participants' portfolios of participation evident in the interviews I was simultaneously conducting. The main advantage of data curation, in addition to demonstrating research rigour, is in familiarising the researcher with their own data set and seeding ideas for the ways it is possible to interpret and work with it. From the data curation, it was already clear to me that I had a diverse social sample that was globally distributed. I also knew that I had data that was able to provide insight into the technical layer of technology, place and the built environment and data that would support a comprehensive discussion of social capital in the community that aligned with the social layer.

5.5 Conclusion

As can be seen in this chapter, the use of quantitative methods requires that sensitised knowledge of the community is needed at the construction and design stage of empirical research, and is further developed in gathering and preparing a data set for analysis. Section 5.2 provided a discussion of the characteristics of the case study population that suggested that an online survey would be an effective data collection tool. Section 5.3 highlighted how knowledge of the community was drawn upon during the design and development stage of the survey and Section 5.4 demonstrated how this knowledge was strategically applied in preparing the data for analysis. This level of familiarity and rigour in developing, deploying and curating the survey data gave me the capacity to proceed with the analysis and the confidence to experiment with new tools for data analysis and visualisation.

Chapter 6
Sensitising Qualitative Methods to the Research Population

6.1 Introduction

This chapter presents the considerations for demonstrating research rigour within qualitative methods, and in doing so, looks at what means to achieve validity within qualitative analysis. Drawing from the case study of the herper community, I consider how the qualitative methods used for data collection, of participant observation and semi-structured interviewing, were sensitised and responded to a community through the relationships established and maintained by the researcher. Section 6.2 draws illustrations from the case study to discuss how ethnographic immersion within a community prompts an evolving relationship between the researcher, the community and the research directions. Essentially acting to begin the sensitisation process. Section 6.3 outlines the strengths of ethnographic practice, its relevance to an environmental approach to data collection, and presents where and how this was conducted within the case study community. Section 6.4 discusses the particular considerations for the conduct of semi-structured interviewing within the context of participant observation and Section 6.5 reviews the practices deployed in the case study research to demonstrate research rigour and techniques for balance and transparency associated with the use of qualitative methods. The following discussion of the use of qualitative methods within the case study reveals the voice, biases and rigour that the researcher brings to the collection and interpretation of the data. Methodological techniques for achieving transparency, congruency and rigour for qualitative research include considering researcher positionality, such as insider-outsider researcher dynamics, and the development of emic-etic perspectives through the research practice. These techniques represent the means through which the researcher establishes closeness to and distance from the subject under study.

Presenting the researcher voice and community voice as a methodological discussion is a delicate balance between revealing social dynamics, maintaining respect for the community and demonstrating the integrity of the research practice. Consequently, the methodological discussion of the case study presented below considers the ethical approaches to preserving participant anonymity when conducting research within a socially marginalised community.

It also reviews the practices of researcher reflexivity, gained through peer-debriefing. Reporting on these practices for the purposes of balance and transparency within the conduct of the research is constituted by how the researcher negotiated the line between personal and professional practice. This line often blended through the immersion of the researcher into the community under study. By example, presenting this discussion from the case study provides for the community researcher one way for how this line can be articulated when bringing scholarly knowledge to the public domain.

6.2 Immersion and the Researcher's Community Connection

Qualitative methods such as interviewing and participant observation allow the research trajectories to follow and critically engage the researcher's evolving connection with the community. What we see and hear as researchers' influences the questions we ask and the themes we begin to develop. For me, when conducting the case study research, it was the surprising repetition of social patterns that always caught me off guard. This repetition is referred to as 'thematic saturation' within the analysis of qualitative data and feels like social saturation during the practice of immersive field research. What this reoccurring and often spooky sense of déjà vu suggests is the capacity for participant observation to bump the researcher into the macro social structures that shape and direct people's experiences and opportunities. Finding repetition and structure within social experience, whether spoken or behavioural, is only surprising because immersion in the mundane and chaotic processes of life tends to shroud and diffuse the immediacy and influence of social structure. This is one reason for the disconnect within research practice and analysis between a discussion of the micro-processes of life, such as those found within symbolic interactionism (Blumer, 1969), with the macro perspectives towards systemic structure and function, such as the conceptual approaches of Marx, Weber and Durkheim.

An example of this dialectic revealed by researcher immersion within a community can be seen from my research practice within the herper community case study. For Herpers, there was a clear articulation of the structuring influences of geographic context upon animal consumption and access patterns evident in the narratives of interview participants. As I spent more time with Herpers and conducted the interviews, I became more interested in how the local geographical context of a given Herper shaped their experience of the pet market and the types of animals they were likely to prefer and have access to. This was despite regionalised, perhaps even globalised, marketplaces and accessible information sources online. This suggested that within the herper community, there was substantial resistance to the homogenisation of social experience through a deeply entrenched set of cultures and submerged architectures that were geographically tied. This action speaks to the globalising forces of the market and borderless nature of information articulated through George Ritzer's (1996) 'McDonaldsisation' thesis and raises the continued tension between the local and global that is enacted within community structures and practice.

The contrast between geographically contextual articulations of the herper community culture was clearly articulated between the US and British reptile and amphibian consumption cultures. In the US, both online and as evident at reptile expos, these animals were valued more for their morphological novelty; how a reptile or amphibian looked in its size, shape or colour patterns on the skin. In contrast, the European consumption cultures, evident in Belgium and the Netherlands for example, more generally valued the taxonomic and geographic authenticity of animals collected; this refers to the closeness and specificity of the genetic profile of the animal to those from its native habitat. Other articulations of the influence of geography upon what is essentially a mediated culture conducted across international borders, could also be seen in the anomaly of the insular nature of the French marketplace consumption culture. This particular marketplace saw a relatively narrow range of Herps retailed and collected, in comparison to neighbouring European countries such as the Netherlands and Belgium, which had a proliferation of animals from all geographic regions of the world. While this is likely to be a product of national, regional and local legislation, it is also a product of what animals the local Herpers are interested in collecting and the knowledge-bank they can easily draw on to keep these animals (and themselves) alive. As situated through the participant observation conducted for the case study, these trends appeared resonant with the country cultures and markets themselves, but did take what felt like unusual manifestations within the herper community. Being able to view these patterns represents the development of a macro view of the community through immersion within the world-view of a population (the micro view) in geographically distinct locales. This is the particular strength of qualitative methods and one reason why ethnographic approaches remain a prominent technique for data gathering and analysis within community studies.

6.3 Illustrating the Heart of a Community Through Ethnographic Practice

As discussed in Chapter 2, Section 2.2 the early community studies of the Chicago School employed inconsistent theoretical frameworks; however ethnography appears to be the general method of choice. From the work of the Chicago School tradition, it is clear that the ethnographic approach provides excellent insight into the meaning of social relations and their culture-specific configurations. Herbert Gans (2009), in a retrospective article on his career as a sociologist, discusses ethnography as follows:

> I was turned on by field methods, more properly called participant observation and now also called ethnography. Like all other research methods, it has its shortcomings, and it is suitable only for some research questions, but I still think it is the most scientific of the available sociological research methods because it brings researchers into close and continuing contact with the people they are studying and the groups and institutions in which they are embedded.
>
> (Gans, 2009, p. 5)

Therefore, ethnography helps us to see what people think about their environment, how they make meaning from it, and the life strategies they employ to navigate the social world. This speaks to the generational of a mediating culture. Ethnographic work also provides practical details of where people actually go and why they go there, i.e. the spatial aspect of social relations. Ethnographic observation takes away the guesswork as to the populated spaces of a social environment and it usually adds to the understanding of the mobilities within space (people go where they want to go and when they don't like it anymore, they go somewhere else). These kinds of details are difficult to catch in a statistical snapshot, as they are more intuitive and episodic. In addition to these established virtues of ethnographic research, participant observation continues to play a very important part in Internet research. By its very nature, engaging with a community through in-person participant observation includes going to places where people are disconnected from the Internet. This in person contact and interaction with a community acts as a valuable data collection counterbalance to the respondent population that an online survey is likely to reach.

Ethnographic methods, such as participant observation and interviewing, also allow for an historical understanding of group experience to develop from the research practice, often defining the 'genesis' story of the community. This is a pivotal element towards the definition and identification of the community as a coherent whole which exists beyond the research framing. This 'genesis' story provides a symbolic understanding of how the community came to be situated within the wider social context. The Herpers, for example, had evolved from the collector culture fed by early explorers returning from afar with exotic animals, amongst other bounty. These collector cultures were associated with the creation of private museums and then public bequests of these collections. Within these cultures public museums arose, and with them locally organised societies or reptile clubs organised members as professionals and amateurs. Over time, these societies became more specialised in the animals they considered and the people who affiliated with them. Reptiles and amphibians were grouped together by their taxonomical relationships, despite their distinct differences in life-cycles and environmental niche; the scientific study these animal grouping and relationships being referred to as Herpetology. The taxonomic association between reptiles and amphibians brought together what may be considered two distinct types of people, those interested mainly in reptiles and those interested mainly in amphibians. One reason that social divisions aligned to the animal divisions are that the knowledge and care practices between reptiles and amphibians are distinctly different and challenge the capacity for a person to be a specialist in both. From this set of uncomfortable bedfellows, herpetological societies emerged and formed the localised backbone of the early communities of people interested in reptiles and amphibians. Seeded by these early beginnings, the scientific study, live public display and pet-trade of these animals have drawn together a group of people who variously refer to themselves as Herpers. From this genesis story, we can see that Herpers have been variously positioned as a knowledge community, a hobby group and as an artefact of alignments between social institutions. This historic perspective provides insights into the ways through which a comparative understanding to other communities that have similar or resonant genesis patterns can be developed through the research findings. Rather than generalisability, the strength of qualitative methods is their dynamic and responsive nature and their capacity to illustrate this historical context and meaning-making used by members to develop a collective identity within the community. They also cultivate an orientation towards serendipity, learning and laterality during the data collection process, which a non-responsive or strongly predefined research approach may stifle.

Alongside the quantitative data collection, I conducted semi-structured interviews with people I met while I travelled through the key places within the network. The findings reported in the herper community case study cover the period of immersion during 2006–2007. During this time I attended Europe's largest reptile expo in Hamm, Germany, and asked people why they were there. I observed the workings of a Parisian pet shop, a small-town Dutch pet shop and a Norwegian private zoo specialising in reptiles and amphibians. I went to a well-established scientific reptile conference in Australia and spoke with people about the sense of community that they shared there. I fraternised with private keepers, academics, museum curators, doctors, paramedics, veterinarians and zoo employees in Australia, the UK, Italy, Luxembourg, Germany, Holland, France, Switzerland, Norway, Singapore and places in the USA including several locations in New Mexico, Massachusetts, Nebraska and Oregon. These sites and places were all heavily connected with the English-speaking Internet, but through contacts and adventures, I also found myself on a farm in rural Holland with no Internet (although they did use mobile phones when travelling across Europe selling reptile cages), where they did not speak English. In such cases, I was able to overcome the language barrier with the help of contacts who acted as interpreters translating, at the time of the interview for me, to and from Dutch, French, or German. I also found myself in a valley in remote Arizona interviewing a contact in heavily localised English. Sadly, the batteries on my audio recorder had gone flat without my knowledge and I am left only with the memory, a few scribbled notes, more knowledge about rattlesnakes and the wonder of witnessing a young man chew tobacco and spit the juice with the accuracy of cowboys in old westerns.

Through this in person exposure to the diversity and similarity of community experience across locals, regions and countries, I saw in action the kinds of differences and distances that kept people from connecting with each other, the rise and fall of key figures and societies and the tragic death and loss that people experienced through their animal collections and their friends. I saw romance bloom and relationships break (both friends and lovers) over and around reptile and amphibian collections. I spoke to people jailed because of their interests in geckos and people who made huge financial profits and losses because of their investment in these animals and their by-products.[1] I knew that I needed to ask about what people got out of connecting with others online, how they met other people with reptile interests, why they were members of societies, what animals they had collected and how they had been involved in the network over time. This gave a sense of time, context and meaning to the social experience of the community from a range of different types of involvement and perspectives. These social histories form the heart of my understanding of community experience in these environments and helped me to make connections and verify the data.

6.4 The Methodological Considerations of Semi-structured Interviewing

Alongside the practice of ethnography, semi-structured interviewing has methodological considerations of its own. This is because the interviewer extracts the participant from their environment, to some degree, and proceeds to ask a structured set of questions that do not reflect the usual patterns of conversation and social exchange due to their bounded, inquiring and directed nature. Within the case study research, interview participants were initially respondents were asked what their interests and involvement in herpetology were. From this point, the interview branched out and questions covered

1 Illegal smuggling and keeping reported here had been prosecuted in relevant jurisdictions before the conduct of the research and was not an outcome of or related to the research practice.

current involvement practices, historical patterns of participation, community experience and Internet use. This structure of questions provided a sense of the type of role that the person occupied in the network, their animal preferences and whether they were an active reptile keeper or involved in some other way. After this baseline of the persons participation profile was established, the interview usually moved to more personal and responsive probes that sought to establish the participant's reasons for participating, their identity development and social interactions with other Herpers. This covered questions such as who introduced them to their reptile and/or amphibian interests, who influenced them in their keeping/research/ or other practices and how they had pursued their interest over time. These questions provide insights into the channels of introduction into the community, illustrating its social edges and 'newbies' space. They also provided information on the types of social influences that engage people and maintain their involvement, and the dynamic social signal a person gives off in a system by their changing commitment levels and involvement types over time (the historical perspective). Often these questions linked into discussions about societies that people were members of and organisations they had joined, thus providing information on the formal institutions that shaped the network. If the Internet and mediated interaction had not already come up during the course of these discussions, it was then highlighted. Interviewees were asked how they engaged with their interests online, where they went in their digital environment, what they thought about the information they obtained and people they met through the Internet, and what their usual communication channels were with other people with herpetological interests. These questions provided a sense of how the interviewee navigated the online environment and what this meant to them. Respondents were then asked to discuss whether their herpetological involvement felt like a community and to discuss their herpetological identity. If the respondent had mentioned anything to this effect during the course of the interview, it was then referred back to and discussed at further length.

Most face-to-face interviews were conducted within a herpetologically related context such as conferences, expos, zoos, pet shops, museums, universities, field trips and the homes of people with reptile collections. Therefore, it was usual that there was engagement with the interview subject outside of and around the interview. This provided a level of context to what was discussed, and allowed for additional interpretation and observation of the person. In addition, this environmental context to the interviews meant that the person presented to the researcher in a way that was shaped by the role that they performed in that context and the purpose that they had for being there. For example, academics attending a herpetological conference generally began the discussion of their herpetological interests in the context of being an academic known for their contribution to a specific aspect of herpetology. Likewise, zookeepers interviewed on zoo grounds at some point during the interview were likely to explain how it was that they came to be a reptile keeper in that zoo.

6.5 Demonstrating Research Rigour: Techniques for Balance and Transparency

This section reflects upon the techniques for balance and transparency used in the research practice and data collection approach of the case study research to illustrate research rigour. The discussion of the ethical approach, in respect to participant anonymity, considers how this was enacted within the practice of the ethnography and across the mixed-methods approach. The theoretical approach that I brought to the research, and how that was likely to influence the way I saw the data and engaged the community, provides for the reader my own personal intellectual bias and assists in their assessment of the validity of the findings. The reflexivity and self-awareness that I developed during the data collection and analysis is also detailed to demonstrate how balance and transparency begins within the process and conduct of engaging with a community, rather than solely through the intellectual approach taken by the researcher the practice of research rigour and peer debriefing allowed me to reflect on and refine the insights I was able to bring to the analysis.

6.5.1 Participant Anonymity and Ethical Research Practice

The key ethical consideration of the case study research was facilitating the anonymity of research participants through the data collection practices, research analysis and reporting. Whilst this is a clear and straightforward requirement for the conduct of low risk research, the implications of this resonate throughout the research design and practice of the case study research, as evident in the methods discussion in Chapter 3. While the questions and considerations conducting of ethical research across online and offline environments are wider than this (Buchanan & Ess, 2009; Markham & Buchanan, 2012), the case study research was particularly preoccupied with this issue given the socially marginal nature of the community. During the conduct of the interviewing and participant observation, there was substantial discussion with participants and the wider community about how their anonymity was achieved through the research practice and results communication in light of a mediating culture characterised by secrecy and competition discussed in Chapter 9. While it is impossible for an in-person interview to achieve the same level of anonymity as an online survey between the researcher and the participant, disconnection of participants' identities across the data collection methods and the level of detail the participant are asked to provide about themselves and others during the conduct of the interview do contribute to this consideration. In addition to these practices, interviews were conducted during participant observation, which meant that the recruitment process did not require extended identification and authentication of participants. Achieving participant anonymity within research conduct, as alluded to above, is enhanced by not pursuing and recording in detail a discussion and characterisation of a person's social networks. Consequently, the need for discontinuity between participants and their social networks within the data collected led to a related methodological consideration of how it was impossible for me to sample the entire breadth of the population and to follow through all known networks. In particular, this concern speaks to the idea, and practice of law enforcement, that a person's social networks and their relational configuration can be used to identify a person. Within a community where reputation is highly mobile and identity is developed through association with key figures and roles, social networks were very identifying of a person to the research population itself, which was the greatest immediate concern for participants. These initial concerns for participant anonymity, whilst not insurmountable, made the use of both quantitative and qualitative social network analysis less effective as these tools are usually based around a discussion of known social networks. Consequently, while the research construct rests on a framework of network theories, the method was not used through either modality of data collection. In light of these considerations, I embedded participant anonymity through the discontinuity of participant identities across data collection methods and their social relations, into the case study research design as a practical enactment of ethical research conduct.

6.5.2 Theoretical Confession

I began the case study research through a series of events that have challenged my perceptions as a social scientist. This section will introduce you to the personal experience that generated and shaped this research. These shaping events can be thought of as the theory-practice shock that pushed me into the search for the notions of emergent form and online sociability within the literature. Another shaping event can be seen in my experience of the macro-micro concatenation of structure and agency, which sent me scuttling into the literature for alternative ways to conceptualise the space of social agency and the way these patterns of social interaction interact with an environmental notion of social structure. The result of this search is the concept of social ecology as constructed through ICT use patterns, patterns of social participation and social resource exchange. Finally, I could never understand how all the individual differentiation and disconnection that I observed actually led to social connection. This experience led me to the notion of networked individualism and portfolios of participation in the literature, which form the mechanics of community experience in the case study community.

The 'community question' (Wellman, 1979) came electrically alive for me in a theory-practice shock that I experienced shortly after I was introduced to the herpetological scene. This event happened in the lounge room of a nondescript 'brick and tile' home in the thick of Australian suburbia. In this lounge room, I had my first close encounter with a Monocled Cobra in full display and a Gaboon Viper, which has the longest fangs and highest venom yield of any snake. Apart from a very healthy fear response, my first thought was wondering how on earth these men had obtained these animals and how they were keeping themselves and these animals alive. What I found out was that these men sat in an active network of social contacts around the world that fed them information and supported them in this endeavour. They were constructing their own personalised experience of community in very unique ways that had not yet been described adequately in the sociological literature. Developing insight into how to describe such a social world provided the initial challenge of this research.

I found out that these animals had been illegally posted into Australia in a box that was packaging for a child's toy by a contact in Switzerland that the two men had met over the Internet. These were the early and heady times when the Internet expanded people's contacts globally and Internet regulation and customs surveillance was yet to catch up. It was clear from the story of these two men that these contacts were not randomly made but occurred in online social spaces dedicated to people who were passionate about reptiles and amphibians. Consequently, the two men travelled throughout Europe, meeting in person the people they had contacted initially over the Internet. In doing so, they embedded themselves in a wider, broader network than could have been predicted by their demographic profile. These men were operating outside of any social parameters that I knew of. These actions began to expose an invisible, unbound and unknown community that was actively demonstrating the strength of weak ties (Granovetter, 1973) and providing a space for people to explore and create their identities, pursue social roles and participate in social exchange across a physical-virtual environment.

The two men legally bred Australian reptiles and then sold them using Australian Internet forums. They were also active members of local and regional Herper societies. Both men knew a broad spectrum of people, from academics to biker gangs. These networks kept them well connected to an unusual range of far-flung contacts. This was despite both men keeping a low social profile due to their illegal activities of growing and selling cannabis, importing exotic animals from overseas and exporting local animals to overseas dealers. Their Australian Herper friends were unaware of these illegal activities. One of the men rarely went out, and spent most of his time tending to the plants and animals, smoking bongs and surfing the Internet. On the surface, this did not appear particularly social to me. However, when they were not tending to their 'enterprise', the two men were out poaching and networking across Australia and left their girlfriends to mind the extensive animal collections in their absence. Through this combination of activities they acquired contacts, photographic skills and knowledge to the point where they became contributors to local Herper society publications and presentations.

There are two further experiences after my practice-theory shock that shaped how I have approached the ethnography of this research population. The first happened at a reptile expo in Hamm, Germany, and the other is based upon my exposure to the animals themselves.

The experience of macro-micro structural events came alive for me during my participant observation at a very large reptile exposition in Hamm, Germany. I had travelled to Hamm from Italy in a campervan with three men: two Italian reptile owners and breeders and one American-Australian scientist. The campervan afforded us a prime position next to the gates of Hamm Expo. This reptile expo is one of the big reptile trading experiences in Europe. It is a networking and trading event with 15,000 people through the doors each day. This was a macrostructural force in the networking and connecting of people with herpetological interests from around the globe.

Not long after cruising into the teeming throng and checking out the venomous snakes' room, we met a man that the Italians knew. He wanted to show us the beauty of the Australian tiger snake he was selling, but was not displaying it as an official vendor in the room. In the close confines of narrow trestle tables, stressed and weaponised animals displayed in click-clack boxes and a steady flow of curious onlookers, it was against regulations to free-handle snakes in the venomous reptile room; and besides, this one was not legally owned. The room was heavily regulated, gate-kept by two burly paramedics at the door (who doubled as 'crowd-control') with only the higher-profile, legitimate venomous-reptile sellers selling at the trestle tables. Everyone else just had snakes in bags in their cars. All three men were keen to see an apparently beautiful specimen of one of Australia's unpredictable and deadly venomous snakes, despite having seen many of them before. It did not appear to be an obstacle to these men that if anyone got bitten by this venomous snake, medical treatment would be difficult to obtain. And yes, they had a space to go to – the campervan. So we returned, one of the Italians snorted cocaine on the dashboard, and they all got into the back of the campervan to watch the snake being taken out of the bag, free-handled and admired. I felt a unique moment of fear at this intersection of unlikely events, noting that for these men, this was a normal and expected pattern of behaviour. I looked out the window and saw several such posses sauntering off into their own spaces with an inconspicuously held wriggling calico bag. We were not the only ones experiencing this. I was in the middle of an event that seemed unique to me, yet it was continuously replayed throughout the course of the expo. These intersections were not momentary: the same people often attended year after year and maintained contact with each other through the Internet in between meetings. These networked social patterns became the motif that guided the methodological and theoretical framework of the research.

I have thought long and hard about why people are (or become) interested in reptiles and amphibians and seek each other out to discuss these interests. What I have come up with to view this type of sociality is a paradox of connection. The paradox begins with understanding the nature of the animals themselves. Donna Haraway points out in her book on companion species (Haraway, 2008) that non-human animals 'look back' at their human counterparts and our relationship with them is perhaps best framed as 'becoming with'. She argues that humans and non-human animals are knotted together in encounter and enter the world of 'becoming with', 'where who and what are is precisely what is at stake' (p. 19). She sees non-human animals as meaning-making figures that gather up those who respond to them into unpredictable kinds of 'we' (pp. 4–5). This emphasises the grouping nature of these animals as a focus of activity, the organising concept of the community under study.

As Haraway observes, these animals are agents that cause people to reorient towards them, which in turn causes the dynamics of interaction to change. The animals get pregnant and have babies; escape from enclosures; fight with each other and bite, strangle, slap and scratch people; die as individuals or become extinct as species. These characteristics affect their value as commodities and impact upon their connection with people. However, these animals are, by and large, vulnerable and are directly affected (threatened even) by the actions of people. One aspect of these animals is that they tend to suffer if they are exposed, handled, poked, prodded or not given the right living conditions. They are fragile, unpredictable and occasionally dangerous animals.

These animals behave in an instinctual way in the environments that they find themselves. There is no reflection upon, or prior to their actions and very little capacity to connect with another animal outside of predator, mate or prey relationships (see Krause, Croft, & James, 2007; Matessi et al., 2010; Sih et al., 2009 for discussions on sociality that occurs within non-human animal networks). Without domestication, their basic response to people is fear and occasionally defence or aggression (see Plumwood, 1995 for a reflective essay on this). In other words, most reptiles and amphibians encountered in this network do not connect with people in a positive way. They cannot be hugged, they do not 'give' love, do not seek company and in no way substitute for a dog, cat or even a bird as a companion animal. The behaviour of these animals can largely be characterised as reactive, opportunistic, non-self-aware in a human sense and exhibiting no compassion.

Despite this lack of emotive engagement, people often anthropomorphise their behaviours to provide a sense of ascribed intimacy. This leads to an apparent contradiction: despite the high levels of social reciprocity in the case study community, the emotional connection that people have with these animals is one-way. What people give, the animals do not reciprocate. What people get from this relationship does not come directly from any affective behaviour of the animal itself, but lies in what can be done to or with the animals. It is a control relationship characterised by a dynamic of disconnection, the result of which is an egocentric relationship in which the self is the controller of the other. One way of viewing this interest in animals is to think of it in terms of a sort of isolation in which the collector is consumed by their collection, over which they have the most control. And yet, dense levels of social communication and reciprocal relations exist between Herpers over these same interests. Hence the apparent contradiction: a disconnected and controlling relationship with reptiles facilitating reciprocal relationships between people.

The case study community struck me as a network of symbolic exchange. The literature on gift economies (cf. Bergquist & Ljungberg, 2001) argues that people are symbolic traders, where the value in an exchange is in the meaning of and social mores surrounding the objects rather than the objects themselves. For Herpers, these symbols were easily disconnected from their physical origins (the animal) and exchanged over the Internet in forms of interactive chat, pictures, commodities and ideas. But these symbols were not warm, cuddly and emotionally connective, like some other types of pets.

These ideas slithering around my head have led to a focus upon ego-centred individualism that operates as a site of differentiation, multiplicity and connection in a group. Within the literature this idea is captured in the concept of networked individualism (Rainie & Wellman, 2012; Wellman, 2001b; Wellman et al., 2003). Networked individualism is derived from the personalisation of communication devices and platforms; it is also about the customisation of self-image over the cultivation of group identity. However, herper community case study did not develop a discussion of the herper identity in this context, given its focus upon the social ecology of the herper network. The discussion of networked individualism (see Chapter 3, Section 3.4) is linked to the social trend of structural individualisation, in which the individual is the site of the resolution of contradictory social forces, rather than resolution being the responsibility of a group or institution (Woodman, 2011). The networked individual maintains continuity within these contradictory forces through his or her portfolios of participation. This is connected with the idea that intersections of multiple networks at the site of the individual provide the space for ambiguity, (re)configuration, connectivity and support (Foth & Hearn, 2007; Wellman et al., 2003). These ideas are used in this book to provide the mechanics for explaining interaction and participation in the social ecology.

6.5.3 Establishing the Researcher Profile and the Role of the Insider Perspective

This section will discuss, in the context of the 'insider' methods literature, how I established my profile within the network and how an insider perspective affects the data gathering and analysis. Acceptance, context and perspective are the key elements to ethnographic research of a social group. The researcher needs to achieve acceptance by the community in order to obtain exposure to the culture and people and generate well-connected research insight to the community experience. The process of gaining acceptance is usually begun in ethnographic research through a series of introductions by gatekeepers and informants in the community, as demonstrated in the Gangland study conducted by Frederic Thrasher (discussed in Chapter 2, Section 2.2). In addition to this, the rigour of ethnographic research is enacted through the researcher being able to see how they are positioned by and towards the group. The researcher needs to be aware of how this positioning may influence the data gathering and analysis.

Kanuha (2000) discusses the fine margin that she walked as a researcher who was 'of' the population that she studied. Her perspective is informative in this case, as I had personal exposure to this network for eight years through my partner of the time and was already 'known' to the population through this role. As discussed earlier, one of the motivations for studying this population was that I had personal access to them, had engaged with them as a participant and had observed social trends that could not be explained through the theoretical frameworks of the time. As LaSala (2003, pp. 17–18) argues, there were four main advantages to my insider research. Firstly, I was better able to elicit and understand the importance of emic perspectives because of my familiarity with the culture and language use of the community. Secondly, I knew where to find Herpers and was likely to be in the same places as they were accompanying my partner. The third advantage was to be seen as a credible person and researcher by the community, through their existing familiarity with who I was. This level of familiarity and trust opened the community's capacity to believe that I was not intending to vilify them and was likely to produce a portrait of the community that would identify and speak to their values. Because of this open reception by many of the community members, I was able to engage informants, and establish the rapport and trust necessary for honest reporting, the fourth advantage of insider researcher argued by LaSala.

Another aspect raised by LaSala is the line between when a researcher is personally and not personally involved in a community. Whilst I am not personally interested in reptiles and amphibians and had no history of this in my past, I was personally involved in the network as I had 'married into' it. I joked with participants that it was like marrying into the Mafia, which appeared to appeal to their sense of humour. At the same time, I was exploring social theory on community and the Internet, participating in scholarly discussions and conducting a mixed-methods study to assist me in understanding the social patterns that I was observing. When all of the above is taken into account, I could be seen to hold a dual perspective that was both emic and etic (Pike, 1967, 1990). Kanuha (2000, p. 441) describes the emic perspective as a subjective, informed and influential standpoint, and contrasts this with the etic perspective, which she describes as objective, distant, logical and at a remove from one's project. LaSala expands on this to describe emic and etic as the difference between the participant's point of view and the theoretical standpoint towards their experience.

> The emic perspective is the viewpoint of the members of the group or culture being studied. Behavior and events are described strictly in terms of what they mean to the informants. From the etic or outsider stand-point, behavior is explained using theories that are thought to be applicable to all groups and cultures.
>
> (LaSala, 2003, p. 16)

The universalist standpoint that LaSala ascribes to the etic perspective is probably an overstatement as most theories do not attempt to be applicable to all groups and cultures in the aftermath of postmodernism. However in this statement he does highlight that the emic perspective is anticipated to hold the voice of the community, while the etic perspective holds an abstract position that views social action from a theoretical framework. The etic perspective can be seen then to facilitate the ability of the researcher to translate the 'voice' of a community into a broader debate and contextual understanding. Consequently, LaSala argues that good research incorporates an integration of both etic and emic perspectives. In the case study of the herper community, the theoretical frameworks discussed in the literature review of Chapters 2 and 3 informed my experience and insights during participant observation, providing an etic perspective. On the other hand, whilst I was not [directly] a Herper, my closeness to the point of view of participants allowed me a level of emic insight. Through the closeness of my association, I was able to acknowledge people's passions for reptiles and discuss these with them in a knowledgeable way, but I could not share their passion with them. I was caught between being on the outside and inside, being subjective and objective, but with few tools to discern when I was one or the other. As Kanuha describes, the critical aspect for a researcher in this position is the need to distance oneself from the project, the participants and the process of studying 'one's own people' (2000, p. 442). Indeed, the need to separate my own experiences and subsequent analyses from those of study participants was the most profound methodological process I had to learn as an insider researcher. In line with techniques suggested by Kanuha and advocated by LaSala (2003), I employed the techniques of self-reflection and debriefing in order to understand the emic-etic dichotomy that I was in. In my case, however, these techniques were not employed during the data-gathering phase, but after all the data had been gathered. During the field research I was continuously travelling between countries and sites, had very limited contact with the world beyond the herper networks, and limited opportunities to debrief and gain perspective whilst immersed in the population. LaSala (2003) argues that this time of immersion is an advantage to ethnographic rigour. From my experience, I would argue that it has provided insight into episodic and unstructured community expression that is impossible to 'plan' observations around. It also facilitated the research time to observe and participate under less contrived conditions and through opportunistic encounters. However, given the emotional labour involved in processing the data collected and negotiating the division between the personal and professional, it has taken substantial reflection and peer debriefing for me to achieve the critical distance needed from the field immersion to provide a balanced and informed interpretation of the data.

Melrose (2002), in her discussion of conducting sensitive research with a marginalised group discusses the impact that emotional labour has on the research practice. She highlights the fine line that the researcher walks between the personal and professional in conducting qualitative research with participants. She highlights that despite the trend towards reflexivity in the research process, dealing with the emotional impact of sensitive research has received little attention. I agree that the emotional labour of dealing with the personal within the professional is the silent partner in participant observation. Melrose articulates this struggle in considering how she believed, before beginning the research, that she would be able to switch between a 'working self' and an 'out of work self'.

> This unrealistic expectation foolishly ignored the fact that my 'working self' is intimately connected to my total sense of self and to fulfil such an expectation, therefore, I would need to be able to dissociate from other parts of myself. This is obviously not a healthy strategy to pursue.
>
> (Melrose, 2002, p. 345)

As this observation suggests, working with research populations can be emotionally confronting for the researcher and role separation provides minimal respite from this. For me, an example of the line between the personal and professional being emotionally charged emerged in the gender analysis of the interview dataset. In the instance I present below, it was the resonance between the overt gendered relations, knowledge dependency and attitudes towards risk and personal safety demonstrated by the couple with the dynamics of my own close relationship of the time that required reflexivity through the research literature and professional debriefing before I was able to treat this analysis with a level of distance from the subject and compassion.

* * *

In conversation, during which her partner was also present, Nellie discusses some of the events that happened for her as a partner to a Herper. Her narrative demonstrates a gender dynamic of personal subordination that is about the authority of the male figure, her anticipatory behaviour change in fear of her partner's anger, the impact of age dynamics and a trust in her partner's ability to protect her. This is the archetypal profile of gender inequality in a relationship, where the woman's actions are shaped by the perception of male authority, domination and protection. Because of this dynamic, Nellie took actions that endangered her own personal safety. There are three other people whom she refers to in the narrative below: Ricardo is her partner, Sally Ann is her sister and John is her sister's partner. These people were all involved in the maintenance and retail of Ricardo's private herp collection.

> Nellie: They took off one time and we [Nellie and Sally Ann] were left with the red-belly babies [venomous snakes]. We accidently sprayed them with disinfectant instead of the water one time. And we'd gone, 'Oh, shit', and we've just picked them all up, dumped them in a fresh bucket of water and then we just scooped them all out with our hands. Our whole problem was these guys [Ricardo and John], it wasn't the animals we were dealing with. It was what they would do to us if they came home and we go, 'I'm sorry we killed all the red-bellies' or, 'We lost an adder'. Like Sally Ann tailed an adder one time because it got out of its tub and her first thought was, 'John's gonna kill me', and she just tailed it and threw it back in [a very dangerous act with this species of snake]. But that's how we were. We just thought they'd kill us if we fucked up … . It was about four years later when we confessed a few things. We were terrified of them. We got told off one time [when they were travelling together on a animal collecting trip/ holiday]. Johno cracked it – we weren't even allowed to talk to each other in the car and we were on holidays! Because we were younger than them and I'd just turned 21 when I met Ricardo and my sister was 19.
>
> Alexia: So you girls had fallen in with an interesting bunch.
>
> Nellie: Well, my mum has said, 'Did I do something wrong?' She likes them [the men], but she doesn't understand the attraction [to reptiles]. She's still of that mindset that snakes will hurt you. You know, what you are told.
>
> Alexia: How did you lose that mindset?

> Nellie: I think the more you learn about them, the less you fear about them. […] Just seeing how Ricardo interacts with them, it desensitises you, I suppose. He's handled 300 snakes today and I've handled 20 and we're still fine. I've seen him being chased around the bedroom by cobras and I used to sit up on the shelves. It was just so much fun. I didn't realise … it was just fun for us. […] But I've always trusted him. Like a cobra has come for me before and Ricardo has just lunged in front of me and grabbed it. So I know he'd put himself at risk to save me, so I feel totally safe.

From this excerpt we can see that Nellie has been socialised into accepting this level of risk and danger through emotional bonding and identification with the perspectives of her partner. During this discussion Nellie demonstrates that she did limited personal research in learning about the toxicity and dangers of these animals in order to gain some critical perspective on them and what she was doing. It is clear from her narrative that she has experienced danger and desensitisation to the risk of a venomous snakebite through the attitude and behaviour of her partner. Consequently, her way of perceiving these events is from a subordinate position in the relationship where her point of view and perception of safety of her actions has been subsumed by her partner's perspective, skill-base and knowledge authority. During her early years with him, this subordinate role placed the site for authority (in knowledge and behaviour) and discipline (through fear and anger) in her partner. It is to be noted however, that she was not in personal danger from him. What she was in danger of was the subordination of her own intuition and perspective to the ideas of her partner that is common to many women in gendered dynamics. This warped her actions to the point that she allowed, and put herself into, life-threatening positions with deadly animals through the structured patterns of her relationship. This transfer of identification away from self-generated perspectives to those of another (i.e. the loss of critical distance to a subject and the loss of a sense of the primary position of the self in relation to a subject) can be seen in the observed phenomenon of victims taking on the perspective of their captives, referred to as the Stockholm syndrome (Fabrique et al., 2007). As she discussed during her interview, Nellie had limited idea of the extreme toxicity of the animals that she was first exposed to, cobras and Gaboon vipers, and took the comfort that her partner felt in handling and working with these animals as a guide to her own behaviour.

More generally, sexism and role typing was experienced by the researcher mildly through verbal interaction during fieldwork, however with the researcher being married, these interactions were more focused on gendered positioning as the cook, cleaner and first-aider during fieldwork. However, I was often grateful for the social illusion of 'protection' that being married brought with it in this network while moving through such heavily male and often dangerous domains. These domains were physically dangerous for the researcher as they involved being exposed to and needing to know how to handle, escape, or not alarm fearful and consequently aggressive animals. The risk of mortality or morbidity was increased by the alacrity, incomplete knowledge and skill levels with which participants handled their animals or engaged with wild animals. Their skill and safety self-awareness was often impaired by excitement, denial, intoxication, and a false sense of security with these animals. I believe that having my partner present, or even his reputation present, at these times mostly reduced the need for the participant to impress (scare) me and for me to actively demonstrate animal-handling skills.

* * *

As is evident in the above discussion, these kinds of role expectations and gendered social relations do have their disadvantages and dependencies that may not result in healthy or sustainable behaviours. In an unresolved state within the researcher, they are also likely to influence the researcher's treatment of the data and impair their ability to recognise and reveal social patterns. For me, a lack of acknowledgement of my own gendered and role-based position inhibited me for a long time in presenting the culture of the community as heavily masculine and competitive, a 'no brainer' on the surface of things. It also impaired my willingness to explore of the types of roles that women did occupy and handle the petty, prejudiced and intentional violations they may have experienced socially in a treatment of the data. In a knock-on effect for the overall research concept, my understandings of social cohesion within the community remained partial due to my lack of willingness to acknowledge the absence and invisibility of women in the community. This was particularly remiss in the face of the strength of women to knit together stable infrastructures of support through trust-based relationships and introduce alternative perspectives towards the animals and each other than those dominant in the community.

Kanuha discusses Aguilar's (1981, p. 26) suggestion that biases or predispositions that are often disproportionately attributed to the insider researcher might be sources of insight as well as error. LaSala (2003) suggests that error occurs through mistaken assumptions by the researcher about common cultural understandings with interviewees and the failure to explore their respondents' unique perceptions. This can be a case of not being able to notice the familiar. Kanuha (2000, pp. 442–3) also suggests that it is dangerous to assume that being an insider within a cultural group necessarily means that the insider researcher has intimate knowledge of the particular and situated experiences of all members of the group, or that generalisation can or should be made about the knowledge the researcher has about her own culture. Unlike Kanuha, who researched her own social identity group, I was not personally interested in reptiles or amphibians but did hold a strong conservation stance and concern for animal welfare. In the case of the herpetological network, it was clear that I was situated by my gender and my exposure to venomous animals and snakes through my partner's research practice as a molecular geneticist and venom specialist. However, what this also meant was that my personal knowledge and involvement in the network constituted a niche interest in terms of animal affiliations and the most socially invisible role in the network, 'the wife'. Being generally oriented towards and educated about conservation issues was an asset in creating rapport with participants. Being Australian and travelling to other countries meant that I also did not operate within the same legislative regulations for keeping animals as many interviewees, and therefore needed participants to explain their experience to me in their local context. This mobility of travel and seeing the network in different locations also minimised 'the familiar' (LaSala, 2003, p. 19). I was clearly of a different gender, role and country of origin than most people whom I interviewed, and this helped me to retain relative objectivity and 'foreignness' in relation to the language and experiences of the participant. These were some of the advantages of an extended period of exposure to the network of people with interests in reptiles and amphibians. At the same time as conducting participant observation, I was also designing survey questions and constructs. This practical engagement with research methods through data collection and design, being active in the field and developing social pattern measures for the survey, assisted my access to the etic perspective while immersed in the community. Engaging with the community at these two levels is an advantage of mixed-methods for the researcher.

During data collection, I worked to blend appropriately with the community through observing the social mores, such as clothing, being across key topics of discussion and make myself generally useful in terms of accepting appropriate roles and tasks. When moving through a Herper social space, I tended to wear gender-neutral clothing that was similar to what many Herpers wore in terms of function and colour palette: usually khaki or beige cargo pants and outdoors-style shirts commonly sold in hiking stores. This was intended to provide a sense of familiarity and was usually applicable clothing for what I was doing during the participant observation at the time. In addition to this clothing sensitivity, during and around the interview I was able to talk intelligibly with participants about their experiences and thinking on animal taxonomy, biology, genetics, handling and husbandry techniques. As we moved into the interview, participants were self-conscious, as they were not used to being part of a social study. In terms of recruitment, I was visible in situations where women were not usually visible, as I sought to meet and expose myself to the wider range of places and people involved. In order to not seem out of place, I accepted roles that also reflected my external position, but were nevertheless useful to participants: that of the first aid officer, tool holder, backup handler, risk assessor, lab assistant and photographer. I also participated in animal documentaries during the data-gathering period, which some participants may have seen. However, the experience gained through participating in animal documentaries provided me with insight into how a television crew produces documentaries about reptiles and amphibians, and who they thought the audience was. This added another dimension to how I was seeing and experiencing the herper community and meant that moving through them as a research observer was relatively smooth and informative.

In terms of my positionality in the research, whilst the type of ethnography that I conducted was immersive and constituted the insider experience, this notion of 'the insider' in itself is argued by Dwyer and Buckle (2009) to reflect an unduly narrow binary:

> Although a researcher's knowledge is always based on his or her positionality (Mullings, 1999), as qualitative researchers we have an appreciation for the fluidity and multilayered complexity of human experience. Holding membership in a group does not denote complete sameness within that group. Likewise, not being a member of a group does not denote complete difference. It seems paradoxical, then, that we would endorse binary alternatives that unduly narrow the range of understanding and experience.
>
> (Dwyer & Buckle, 2009, p. 60)

This binary of insider and outsider is limiting as a way to understand the ability of the researcher to be able to authentically access and reflect the voice of the community whilst also seeing it in its social context and through a theoretical lens. As the discussion above has indicated, taking a mixed methods approach alongside observing social mores of the community and accepting appropriate roles and tasks during field work were crucial to the development of research insight. The act of peer debriefing assisted in the untangling and sense-making of the subjective, immersive and personal experience that engaging with a community brings.

Although this binary can be seen as a limiting perspective, Labaree (2002) highlights the hidden dilemmas of entering the field of positioning and disclosure, shared relationships and disengagement. Positioning and disclosure occurs between the researcher and the research population through the transparent establishment of who the researcher is understood to be by the community and the level of disclosure they provide about how their activities and interactions with community members will be recorded and presented as research findings. Positioning myself as a researcher and partner to a prominent figure within the case study community discussed above documented the establishment of familiarity, trust and rapport building during participant observation. Labaree suggests that the hidden issue of shared relationships, while unavoidable in the development of meaningful relationships with informants, holds both benefits and challenges to the research. The challenge in particular being highlighted that a pre-existing relationship, when utilised instrumentally for the purposes of research data collection, networking and knowledge of key events may be damaged when used for these purposes. Another challenge of these social bonds and intimacies created or utilised for the purpose of research is that the social standing of the informant within the community may affect the access the researcher has to certain people and activities, alongside aligning the researcher with the perceptions the community holds towards the informant. This may become particularly complicated if, as suggested by Labaree, suspicions of hidden agendas held by the community towards the researcher arise through the associations the researcher holds within the community. While the experience of being tarred by association was rarely an overt case for me during the conduct of the case study research, I did need to navigate carefully my association with a character who afforded access to the shadier sides of the community. At the outset of data collection in his local area, I was unaware of the level of social stigma associated with this person; however the time and tide of conversations quickly revealed that I would need to demonstrate social distance from them. At the time of my research practice, this person held a balance of being instrumentally useful to many people, and was relatively well connected. However during the course of the data collection, informants and community members would clearly inform me to not bring this person along when visiting with them or their private collections. Due to my mobility between places and countries, I was able to disconnect and distance effectively and respectfully, however this was an important lesson in the impact of association upon social access.

Other undetected biases may also exist within the interview data and participant observations due to the implicit agendas of those who chose to engage with me. While these may have been invisible to me, it is likely that some participants in the research felt that it was an opportunity to build credibility within the community by association. This is particularly the case when considering the impact of my significant relationship with a key figure in the community. Most participants knew me for who I was at the time: the wife of an academic who had research and personal interests in reptiles and amphibians, with a particular bias towards snakes and venomous animals. As Labaree (2002, p. 113) argues, and evidenced within the case study research, close association with an informant, such as marriage or an intimate relationship, both provides access and closes access within the network. One clear impact of my marital relationship is that data on people with interests in venomous snakes, large lizards and other dangerous animals (such as crocodiles and large goannas) is over-represented. Also, people who had an aversion to either my partner or venomous animals were less predisposed to talk to me. In order to address these biases in my exposure and access, I networked at conferences and expos and attended events held by local herpetological societies. In addition to these efforts, the animals that my partner dealt with expanded from venomous snakes and lizards to include a wider range of snakes, lizards and amphibians. Consequently, I moved from meeting people through him who were specifically associated with venomous-animal research to meeting people who were interested in a wide range of reptiles and amphibians.

In terms of shared relationships within the case study research, most relationships I held with participants were discontinuous, due to the episodic nature of engagement. The pace of travel and exposure to different cultures in different countries made episodic engagement more or less inevitable. The key implications of this style of convenience sampling, while addressing concerns to do with the influence of shared relationships upon data collection, is that data collected and people engaged in one locale were less likely to characterise the experiences of people in another. This consideration of data continuity and applicability was addressed in the research project by embracing these patterns and pursuing a diverse array of location and event types (from public to private) to create a broader perspective upon experience and engagement in the network. In addition to these biases, people who are willing to be interviewed for research purposes tend to have a desire to share their story and experience to a wider audience or hold value for the practice of scholarly research. These participants also tend to be more outgoing and more invested in the community itself, but not exclusively so, with some participants more engaged by the novelty of having free reign to discuss their interests with a female researcher who intended to use their experiences constructively. This speaks to an agenda for social contribution that was generally somewhat altruistic and evident in the reasons participants engaged with me.

A final hidden dilemma highlighted by Labaree is the process of disengagement from the field for the researcher. This process is fraught for several reasons. The first being that when a community member leaves a community, there is a sense of loss felt by both and an artificial disconnection that is usually enacted only through social ostracism or self-exile. This leaves a silent hole for both the researcher and the population. Withdrawal of the researcher also tends to highlight the utilitarian nature of the connections made by the researcher for the purposes of conducting research, which is at odds with the sense of membership, identity and connection that participating in a community usually generates. As noted by Snow (1980) in his critical consideration of researcher disengagement from participant observation, the community impact of this depends upon whether the community itself is used to membership turnover, which the case study community was.

For the researcher, exiting the field however is as important in terms of critical reflection and distance as it is to signal the close of data collection for the research participants. Snow highlights that community disengagement usually results in a period of disorientation and decompression from the intensity of the interpersonal ties between fieldworkers and informants. Within the case study research, as I was intimately involved through my relationship with my partner the process of disconnection and reflection was not fully achieved for me until the close of that particular relationship. This proved to be a personally fraught disentanglement to navigate while conducting data analysis and required peer support and debriefing. My experience does raise for me the concern that engaging with a research population through a close or significant relationship, while advantageous in terms of connection and acceptance, may impede the researcher in terms of gaining reflection and distance to the subject. In this instance I argue for the assistance of peer debriefing to gain a reflective and critical stance to events and people and a return to an alternative pattern of living or 'normal life' that is congruent with the researcher's own personal practices and values and somewhat removed from the practices of the community under study. Consequently this course of action requires planning and awareness and should be weighed carefully by the researcher considering embarking on research with a population with whom they are personally connected.

Disengagement from the field also holds with it the expectation that the researcher will contribute their research findings back to the community from which they gained them. As Snow (1980, p. 114) highlights, the researcher often disengages from the community with a strong sense of guilt, obligation and indebtedness to the community itself. I also experienced this through the case study research and felt that it was my obligation as a researcher to complete the research, which became a key motivation for my persistence in completing the work. In addition to completion, I consider making the work accessible and in formats that are relevant to the community as well as to my scholarly peers and the wider public another way that I can attend to this community contribution. Although it was clear that the Herpers who participated were unsure exactly what application the research results would have, they appeared to hope that it may assist to legitimate their interests in the public domain. As Snow (p. 114) poetically observes, the ethnographer is typically ensnared in a web of multiple loyalties and competing claims, some of which requires them to weigh up the public's 'right-to-know' against the 'right-to-privacy' of those studied. When weighing up these agendas, the researcher may publish findings that do not align with or respect the framing through which a community sees a set of events. As was highlighted by the experience of Scheper-Hughes (2000) in returning to her population after publishing her research results, the clash of these two agendas does not always work out well and at times can result in the loss of access for the researcher to the community. In terms of the case study population, it remains unclear how the publication of these results will be received, however the agenda of this book to focus on a research methods discussion has at some level alleviated some of these concerns for me and de-emphasised the role and relevance of some of the more private and confidential data and social interplays that I may have been privy to during the ethnography. Regardless, the work is written in respect, compassion and gratitude and I have turned the tools of my trade to it. Working with social research methods and concepts has rapidly expanded my abilities to collect and analyse research data in a balanced and nuanced manner. This, for me, is the contribution of the work to my research practice.

6.6 Conclusion

This chapter has provided an overview and introduction to the methodological discussion of qualitative research practice. This included a discussion of the efficacy of ethnography to provide both macro and micro perspectives into the community as well as its capacity to illustrate the heart or mediating culture of the community. From this discussion, the chapter then provided a consideration of the practices within the design and conduct of data collection of the case study that contribute to the validity and capacity for insight and congruency of research findings. The researcher positionality, a crucial component to transparency within qualitative research process was discussed through how I, as the researcher in the case study, was perceived and positioned within the community and how this may have influenced the types of data I was able to collect and the social practices I was likely to observe. As an insider researcher, the discussion of researcher positionality also considered how the influence of shared and significant relationships was likely to impact the data collection and how I addressed these concerns within the research practice. In terms of gaining distance and perspective from the immersive and consuming experience of field work, I highlighted in this chapter the pivotal nature of the process of disengagement from the field and the role of post data-collection debriefing to balance research insight. The chapter also considered the emic-etic tangle that is entered into by the researcher during immersive field-work and how the conduct of mixed-methods research can be considered an advantage to the balancing of perspective and biases introduced through this close and intimate connection with the community under study.

Despite a research methods discussion being a somewhat detached way of looking at research practice, this is my most personal chapter. In it I have shared the insights I gained from conducting the qualitative methods for the case study research, both to state the importance and presence of subjectivity within qualitative research and to underscore for researchers considering these methods the benefits and challenges that immersion within a community raises for research design, practice and publication.

PART II
Illustrating the Connections between Research Methods, Concepts and Analysis

Chapter 7
Community Place

7.1 Introduction

In this chapter, I discuss the methods used to explore the environment of social interaction and exchange within a community that articulates its place. Data presented in this chapter from the herper community case study is both qualitative and quantitative. Section 7.2 unpacks the spatial imprint of the community that exists through the channels of mediated sociability used. Initially this section presents a discussion of the survey data from the case study to consider what the communication hotspots are and how they span in-person to online communication channels. The spatiality of the online environment is explored through a hyperlink map of the online issue network of the herper community. This map is constructed from a co-link analysis of website addresses collected through the survey tool and visualised using the hyperlink analysis tool hosted at issuecrawler.net. The spatiality of the social layer, presented in section 7.3, is reconstructed through the connections between social networks and geography collected through the survey instrument. Section 7.4 reviews the mediating culture of the case study community and explores the qualitative data on how the Internet has influenced this. Through consideration of the case study data, I present a practical discussion of the findings of the mixed-methods approach that demonstrates how regarding the community through an ecological lens has allowed the analysis to move beyond the place-based boundaries and online and offline dualism identified in the literature review. From this, the research practitioner is drawn into the characterisation of an open social system that fluidly operates across an identifiable technological, spatial and social terrain.

The place of a community is the environment the community operates in. So if my question is 'Where do I find Herpers?'. I would very quickly be asking 'What's their environmental niche?'. If the environment where their social activity and exchange takes place has both physical and virtual dimensions, as was the case for the Herpers, then the definition of community place needs to incorporate both of these spaces. In his discussion of the social impact of communication technologies and the Internet, van Dijk (2006) reconceptualises the notion of place to be a co-ordinate of social interaction in time and space. For research practice, the operational face of this approach to place allows the incorporation of methods that can be deployed to collect data on social engagement both online and offline. Using the notion of a co-ordinate to locate the community in space also allows us to draw on topological understandings of social space. It allows the researcher to consider mapping location co-ordinates of physical spaces within the community through publically available GIS software (Batty et al., 2010; Haklay, Singleton, & Parker, 2008; Haklay & Weber, 2008) and relational data within the online space of the community through citation-based, issue-based and social hyperlink networks (Ackland, 2013; Rogers, 2009a, 2009b, 2010a, 2012; Thelwall, 2009). The possibility that digital trace data can be used to articulate these environments was raised while I was exploring how to equate my global respondent population demographics in the survey design and how to represent the hyperlink space of my survey participants. Within the commercial sector, global geo-demographic datasets are derived from merging datasets linked to post-codes (Burrows & Gane, 2006; Parker, Uprichard, & Burrows, 2007). Within the domain of Big Data (boyd & Crawford, 2012; Mahrt & Scharkow, 2013), other social practices of digital territories are being developed through locative media that also hold spatial understandings of community behaviour for the researcher (Lemos, 2010; Power et al., 2013; Rodríguez-Amat & Brantner, 2014; San Cornelio & Ardevol, 2011). However the research journey into such evolving practices is not always smooth, with data interpretation providing new challenges (Nafus, 2014). These forms of locative and relational information analysis visualise a digital imprint of the environment within which the community is fertile. This reveals a form of materiality to the space of the community for the researcher to view and think about. As we know the location of place evolves through technical innovations, our concepts used to describe it need to be future focused to connect with this. This approach allows for the researcher's choice in methods to evolve alongside social practice, existing knowledge and available tools for analysis. I argue that incorporating evolving methods and data contexts such as these within research practice is what turning a definition of community place into a community environment enables in the research methodology.

Through the time-stamped nature of this locative imprint of social space, it also allows us to understand the place of community as dynamic. Through the literature review in Chapters 1 and 2, we can see that the dynamic nature of socio-technical space is brought about through innovation, adaptation, appropriation and disruption. As the Herpers demonstrated for me, locations where a community gathers fall in and out of favour, get disrupted through technical and social conflict or cease to exist; but this does not mean participants in these spaces cease to stay connected. Some connections remain and new endeavours begin over time. From this understanding we can see that the community curation and response to social space develops a 'niche' environment with a unique and evolving shape, which the researcher can find and follow for the duration of the research. For me, the analogy of 'lighting a beacon' when research is begun draws upon this morphological and dynamic notion of space. It is about attracting community members to engage with you from within the environments that they are socially interactive and willing to engage with people they may not know. This is a point-in-time place where they gather, which usually becomes a regularised location that people remember and come back to. The continuity of social experience across the dynamic spaces of the community occurs through the connections established in these fertile places. These connections, rather than static locations, support the flourishing of the community more generally. From this discussion, I argue that a flourishing community is one that is perpetually in the process of becoming, and the act of becoming usually has a co-ordinate.

7.2 Technology, Place and the Built Environment

Knowing that a population is socially active in physical locations and virtual locations is one thing, but working out how to isolate and analyse these behaviours into a sense of the spatiality of the community is another. While I was able to observe the population socialising at society meetings, pet shops, reptile expos, at their work sites such as zoos and museums and meeting informally together, I had no idea of the balance to which their social activities ranged across in person networking and online engagement. Conceptually, the technological layer and its associated ICT environment is the combination of different types of technologies people use to communicate with others. The survey and associated quantitative analysis allowed me to observe the mediated sociability of the network and the consequent interconnectivity of places and online spaces through the geographic reach of participants' social ties. This reflects the multi-spatial, multimodal nature of a social ecology that was discussed in the literature review through the globalisation and networked sociability literature.

The question of ICT use patterns within the Herper community initially focused upon how people in the respondent population used the Internet. This enabled a consideration between the findings of this case study with discussions of Internet use, virtual community, online sociability and computer-mediated communication within the literature more generally. It also connects the case study with notions of the Network Society in which Internet access is a pivotal facilitator of sociability and information exchange. In contemporary literature the idea of 'the Internet' being central to online sociability has been replaced by the idea that the use patterns of ICTs are converging into a communication environment (Jenkins, 2006; Schroeder, 2010; van Dijk, 2006). This speaks to the notion of the communicative ecology that forms the basis for understanding social space in a social ecology. Whilst still covering distance and mediated by mobile hardware and different software approaches to sociality, the research reporting here includes social interaction over the telephone, email, video (Skype for example), forum interactions and instant messaging for example, and does not exclude face-to-face interaction. However more contemporary research on ICT use focuses on the web 2.0 technologies such as SNS sites (boyd & Ellison, 2008). The Internet remains at the backbone of this trend because of its singular capacity for high-volume, real-time data transfer and the mixed between centralised and decentralised, many-to-many connections (Fuchs, 2005). As Shen and Williams (2011, pp. 126–7) argue, the Internet is a malleable medium that allows for both social and asocial use. In this context people are not passively dictated to by technology but actively appropriate technology to accomplish their own goals. The authors see this as consistent with the idea that social relationship developments coalesce in computer-mediated and face-to-face contexts over time because users actively appropriate and develop adaptive strategies to use communication technology to suit their relational goals. This is referred to by Dutta-Bergman (2004) as channel complementarity. Hence the environment of ICT convergence through social relationships is well supported in the research literature. This facilitates the efficacy of the idea of 'channels' of communication to be introduced as the place of a network.

The literature suggested initially that I would need to know their technical capacity to access the online environment in order to establish if this population was digitally immersed. To do this, I incorporated into the survey a measure derived from the literature was web-oriented digital literacy (Hargittai, 2005). Hargittai (2005) discusses web-oriented digital literacy and includes self-perceived skill levels as one indicator of this. Whilst her research proposes a digital literacy measure consisting of seven items, this measure was not feasible to include within an already long survey. This proposed measure is based upon a participant's recognition of Internet navigation tasks. Given the constant rate of technological innovation, these terms tend to become outdated over time. Because of this, measures testing familiarity with terminology and tasks cannot provide comparative data between studies. However Hargittai contributes the predictive power of self-perceived skill when regressed on actual skill levels. In her study the adjusted R^2 of self-reported skill levels was 0.239. This is in comparison with the adjusted R^2 from the recommended seven-item measure of 0.321. This suggests that self-reported rating of Internet skills has less predictive power but remains informative. The self-reported rating of Internet skill discussed in this article and used in the survey was:

In terms of your Internet skills, do you consider yourself to be . . .

Users were asked to answer this question measured on a five-point scale ('not at all skilled, not very skilled, fairly skilled, very skilled, expert'). The mean self-perceived skill level in Hargittai's sample was 2.88 (SD = .73). The average perceived skill level that respondents reported in accessing and using the Internet of the respondent population is fairly skilled (M = 3.55, SD = .84, N = 1557, Median = 4, IQR = 1) with the median response being very skilled. This suggests that the sample perceived themselves to be, in general, more skilled in accessing and engaging in the online environment than the established average in the study conducted by Hargittai.

In addition to skill levels, the literature suggests that there are other factors that influence this technology use, such as people's years of experience in using the Internet, time spent online and the quality of the Internet access they have (computing power and connection type). All of these factors influence how immersed a person is likely to be in the digital environment. For the survey respondent population, the median number of years online for participants was 9 years (M = 9.07 years, SD = 3.79, Median = 9, IQR = 4.5). Upon inspection of the data, there was a substantial proportion of participants who had accessed the Internet for 10–15 years (Skewness = .87, Kurtosis = 3.04). Participants were also asked how many hours they spent on the Internet in the last seven days. Similar wording was used to the question asked by the original HomeNet study (Kraut et al., 2002; Kraut et al., 1998) and a more contemporary study conducted by Shen and Williams (2011) on an online gaming population (high Internet users). The median number of hours online in the previous seven days for the sample was 15 hours (M = 19.92, SD = 20.33, Trimmed mean = 17.49, Median = 15, IQR = 18). These results suggest that the respondent population is Internet-active in relation to pursuing their interests in herpetology online. The online gaming population surveyed by Shen and Williams (2011) spent an average of 29.57 (SD = 20.57) hours online every week in 2011 and the authors described this population as heavy Internet users. Given that online gaming is solely an online activity and the Herpers were accessing the Internet for their interests in concert with other activities in 2006, this suggests that the sample is quite active online.

In reflection upon these results, it appears that respondents had been accessing the Internet for an average of nine years with a substantial proportion of participants having accessed the Internet for 10–15 years. With the data collecting having taken place in 2006, this indicates that respondents were early adopters of the Internet environment (1997 on average being the year in which these users would have started going online). The ethnography suggested that Herpers were early adopters of the Internet-mediated space as a means to interact and share information and these results suggest that participants were actively and autonomously engaged online from an early point of the dispersion of the Internet into the public domain. Consequently, the spatiality of the herper community as incorporating the use of the Internet as a domain of interaction is likely to have been well established within social practices rather than a novel aspect. The results presented below on ICT channels of use and the relational space online also support the idea that the integration of the spatiality of the Internet of increased reach and niche knowledge was deeply embedded within the herper community at the time of data collection. These findings supported the proposition that this community was an effective case study to explore the reconfiguration of community into digital space.

7.2.1 Communication Hotspots

When thinking of relationships across this digital architecture, it is important to keep in mind that they consist of multimodal connectedness (Schroeder, 2010) and are rarely confined to any one channel. Schroeder (2010) argues that narrowly focusing on individual technologies of communication (such as a mobile phone in their case) misses the point that the mobile's usage cannot easily be separated from usage of other information and communication technologies (ICTs). They argue that this misses the social behaviour of distributed maintenance of social ties across devices and refer to this as the concept of multimodal connectedness. Consequently, the media that people use to interact with each other defines the scope of ICT use and the accessibility and reach of social ties across the environment of a community. However it also reveals the nature of sociality within the community, for example whether it is group based or enacted through informal social networks. From the literature, we know that the channels of mediated sociability represent different combinations of factors of use such as cost, familiarity/skill base, who else in a peer network uses it, one-to-one, one-to-many and many-to-many styles of communication (Bolter & Grusin, 2000; Fuchs, 2005, 2008), mobility and convenience. In terms of understanding the results of the communicative environment of the network, it is helpful to take some time to think about the dynamic of each channel. See Table 7.2 for a brief outline of the dynamics of each channel reported on. This table is a synthesis of how these formats of interaction are described in Internet-based and media-based research on the social impacts of new media (cf. Bargh & McKenna, 2004; Chan, 2011; Comunello, 2012; Fuchs, 2005, 2008; Schroeder, 2010; Shanyang, 2006; Subrahmanyam et al., 2008; Trappeniers et al., 2008).

In light of this permissive spatial logic, the participants were asked about all of their possible channels of communication with other Herpers based on ICTs in use at the time of research. In their survey responses, they indicated how many Herpers they contacted via each channel in the last seven days. When looking at the univariate results in Table 7.1[1] below, face-to-face social contact,

1 The trends discussed are annotated by an asterisk * in Table 7.1.

email use and other Internet channels were the most frequently used means to connect with other Herpers. This data is also further reinforced by the fact that much higher numbers of respondents (39.6 per cent, *N* = 486 and 35.5 per cent, *N* = 433 respectively) did not use landline phones or mobile phones to contact other Herpers in the last seven days, in comparison to those who did not use face-to-face, email or other Internet channels. From these univariate results, we can say that Herpers that the environment of the community is constituted by physical places where people are co-located, email threads, where Herpers maintain connections and Internet channels, particularly forums, where they maintain and create new connections through extended and diverse socio-technical domains. As these coordinates of sociability are open to engagement with diverse and unknown others in group contexts and informal social networks, it seems likely that the social spaces of the Herpers were characterised by both of these social configurations from these findings. Consequently, the environment of communication is deeply intertwined with the patterns of social organisation within the community. These findings will be further considered in Section 7.3 on the spatial dispersion of social ties. The following discussion, however, considers what the online environment may look like from a topological perspective.

Table 7.1 Frequencies of face-to-face and mediated interaction between Herpers over the last seven days

Number of people contacted	Face-to-Face	Landline phone	Mobile phone	Email	Other Internet
	% (N)	**% (N)**	**% (N)**	**% (N)**	**% (N)**
none	19.5 (276)	39.6 (486)	35.5 (433)	13.3 (189)	19.5 (258)
1–2 people	44.1 (626)	42.1 (517)	40.6 (495)	28.7 (407)	19.3 (256)
3–5 people	21.8 (309)	11.5 (141)	15.7 (191)	25.3 (358)	17.9 (237)
6–10 people	6.4 (91)	3.8 (47)	4.5 (55)	16.1 (228)	13.4 (117)
11–15 people	1.8 (25)	1.0 (12)	1.6 (19)	4.7 (67)	6.1 (81)
16–20 people	1.7 (24)	0.5 (6)	0.7 (8)	3.7 (52)	4.6 (61)
20+ people	4.7 (67)	1.5 (18)	1.6 (19)	8.1 (115)	19.1 (254)
Total**	100 *(1418)	100 (1227)	100 (1220)	100 (1416)	100 (1324)

** These are separate variables, hence the different column response totals.

Table 7.2 Factors of use of communication channels at the time of data collection (2006)

Channel	Social adoption	Location	Connection costs	Communication style	Format	Contact requirements
Face-to-Face	Oldest form of social interaction.	Must be physically co-located, embodied presence.	High or low.	One-to-one, one-to-many, many-to-many.	Visual, spoken, embodied, synchronous.	Known to each other, not known to each other. During hours of waking activity.
Landline telephone	Widely used and socially integrated.	Fixed locations, not co-located, disembodied presence.	Moderate.	Mostly one-to-one.	Spoken, synchronous.	More often known to each other than not. Need personalised phone number to contact. Can be used to contact people with mobile phones. During hours of waking activity.
Mobile phone	Widely used but newer form of technology.	Unfixed locations within the network provider parameters, not usually co-located. Disembodied presence.	Moderate to high.	Mostly one-to-one.	Spoken, text messages, photo attachments. Synchronous and asynchronous.	More often known to each other than not. Need personalised phone number to contact. Can be used to contact people with landline phones. During hours of waking activity
Email	Widely used, Internet mediated.	Laptop or desktop computer based. Not usually co-located. Disembodied presence. Passive co-presence.	Internet access cost, not scaled by number of people contacted.	One-to-one, one-to-many, many-to-many.	Text, mixed media attachments. Asynchronous. Letter format.	Known to each other, not known to each other, need personalised email to contact person. 24/7 access. Alias-driven
***Internet mediated**	Newest platform for interaction.	Smartphone, Laptop or desktop computer based. Not usually co-located. Disembodied presence, Passive co-presence.	Internet access cost. not scaled by number of people contacted.	One-to-one, one-to-many, many-to-many, Social Networking Sites.	Multimedia (text, sound, pictures and videos). Synchronous and asynchronous. User generated content.	Avatar-driven. Known to each other, not known to each other. Can be used to contact other people using the same software through their username. Do not always need a specific username to contact people (openly facilitating known and unknown contact). 24/7 access.

* Examples of Internet-mediated channels observed to be used by respondent population during ethnography are forums, discussion boards, instant messaging and Skype.

7.2.2 Relational Space Online

Mapping hyperlink networks is a key way to articulate a relational notion of social space online. Ackland (2013) discusses the various tools that are currently available to the researcher to do this. However, within the case study of the Herpers, I utilised the issue network tool issuecrawler.net. The conceptual architecture directing the technical approach of this web crawler comes from actor network thinking in the domain of Science and Technology Studies (STS), rather than from the field of social network analysis. This approach overlaps with the conceptual technicalities of a social ecology, with some key differences, through its articulation of relational space online through hyperlink networks. At the time of the study, it was one of the early easily accessible tools for scholarly data visualisation of online dynamics.

Respondents to the survey were asked to provide the website address of up to 10 websites that they visited that were related to their interests in herpetology. The findings of this visualisation were presented in lieu of a univariate analysis of websites provided by survey participants. As the survey was non-random, there is limited knowledge to be gained from presenting a frequency analysis of website listings as a way to determine the centrality and influence of these websites within the Herper community more generally. A more accurate indication of which websites are influential to this community were achieved through co-link analysis and visualisation of the issue network using the online tool called IssueCrawler (Rogers, 2010b). IssueCrawler is a publicly available crawler system offered by the Amsterdam-based Govcom.org Foundation at http://www.govcom.org. The representation of hyperlink networks through IssueCrawler provides a commentary on both the networked structure of the technology layer of the community and the structuring influence of a hyperlinked environment. As McNally (2005, p. 3011) argues, the importance of hyperlinking online is that websites not linked to by other sites (orphan sites) are not accessible to people who surf between websites through recommended links (referral networks). Rogers (2010a, p. 10) sees the goal of network mapping as revealing non-public relationships in the online environment. Hyperlinked networks can therefore be seen as a representation of visibility, recommendation and flows of people across digital space.

There is an increasing range of studies of web-based networks using the IssueCrawler tool (Bruns, 2007; McNally, 2005; R. Rogers, 2009b; Siapera, 2006). Bruns (2007; Bruns et al., 2011) discusses the culture surrounding the use of the tool, which impacts the quantity and visibility of the data provided. He describes it as operating much like the mainframe computers of the early Internet where researchers using the tool share its processing power and queue up their crawls, which are processed two at a time. The datasets produced from their efforts are publicly available to all registered users of the site (Bruns,

2007). In addition to the queuing process and public availability of data there are limitations to the number of websites that can be entered, which is 500. Rogers, the originating author of the tool, describes the methodology of the mapping procedure as follows:

> The Issuecrawler is server-side Web network location software. Input URLs into the Issuecrawler, and the software crawls the URLs, captures page/site outlinks, performs co-link analysis, and outputs the results in lists as well as visualizations.
> (Rogers, 2009b, p. 5)

From this we can understand that Issuecrawler takes as input a list of webpages and then investigates the links these starting points make to other sites. The process of co-link analysis is described on the website as harvesting a list of all external links from each site that has been initially entered. Then each link from each site is compared to all links of the other sites. If the same link is found, it is put in a set of co-linkees with which the next iteration starts. Websites that are held in common are retained as the core network. The results can be visualised through a spring-based cluster map in which websites that have the highest number of in-links are centralised. As described by McNally (2005, p. 3011), the resultant data is rendered into a map of nodes, which are co-linked websites/pages, and the links, which represent the direction and intensity of the hyperlinks between them.

There are recommended settings for different types of analyses and an interpretive approach to the results of these. Because the aim of using issue crawler in this research was to investigate the most influential networks in the survey response set, the recommended settings for visualising an Issue Network were followed. These settings begin with 'privilege starting points' set to 'off', analysis set to 'by page', and two iterations of the method selected (Rogers, 2010b). These settings mean that websites used to begin the analysis (the seed set) may not occur in the final visualisation if other websites in the data set do not connect to them. Crawl depth was set to two levels in order to reveal the underlying core of websites in the Herper community issue network. This setting is advised for website data that are top-level homepages, as was the case in this research for some of the websites submitted. Interpretation of these results is done both through noting the number of in-links a website has and the type of website that it is (as in .edu, .org or .com). The type of website is an indication of commercial, organisational and educational sectors that influence online connections in the issue network. This approach reveals the key sites of influence for people with interests in herpetology in the online environment.

Figure 7.1 presents the key connecting websites behind the 500 most frequently used websites by survey participants. The mapping presented was undertaken on 2 September 2007, which was the closest timeframe, after data curation and cleaning, to the participants' own experience of the online environment. Subsequent visualisations of the hyperlink information presented different faces of the data. This indicates the dimensional construct of the information and suggests the dynamic nature of these recommendation networks over time. In the visualisation of the spring-based cluster map of core networks, nodes are generated on the basis of indegree centrality. Larger nodes have a higher number of websites linking to them. The crawl identified out-links from these URLs, performed co-link analysis, and returned a network containing 48 nodes. There are 13,684 directed linkages within the core network, but these were not evenly distributed because herpetology on the World Wide Web is a 'scale-free' network in which a few highly connected nodes function as hubs (Barabasi, 2002; McNally, 2005). The number of in-links to nodes from the crawled population ranges from nodes with only 10 in-links, up to 11,911 in-links for kingsnake. com, a reptile and amphibian hobbyist site with forums for animal sales and discussion. Other herpetology-specific nodes with high in-link counts from the crawled population are: http://www.cnah.org/ (572 in-links), which promotes itself as an academic portal to North American Herpetology; http://anapsid. org/ (336 in-links), which is a personal website providing care sheets for Herps; and http://ebeltz.net/herps/etymain.html (408 in-links), which is a database of scientific and common names of reptiles and amphibians in North America. Other highly connected pages are bulletin board software such as www.phpbb. com (with 4135 in-links) and photo hosting websites such as www.photopost. com (with 416 in-links). The number of in-links to these discussion board and photo sharing sites indicates the high level of online interactivity and exchange of images and ideas that occurs amongst people with interests in herpetology.

The colour allocations at the core indicate that commercial websites (.com), organisation websites (.org) and educational institutions (.edu) are the most central connectors of the online network. Central themes to these websites are conservation, research, education and herpetological societies. Also present as more periphery connectors are government websites (such as nbii.gov) and taxonomic databases (such as embl-heidelberg.de). The presence of a diverse range of conservation and not-for-profit organisations, commercial websites and government websites indicate that this is a developed network (Rogers, 2004). These websites demonstrate the pivotal role of the pet trade, not-for-profit organisations, academia, legislation, organised societies and online communities as constituting the referential environment of community.

7.3 The Articulation of Spatiality through the Social Layer

Social factors, such as the numbers of people that a person contacts, the accessibility of peers and the local-global reach of social ties provide a sense of the social spatiality of these mediated networks. When viewed from the perspective of social patterns, this data provides insight into the digital architecture and geographical context of the social ecology. In terms of accessibility, respondents were asked to estimate the number of people with herpetological interests that they see most days, then they were asked to estimate the distance (measured through an estimation of the travel time) between them and the people they interact with. In addition, a sense of cultural similarity is discussed through asking whether these people live in the same country, a neighbouring one or other places around the world. Table 7.3 below provides these results with asterisks highlighting trends in the results. The data profile for variables reported on exhibited a non-normal distribution, with a bias towards fewer rather than more people contacted at each temporal-spatial point measured. Because of this, the median averages for results are reported. In general, respondents saw 1–10 Herpers most days ($M = 1.7$, $SD = .85$, Median = 2, $IQR = 1$), however the response was almost as likely to be 'none'. This indicated that spatial dispersion, in addition to local contacts, is likely to be a characteristic of participants' social networks. In terms of what that spatial dispersion is, generally respondents knew 1–10 people who lived less than an hour's travel away from them ($M = 2.18$, $SD = 1.09$, Median = 2, $IQR = 0$), 1–10 people who lived between 1–2 hours' travel away from them ($M = 2.27$, $SD = 1.33$, Median = 2, $IQR = 2$) and 1–10 people who lived between 2–3 hours away from them ($M = 2.59$, $SD = 1.57$, Median = 2, $IQR = 3$). As can be seen from the mean averages, respondents knew slightly more people living further away from them than closer to them in terms of travel time. This suggests the presence of elongated spatial distribution of social ties, even within a local context of three hours' travel time, in the experience of participants.

In terms of national similarity, in general respondents knew 21–30 people living in the same country as them ($M = 3.72$, $SD = 1.37$, Median = 4, $IQR = 3$), 1–10 living in a neighbouring country ($M = 2.17$, $SD = 1.5$, Median = 2, $IQR = 1$), 1–10 people living in other countries around the world ($M = 2.39$, $SD = 1.58$, Median = 2, $IQR = 2$) and 1–10 people who they knew but didn't know where they lived ($M = 2.34$, $SD = 1.73$, Median = 2, $IQR = 2$). In general, respondents knew more people in their own country, but that these people were a little more likely to live 3 hours away rather than within a one-hour radius of the participant. It is clear from these results that there is still a small but persistent local network effect (60.5 per cent, $N = 883$ had 1–10 contacts living within an hour of them) and over half of the population (51.5 per cent, $N = 743$) were seeing 1–10 Herpers most days. Regardless of these small local cliques, just under half of the population knew 1–10 people 1–2 hours' travel away (45.4 per cent, $N = 652$). This extended reach of social ties beyond the local place is further supported in the slight rise of accessible social ties that respondents had at the 2–3-hour travel mark in those who knew over 30 people

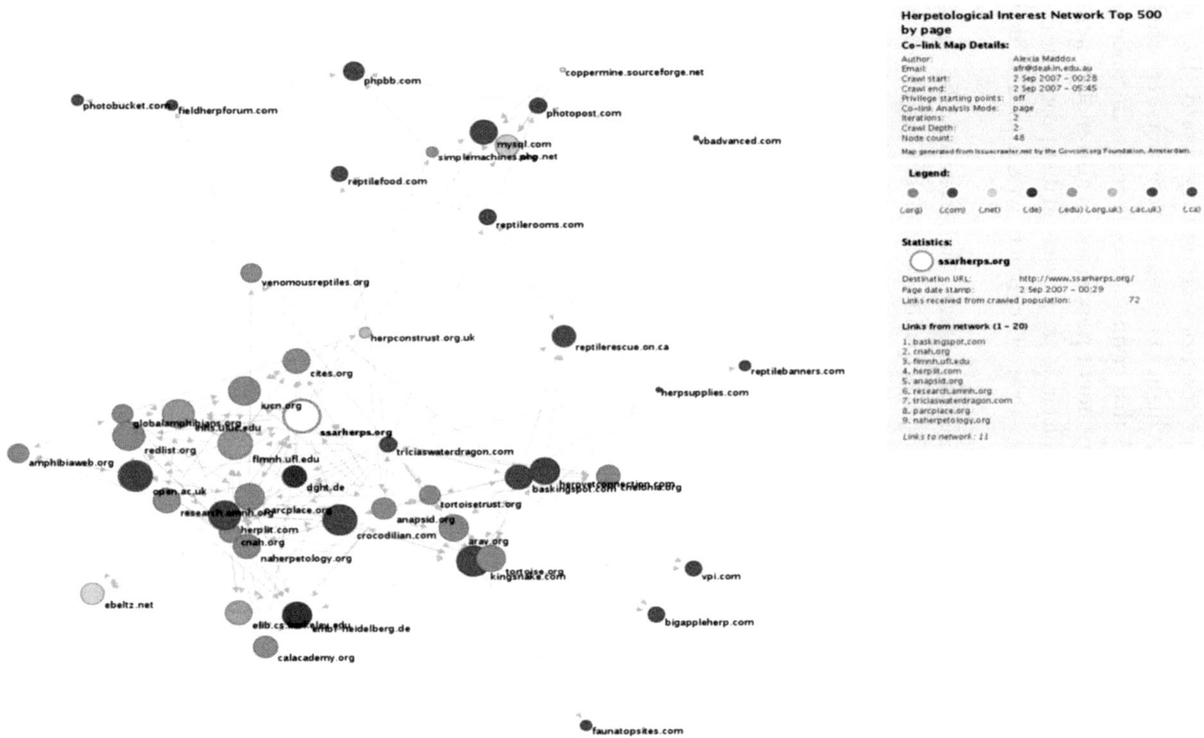

Figure 7.1 Hyperlink analysis of the Herper community issue network

Note: Nodes are websites linked to by two or more websites used by the respondent population. Node size represents 'centrality' in the network, which is the number of nodes in the network that link to the website plus the number of nodes that it links to. Direction of hyperlinking between nodes is indicated by arrows. Node colour represents the top level of the website domain name. See the legend panel on right-hand side of figure for this information.

in the different access zones (1.3 per cent $N = 19$, 3.5 per cent $N = 51$, 4.4 per cent $N = 63$, 11.7 per cent $N = 169$ for respective time zones). It is notable that this trend also reflects the rise in higher numbers of people known (30+) with greater spatial reach across other countries around the world (10.7 per cent, $N = 155$). It is hypothesised that higher numbers of contacts reported is related to the mediating effect of ICTs that connect people across distance and the synergistic likelihood that the respondent population is also mobile across these distances. Regardless of these distance ties, a reasonable proportion of respondents were more likely to know over 30 contacts within their national borders (41.3 per cent, $N = 633$).

Accessible social ties and the nation clearly characterised the spatial boundaries for a large proportion of participants. Reasonably large numbers of people knew no-one outside of their own country. Of the respondent population 43 per cent (42.8 per cent, $N = 610$) did not know anyone in neighbouring countries and 37 per cent (36.7 per cent $N = 532$) did not know people in other countries. This trend also links with the likelihood that for many respondents (in the USA and Australia, for example) national boundaries also contained the social ties that the respondent had within three hours' travel time. This speaks to the continued impact of time-based accessibility and cultural homogeneity upon social ties (in terms of shared national culture, pet market similarity, key figures and legislation). Whilst this impact is clear in the spatiality of social ties, this must be seen in context with the fact that just under half of the total respondent population knew people but didn't know where they lived (45.1 per cent, n=719). This is very likely to be an effect of mediated forms of communication over the Internet that reflects a contrasting trend towards the lack of territoriality for some known social ties. As the dynamic between these two data trends was noteworthy, these variables were explored further through bivariate analysis to investigate their possible influences.

In terms of the spatiality and accessibility of these social ties, the univariate results indicate that there are national, global and 'non-place' elements. This is both a global and locally distributed network that is connected by social relationships, in addition to the connecting nature of organisations and market forces. The place of the network has been argued to span the reach and distribution of these ties. The question here is whether there is an effect of the use of mediated technologies upon the reach and quantity of participants' social ties. It makes sense that the use of ICTs would allow the participant to keep contact with more spatially distributed social ties. However it did raise the question as to whether those who use face-to-face, email and other Internet channels to keep in contact with their social relations were more likely to keep in contact with people who are closer or more spatially dispersed from them. In the bivariate analysis of the variables presented above, respondents experienced fairly elongated face-to-face networks and were networked with small numbers of people around the world or in cyberspace. Local interactions were mediated by face-to-face, email and through other Internet channels. Internationally based interactions were more likely to be mediated by email and other Internet channels. Email connected people in non-place-based relationships, but other Internet channels were slightly more likely to facilitate these kinds of relationships. When this data was placed in context with the demographic data discussed in the following chapter, it is clear that professionals and academics, who were long thought of as the mobile global elite, are not the only cohorts to develop and maintain global social ties. Those who use other forms of mediated communication such as email, but more so for those who use other Internet channels, are likely to have globally distributed and non-place-based social ties in the herpetological network. These findings suggest that quite a diverse cohort of the herper community have globally extended social connections through their access and use of the Internet. The following section draws on the qualitative data to articulate what the impact of the Internet has been upon the mediating culture.

7.4 The Mediating Culture and the Internet

The interviews act as a critique of existing approaches to community and virtual community, discussed in the literature review, through their demonstration of the mix between mediated communication, face-to-face interaction and virtual and physical place in participants' experience of the herpetological network. The co-existence of these sites of interaction are demonstrated through the communication hotspots and social access patterns (global and local) of the survey respondent population. Interview participants demonstrated that an experience of the herpetological network is neither exclusively virtual nor organisation-based, and yet it integrates aspects of both with extended networks of strong and weak social ties.

As discussed in the literature review, the Internet facilitates outward connectivity and an eclectic information environment of prosumers through the software it offers, its decentralised networks and its global, real-time infrastructure. Participants regularly discussed the impact of the Internet on the herpetological network as increasing its profile and engaging a broader range of people. Lionel, a key figure in the zoo and hobby scene of the network, saw the effect of the Internet in Australia as increasing the diversity of people and their reasons for involvement.

> The hobby […] has a lot of things that were profoundly influenced by the development of the Internet. […] When we first got the licensing system going before 1990 there was probably 100 serious reptile keepers or 100

Table 7.3 Frequencies of accessibility and global reach of social ties

Numbers of people	See most days	Live within an hour's travel	Live within 1–2 hours' travel	Live between 2–3 hours' travel away	Live in same country	Live in neighbouring country	Live in other countries around the world	Don't know where they live.^
	% (N)	% (N)	% (N)	% (N)	% (N)	% (N)	% (N)	% (N)
None	43.1 (622)	20.3 (296)	28.9 (415)	27.5 (396)	*2.3 (35)	*42.8 (610)	36.7 (532)	*48 (663)
Some (1–10)	*51.5 (743)	*60.5 (883)	*45.4 (652)	37 (533)	26.6 (408)	33.8 (481)	*33.6 (487)	*22 (304)
A few (11–20)	1.7 (27)	9.4 (137)	11 (158)	10.1 (146)	15 (230)	7.9 (112)	8.4 (122)	7.1 (98)
Several (21–30)	1 (15)	3.3 (48)	5 (72)	6.5 (94)	11.8 (181)	2.5 (36)	4 (58)	3.5 (49)
A lot (over 30)	1.3 (19)	3.5 (51)	4.4 (63)	*11.7 (169)	*41.3 (633)	5.7 (81)	*10.7 (155)	*9.9 (137)
Don't know	1.2 (18)	3.0 (44)	5.4 (77)	7.0 (101)	2.9 (45)	7.4 (105)	6.7 (97)	9.5 (131)
Total	100 (1444)	100 (1459)	100 (1437)	100 (1439)	100 (1532)	100 (1425)	100 (1451)	100 *(1382)

* Notable trends in data discussed in text.

^ This is likely to be an Internet-related social phenomenon.

> keepers full stop, and there is 14,300 licensed keepers now and a lot of that had to do with the Internet. The Internet has Americanised the hobby. […] The Internet will continue to expose people to the hobby, but it's also brought in a different sort of person that's fascinated with reptile keeping. It's not that very small group of people who were just really passionate about wildlife. Now they're exposed to how cool it is to keep reptiles, but they're coming from somewhere else.

This insight into the impact of the internet in the Australian herpetological scene is reiterated by Sam in his interview. He has been active in the online herpetological networks for many years and has seen the change of the population who engages with their reptile and amphibian interests online. He believes that it is the increasing visibility of people with herpetological interests online that informs others that such a pursuit is possible.

> The Internet is largely responsible for the proliferation in the interest in keeping reptiles in Australia for example. […] When people can do a Google search and find that there are lots and lots of people who are keeping these things through an easy medium, that's probably going to be what gets them interested themselves. I would say that the Internet is probably the catalyst for the booming interest in Australia, more than anything else.

As we can see from these two excerpts, the visibility of the interest in the online environment has created a more socially diverse environment in Australia. From the interviews, each country appeared to have its unique engagement with the effect of the Internet, but this increasing diversity of participation and values was the consistent outcome. In these excerpts, we can see the Internet influencing a change from a small group of people with a natural-history focus to encompassing people who have learnt from the internet that it is possible to have them in their homes. This reflects a contrast to the closed social networks that were evident in the narratives of participants talking about their pre-internet engagement with the network. These narratives portrayed a more classical example of community as closed, with known others who shared the same values. This perspective is in keeping with the social origins of the herpetological interest network in the geographically and organisationally bound museum-based, naturalist societies (Jardine, Secord, & Spary, 1996). In the past, the network was much more focused on the experiences of collectors concerned with the natural-history context of the animals they collected. In the present-day context, Lionel demonstrates a tolerance for this diversity of values towards the animals, but holds an undercurrent of hoping to engage these people in the original discourse of natural history that pervaded his early experiences of this network of people.

In addition to the impact of the Internet on the hobby creating social diversity, participants also discuss the global reach and geographic equalising features of the Internet. James, an academic who has been involved in the network for most of his life, experienced the Internet's impact through spatial equalisation and real-time communication that the Internet connectivity facilitates.

> It suddenly put me on a par with the guy in San Francisco, in terms of the rapidity with which I could communicate and submit articles to journals through web-based systems. […] Australia, being the arse-end of the world, it used to be a huge issue in maintaining that intimate, rapid contact with collaborators, colleagues or just catching up with new ideas. […] The friendships are maintained more easily.

In his experience, the key features of the Internet impact were the disembedding of time and place articulated by Anthony Giddens. His experience also highlights the 'global village' experience of the Internet put forward by Harold Rheingold, in which interaction is synchronised and disembodied into a collective space. This collective space is the imagined community that Anderson (1991) proposed as a way to understand national identity and danah boyd (2007b) has appropriated as a way to understand networked publics in the networked technology environment. These ideas and how they relate to the notion of a social ecology are discussed in the literature review. However, James' experience is also about communication as well as real-time connectivity. Communication is about language. As we have seen from the experience of Sven, the linguistic framework of the Internet for the herp world is English. Sven's use of the English-speaking forums to find information is re-voiced in the experience of Louis who says that for him, English is the language of business and social exchange across the network both online and with the people he meets at expos. Participants accessed forums in languages different to their native tongue. They discussed online forums that had country-specific content; however others appeared to be more topic-focused. The website kingsnake.com, for example, was known by most Internet-active participants.

As we have seen, participants' experiences exposed the geographic 'equalising' of the Internet that is linked to the real-time, global reach of its infrastructure. Socially, global reach is facilitated by a common language of exchange across the network. Participants also demonstrated exposure and emotional engagement to the actions of visible figures online regardless of their geographic position. This exposure often occurred because of the common spaces online to which people would go to gather information and get online support and interaction, participating in the buzz. The effect of the Internet on the composition of the network has been to increase the numbers of people who engage and also to increase the diversity of values that people bring to this engagement. It has also produced a social process of 'figuring things out' that is about the slow articulation of key networks. The resulting social architecture of the network, now based on the Internet, is decentralised and pervasive. It facilitates an increased exposure to the diversity of perspectives and overlapping values, rather than shared ones, through which people engage with their herpetological interests and each other. Consequently this social architecture is more malleable and porous, allowing it to be more tolerant of disruption and capable of incorporating change and differences. Its form can be identified through its transient emergence and social expression rather than through overt hierarchical structures of order and place. The common elements in the narratives of participants demonstrated how the global reach afforded by the Internet architecture has resulted in the opening up to social diversity of a previously closed social group.

7.5 Conclusion

In the above presentation of the case study methods of research and their key findings, the environment of the Herpetological community has been expressed through physical interactions and digital engagements and online relational architectures of influence. Survey respondents experienced fairly elongated face-to-face networks and were networked with small numbers of people around the world or in cyberspace. Local interactions were mediated by face-to-face, email and through other Internet channels. Internationally based interactions were more likely to be mediated by email and other Internet channels. Email connected people in non-place-based relationships, but other Internet channels were slightly more likely to facilitate these kinds of relationships. When this data is understood alongside the demographic data discussed in the following chapter on the social composition of the network, it is clear that professionals and academics, who were long thought of as the global elite, are not the only cohorts that have global social ties. Those who use other forms of mediated communication such as email, but more so for those who use other Internet channels, are likely to have globally distributed and non-place-based social ties in the herpetological network. Participants who communicated online and contacted larger numbers of people this way reported more strong and weak social ties and experienced a greater spread of social ties both locally and globally. We see fewer professionals using other Internet channels, but we see a broader range of the sample having spatially distributed ties than might be expected. These patterns counterbalance the apparent homogenising effect of online channels, given that the people being engaged with are not necessarily in the same locale or country. This suggests that the space or place of the ecology is a global network of local clusters linked through sparse networks of spatially elongated social ties that cross national and continental boundaries.

I argue that these results suggest the continued relevance of the nation-state (the local and the regional place) in patterns of social organisation within contemporary community formats, but that the Internet has an equally proportional affect upon the spatial distribution and diversity of social ties. This is represented by the co-existence of global connections with local connections and social diversity and exchange within the survey sample discussed in subsequent chapters. Within the hyperlink visualisation, we can see that this is a well establish online network that has been continuously active over time. This understanding is reinforced by the discussion of the impact of the Internet upon the mediating culture of the community within the ethnographic data. The qualitative insights have demonstrated that the impact of the Internet has been to open up what was previously a closed community and increase network resilience through social diversity. This allows us to see the digital and global space of the community as influential factors that imbricate with the patterns of social organisation in the network. Methodologically speaking, these insights into the spatiality and environmental imprint of the herper community would not have been possible if I had pre-determined the location of the population at the outset of the research.

Chapter 8
Social Composition

8.1 Introduction

This chapter aims to illustrate how the social composition of a digital community is articulated through an environmental approach. Section 8.2 presents the technological layer and its relationship to social composition through a discussion of the herper community case study and the presentation of the characteristics of a networked individual within the community. This section describes the portfolio of participation of community members and how this articulates the population composition of the network. Section 8.3 profiles the social layer of the case study community through its demographics and reviews the data suggesting how this is influenced by the use of information communication technologies (ICTs). Section 8.4 presents data on the mediating culture of the case study and considers how this interacts and influences the social composition of the community within the case study.

Knowing what the social composition of a community is answers the question as to who is eligible to participate in the research. It also provides insight into the broader social context of the community. Within research methods, the social composition of a community is initially established through a discussion of demographics and community roles. Consequently, the membership profile of a community is approximated through society memberships, organisational roles, and ethnic or religious identification derived from public or government records such as census data. These information sources provide insight into those enacting the community within its spatial environment. From this understanding, we can immediately see the relationship between the place of the community and its social composition. Conventionally, the relationship between place and social composition is mediated by the structures of society, including organisations and institutions and physical infrastructure such as roads. However the many-to-many social architecture that the Internet brings, and the cross-pollination between social networks, organisational roles and engagement profiles across the online and offline environments removes the directness with which the researcher can establish the social composition of a spatially dispersed community. The implication of this for research practice is that the inherent territoriality and organisational origin of available information on social composition does not match the spatiality of an open social structure. Because of this, I argue that insight into the social composition of a digital community can only be established through collecting information on the co-ordinates of social activity within the community once the research has begun. As the social ecology approach highlights, these social records may be utilised within the practice of the research to develop insight into the social composition, rather than defined at the outset of the research design. When investigating a community that comes together through foci of activity, it is already clear what the inclusion and exclusion criteria of community membership is; rather than homogeneity of social composition it is based around the topic of interest. In the case of the Herpers, the imbrication of communication technologies with sociality opened up what was once a closed and fairly socially homogeneous group and enhanced the establishment and maintenance of global social ties beyond the global elite.

Social heterogeneity is a key theme that emerges from the combined dataset of the case study and is of interest for a methods discussion because, theoretically, social homogeneity is an identifying characteristic of community composition and social cohesion. The social theory behind this is that reciprocity and exchange occur due to a similarity of experience and shared values. The space of trust, obligation and reputation that defines community cohesion also differentiates and articulates the boundaries of a group and creates the parameters for collective identity. Within these group boundaries, the individual identity project and social roles are given meaning through immersive socialisation in the group culture and hierarchy. The social experience of homogeneous population compositions of communities is well documented within the scholarly literature, largely because of its connections to the discussion of social mobility and social stratification. In the early Chicago school community studies, the experience of social stratification and its relationship to social mobility and authority were explored through focusing on disadvantaged social groups. These groups were considered socially marginal and liminal to society, with examples being ethnic minorities or ganglands. An example of this is Herbert Gans' (1962) work with the Italian-American migrant community. He conducted research into an ethnically homogeneous and economically homologous neighbourhood community, which he situated within a class-based schema. Through this research he developed the notion of a 'Peer Group Society', which inhibited social mobility but provided social stability for a marginalised community. In this case, the social homogeneity of the community was what sustained and situated it within the broader social context and linked it to poverty and lower socio-economic status.

Social stratification is traditionally a class-based concept that presupposes people who have a similar habitus will experience solidarity and group dynamics. These groups of people are theorised to exist within a social system ordered by an economic and social hierarchy. This system order is delineated by group boundaries and categorised, in basic terms, by lower, middle and upper class; Karl Marx being an iconic proponent of a class-based notion of social order, and seeing the shared values and economic circumstances as created by people's relationship to the means of production. In this way, we see that social homogeneity, community composition, and class analysis are traditionally tied. When the notion of social heterogeneity is introduced as a foundation of social composition in a group or community, the efficacy of these system ideas of social order to provide insight into contemporary community cohesion and patterns of social organisation is put into question. In the broader body of sociological analysis, class and socio-economic consumption profiles remain a way of understanding social order and composition within nation-states. However the experience of community across open social structures occurs both within and outside of the nation-state and appears to be about social heterogeneity rather than social homogeneity. Because of this, the application of the social ecology concept as a way to describe contemporary community experience holds advantageous analytical capacity in that it remains conceptually robust in the face of social diversity.

The leverage of this approach for the analysis of the case study population begins with the technological layer and how the individual is seen to enact across it. In this instance, theories of the networked individual (Wellman et al., 2003) held strong resonance with the social practices of the Herper community. Using the networked individual as a conceptualisation of agency within the community, the participant becomes defined by their portfolio of participation, architectures of interaction and demographic profile. The aggregation of this information provided by participants, who identify with the foci of activity, articulates for the researcher the social composition of the community. The initial section of this chapter provides ethnographic insights into how the networked individual can be seen as a key characteristic of the herper community. This begins the discussion of the impact of the technological layer upon the social composition of the community. From this technical perspective, we then look at the social layer of the population through their demographic and participation profiles gathered through the survey data. When this data is interrogated with insights from the relational online space of the community presented in the IssueCrawler hyperlink visualisation (Chapter 7, Section 7.2.2), it opens up insights into the mediating culture of the community. Turning back to the ethnographic data, this chapter will close with a discussion of how the social heterogeneity of the community is experienced by participants.

8.2 Technological Layer and the Networked Individual

This section will discuss the technological layer of the community from the perspective of the networked individual. This perspective provides insight into how the environment of the community is generated by the individual actions of a participant through their self-directed networking, technological capacities and participation profile. This discussion suggests how the social composition and social profile of the community is articulated through the data collection process. Taking this focus also suggests how the social actor is both a product and co-creator of the technology, place and built environment of the community. To this end, this discussion of the networked individual provides a sense of the social fabric participants experienced when engaging with other Herpers and using ICTs to do so. Because of this overt relationship between place and technology within social action, it is initially worth spending time unpacking the notion of networked individualism to make clear the conceptual link between this ego-centric idea of the social actor and collecting data on the social composition of a community.

Networked individualism is a theoretical concept introduced by Barry Wellman to describe how people personalise their social networks through portfolios of participation rather than through a place-based group such as a neighbourhood (see Chapter 3, Section 3.5). A particular feature of this approach is how people engage with ICTs that allow personalised and customised networking of the individual, such as text messaging on mobile phones, email, forum use and instant messaging via the Internet. This concept represents a shift from reliance upon a geographically bound core group for support and exchange to a focus upon individual relationships as the links in multiple networks of strong and weak social ties mediated by ICT use and social media. This produces a relational interpretation of community experience. In the experience of the participants, this form of mediated interaction is driven by the individuals' access to computers and mobile phones in their homes, workplaces and other spaces, as well as by their digital literacy and comfort with social media. The patterns of ICT use in the respondent population are an example of the way networked technologies alter how information flows and people communicate (boyd, 2007b). Because of the affordances of the technologies used, participants were able to contact other individuals and groups of people that may be geographically distant from them for support, information and interaction. The use of this digital environment is therefore linked in the experiences of the interview population with the generation of global social networks and the capacity for anonymous interactions and interactions with unknown others online. This behaviour is foundational to the social diversity of the community.

As discussed in the literature review, the notion of individualism can be conflated with individualistic behaviour, such as the personality trait of being egocentric or selfish. Networked individualism is a concept that draws from the 'ego'-centered approach of social network analysis derived from the field of psychology. This reflects a focus on the individual and their viewpoint out to others rather than group behaviour. Networked individualism can also be conflated with structural individualisation proposed by Beck and Beck-Gernsheim (2002). Woodman (2011) argues that Beck sees this trend in structural individualisation as one where people are left to deal with structural contradictions themselves. Networked individualism is clearly neither of these two concepts but is a mid-range concept that neither contradicts nor harnesses either of these ideas. In terms of the respondent population, participants are independent and do differentiate themselves from others through the specialisation of interests. They embody the marginalisation of their interest and seek people who accept and enhance how they choose to engage with it. The Internet is a contemporary and natural facilitator for this kind of world where knowledge exchange, social networks, organisations and key figures are all important. The focus of networked individualism here is upon the importance of social networks that are cultivated by the individual, the spatial distribution of these ties as both near and far and their capacity to provide support, information and exchange in a technologically mediated environment.

8.2.1 Self-directed Networking

The driver of networked individualism, as an agency based concept, is the ability of the individual to shift time and energy away from their immediate social environment and put this into a portfolio of participation, a somewhat compartmentalising behaviour. In the herper community, self-directed networking is the key mechanism that underpins participants' ability to make connections with other like-minded individuals. To understand why this is so pervasive amongst Herpers, we can start by building up our understanding of collectors. For a discussion on this mind-set as we understand it sociologically, it is helpful to turn to Beer's (2008) analysis of Walter Benjamin's (1999) classic essay on the book collector. In his analysis, Beer describes the relationship between the collector and the object as about the physicality, aesthetics, experience and tactility of collecting rather than about the practice of reading. He argues that:

> Benjamin's collector is immersed in memories and narratives through the connections made with the physical properties of the book. These narratives emerge not through the text printed on the book's pages but through the unique relations that the collector has with that particular object.
>
> (Beer, 2008a)

In this way we can see that the collector is immersed in the meaning-making and tactility of their connection to a physical object, which they collect. This is essentially the aspect of collecting that can be shared between people. Beer argues that for anyone who holds a collection, 'the physicality of the collection is an integral part of our relations with it and the identity constructions it facilitates; this is both how we think of ourselves and how we wish to present ourselves to those that visit the private places where we exhibit our collections'. (Beer, 2008b) Within the respondent population, collectors often shared their interests with others by displaying their collection, making networks that helped them to build that collection and discussing their experiences with like-minded people. Beer describes the collector also deriving a sense of identity from his or her collection in the context of those who share a similar perspective. This was indeed the case for the participants who were immersed in the herper community. An example of this would be those who had private collections of animals (such has private keepers and breeders) and those who collected photos or knowledge about specific animals (such as academics, museum curators and amateur professionals). Not all respondents had the profile of a collector but this is a good place to start understanding how the community is driven by mediated socialisation according to an individual's portfolio of interests. The idea of the collector as influencing the herper mind-set was explained to me by a Japanese importer of turtles and tortoises I met in a Parisian pet shop. Michio introduced me to the idea of the 'Otaku' in his discussions of who he sells these animals to in Japan. We talked about the price tag that he sells his tortoises for in Japan, which ranged from US$3,000 to US$20,000. Given the substantial financial commitment that that price tag represents for anyone in the world for any object, let alone a tortoise imported from another country, I was deeply curious as to who paid this kind of money.

> Alexia: Who buys? What type of people?
>
> Michio: Otaku.
>
> Alexia: So, very rich people?
>
> Michio: No, no. Of course there are rich people. But they spend all money for this hobby ... There are many Japanese reptile otaku ... These kind of crazy ... many Otaku, their life concentrate into only that hobby.
>
> Alexia: What about their family?
>
> Michio: Normally most otaku cannot get girlfriend because they spend all money on their hobby.

This indicates the more compulsive animal collectors that drive the top end of the reptile and amphibian pet trade. However this kind of overdrive towards collecting animals is also expressed in the intellectual pursuits of the community through the focused pursuit of knowledge about one particular type of animal by academics and amateur-professionals. Fabio, the son of a successful business owner in Switzerland, blended his personal interests in collecting examples of certain types of snakes into a personal private zoo. This was in his parents' home and consisted of an amazingly expensive, climate-controlled installation of cages, airflow and water circulation to mimic the climates and ecology where these animals had been collected[1]. In addition to this he ran a webpage providing detailed information and his own research observations into these animals. This is where the line of the collector-hobbyist is blurred with the amateur-professional and herpetologist within the community itself. From here, we can start to see how this focus upon a particular animal interest creates differentiation amongst the Herpers. The passion for what is known and unknown about this specific interest provides a person the space for identity development through specialisation and drive for self-directed networking.

As can be seen from the discussion above, this kind of focused interest in a non-human object both detaches and attaches the participant to people within a certain portfolio of interest. Because these interests are specialised, participants were active in making social connections according to their interests. The slow growth of contacts through this the individual's seeking of others with similar or overlapping interests and knowledge is fairly characteristic of many respondents' experience. For example, an Australian private breeder and pet shop employee, Darren, discusses his slow entrance into the herpetological networks as unfolding through friends of friends.

> It was through that that one of my fellow friends met a guy that had a lot of snakes that was friends with [key figure], [key figure]. So I sort of was just lucky that I got into some of those guys through an associate of mine. He started keeping them and he met them from someone he knew and I sort of got into it ...

Regardless of how people endeavour to meet other people with shared interests, the herpetological networks appear to be very interconnected. As the experience of Adrien, the owner of a pet shop specialising in reptiles and amphibians, demonstrates in the interview excerpt below.

> That's a small world. We all know each other, of course. In France, in Europe, in the world. When I started I had friends in Togo rearing the ball pythons. I

1 A few months before the interview, a grain of sand had blocked the water flow system through the cages, shorted the electrics, flooded the room, damaged the marble floor and resulted in the deaths of many of the rare snakes in his collection. He was devastated.

> had friends in Canada, which was a famous Herper at that time. I had friends in the US also ... I was a member of some association. It gave access to the information and magazines and newsletter and so on. That was helpful.

What appears to be important to this self-directed networking is the associated use of different information channels to keep connections with people open and to be visible in the network. This is what translates the networked individual into a community actor and as integral to the generation of the community environment.

8.2.2 Portfolio of Participation

In presenting the case study findings, it is worth spending a little more time unpacking this notion of the portfolio of participation to further articulate how the following analysis of individualistic data can be understood in its social context and influence the social composition of the network. The portfolio of participation is drawn from Barry Wellman's notion of networked individualism discussed above and documented within the interview participants' experiences and approaches to the community. In this notion, each person crafts an idiosyncratic style of participation according to who they are, what their life opportunities are and how they resolve this across multiple networks. There is a clear individualistic agenda behind the portfolio of participation. When these portfolios are taken as an overall profile of social strategies that the network has the capacity to support, they indicate how networked individualism translates into a group fabric. These strategies arguably constitute the socialisation pathways of the social ecology. This is a unique idea of this research methodology that allows egocentric data to be extrapolated into the process of group interaction and understood as patterns of social organisation. The portfolios of participation allow for the idea that the individual is the site of agency. At the same time, they process this intersection both individually and collectively through socialisation across a heterogeneous environment. This harks back to the notion of structural individualisation discussed in the literature review as the underlying social trend through which networked individualism is enabled. An individual's portfolio of participation is articulated within the case study population through their role within the community, their manner of engagement over time and the animals they are interested in and the types of knowledge they consume and produce within the network. This provides insight into who the herper is considered to be and the social composition of the community from the perspective of its membership profiles. The social layer of the community discussed in Section 8.3 will articulate the demographics of these participants to provide another angle of insight into the social composition of the community.

Table 8.1 Frequencies of patterns of involvement in herpetological interests over time

Tempo of engagement	% (N)
Occasional involvement	2.7 (42)
Sometimes more and sometimes less involved over time	17.4 (273)
Increasingly involved	46.4 (728)
Always been very involved	31 (487)
Other	2.5 (40)
Total	100 (1570)

Survey participants were asked about initially about how long they've been engaged with their interests in herpetology and how active they've been over time with them. The respondent sample had been involved in their herpetological interests for a median average of 12 years (*M* = 16, *SD* = 13.04, Median = 12.17, *IQR* = 18). With the data being clearly skewed to the lower values (Skewness = 1.07, Kurtosis = .55), an inspection of frequencies showed that a large number of the respondents have been involved in the network for 10 years or less (accounting for around 40 per cent, *N* = 626 of respondents). On average, participants were increasingly involved over time (*M* = 3.13, *SD* = .822, Median = 3, *IQR* = 1). Frequency results (see Table 8.1 below) reported that nearly half of the participants became increasingly involved with their interests over time (46 per cent, *N* = 728). Thirty-one per cent (*N* = 487) were always immersively involved and 17 per cent (*N* = 273) were sometimes more and sometimes less involved in their herpetological interests over time. These results provided a foundational understanding that survey respondents were likely to provide a deeper view of community experience rather than a surface understanding.

The animal interest results reported in Table 8.2 indicate that there is a broad spread of animal interests represented in the respondent population with respondents being, on average 'interested' in all of the animals listed. The only animals that were an exception to this were crocodiles, alligators and poison dart frogs that had fewer people who were very interested in them. The animal group that was on the opposite side of this spectrum was the 'other snakes'. This group had a very high level of people who were very interested and low levels of ambivalence, in comparison to the other groups. This group of animals are the non-dangerous, small snakes that are very common on the pet market and are usually very easy to keep. This may explain the high level of interest in them in the respondent population. In terms of the opposite feeling (totally uninterested) newts and salamanders, and venomous snakes in general appeared to generate a lack of interest to a greater level than other animals for the respondent population. These animals may be considered 'niche interest' animals.

In terms of identifying whether the respondent population is characterised by specialised animal interests or broad animal interests, the average number of animal groups listed that respondents were interested in was 10 groups (*SD* = 4.06, Median = 11, *IQR* = 6), however there was a high frequency of people with interests in all of the groups of animals listed (17 per cent, *N* = 271) and only a small group in the respondent population had more specialised interest in 5 or less of the groups of animals listed (13 per cent, *N* = 206). In terms of keeping these animals, 84 per cent of the respondents (*N* = 1335) kept these animals privately. Because a few respondents kept a disproportionality large number of herps privately (1,000, 1,600, 1,900 and 39,000), the median is reported. The median private captive collection size was 14 animals (*M* = 68.06, *SD* = 1081, Trimmed mean = 24.5, Median = 14, *IQR* = 34), with reasonable estimates of personal collection sizes reaching 200 animals. Of those who were not keeping a private collection at the time of the survey, over half (58 per cent, *N* = 136) had done so in the past.

Respondents indicated the kind of involvement that they had in the network (which can be understood theoretically as their "role") by selecting types of engagement that applied to them. These were not designed to be mutually exclusive categories as participant observation demonstrated that people engaged in multiple activities rather than just one "type". Because of this, the following responses are each a per cent of the total population (*N* = 1593) and are not cumulatively equal to 100 per cent.

A majority of the respondent population had a personal interest only (63 per cent, *N* = 1003). This indicates that the more professional or commercial styles of involvement were about 37 per cent (*N* = 590) of the total population. In terms of this cohort, 3.7 per cent (*N* = 59) made their main income from sales associated with their interests (commercial involvement). Other groups in this professional cohort also consisted of 8.9 per cent (*N* = 141) who were employed in an official capacity such as a government official or zookeeper and 13.6 per cent (*N* = 216) were involved professionally as academic scientists, veterinarians or other types of professional herpetologists. The remaining population in this professionally involved cohort is unidentified but may include those who were students of herpetology or herpetologically related fields at university (11.2 per cent, *N* = 180) or had other types of involvements (16.7 per cent, *N* = 266).

Other types of involvement in which there are usually crossover roles between hobbyists and professionals relate to private breeding, public education and offering free services to other people with herpetological interests. Of the respondent population, 40.4 per cent (*N* = 642) privately bred and traded reptiles. In terms of public outreach and education, 34 per cent (*N* = 543) of the respondent population participated in these activities. In addition to this

Table 8.2 Frequencies of animal interest preferences

A) Frequencies of interest in lower-risk animals

	Large tortoises	**Large turtles**	**Other turtles/ tortoises**	**Poison dart frogs**	**Other frogs/ toads**	**Newts & salamanders**	**Other snakes**	**Other lizards**
	M = **2.3**, SD = **1.02**	M = **2.38**, SD = **1.03**	M = **2.32**, SD = **1.02**	M = **2.41**, SD = **1.03**	M = **2.32**, SD = **1.04**	M = **2.62**, SD = **1.16**	M = **1.55**, SD = **.83**	M = **1.85**, SD = **.88**
	% (N)	% (N)	% (N)	% (N)	% (N)	% (N)	% (N)	% (N)
Very interested	21.3 (238)	19.6 (302)	25.4 (386)	*16.2 (253)	21.1 (322)	17 (257)	*60.8 (937)	38.1 (587)
Interested	43 (662)	40.8 (627)	41 (624)	45.9 (715)	43.5 (663)	33.5 (507)	28.4 (437)	44.8 (690)
Neither interested nor uninterested	23.8 (366)	25.6 (394)	22.1 (337)	24.1 (375)	22.4 (342)	28.4 (431)	*6.8 (105)	12.7 (196)
Uninterested	8.7 (134)	10.5 (162)	8.4 (128)	9.2 (144)	9.1 (139)	13.9 (211)	3 (46)	2.9 (44)
Totally uninterested	3.5 (41)	3.4 (52)	3.1 (47)	4.6 (71)	3.8 (58)	*7.2 (109)	1.1 (16)	1.5 (23)
Total	100 (1541)	100 (1537)	100 (1522)	100 (1558)	100 (1524)	100 (1515)	100 (1541)	100 (1540)
Note	Mainly kept in zoos or custom private residences due to large size and length of years lived.		Commonly kept, small to moderate in size.	High conservation status, moderately accessible, difficult to keep, only toxic in the wild (diet related).	Accessible, small in size	Moderately accessible, easy to keep, small in size	Accessible, easy to keep, small in size.	Accessible, easy to keep, small in size.

* Identified trends in the data.

B) Frequencies of interest in higher risk animals

	Crocodiles & Alligators	**Large constrictors (>2m)**	**Monitors & Tegus (lizards)**	**Gila monsters & bearded lizards**	**Rear-fanged colubrids**	**Elapid snakes**	**Arboreal viperids (snakes)**	**Ground Viperids (snakes)**
	M = **2.4**, *SD* = **2.26**	*M* = **1.97**, *SD* = **1.04**	*M* = **2.01**, *SD* = **.94**	*M* = **2.13**, *SD* = **1.03**	*M* = **2.08**, *SD* = **1.11**	*M* = **2.27**, *SD* = **1.26**	*M* = **2.20**, *SD* = **1.18**	*M* = **2.16**, *SD* = **1.18**
	% (N)	% (N)	% (N)	% (N)	% (N)	% (N)	% (N)	% (N)
Very interested	*16.3 (256)	40.7 (630)	32.6 (506)	29.8 (463)	35.6 (549)	31.1 (468)	33.4 (512)	35.8 (552)
Interested	47.3 (754)	34.6 (535)	42.5 (658)	40.9 (637)	37.5 (579)	35.7 (537)	34 (522)	32.8 (505)
Neither interested nor uninterested	24.4 (382)	14.8 (229)	18.1 (280)	19.8 (308)	15.2 (235)	18.1 (272)	18.6 (285)	17.7 (273)
Uninterested	3.4 (54)	7.4 (115)	5.0 (78)	6.2 (97)	7.3 (112)	8.1 (121)	8.4 (129)	8.2 (126)
Totally uninterested	4.1 (64)	2.5 (39)	1.8 (28)	3.5 (51)	4.4 (68)	*7 (105)	*5.6 (86)	6*.4 (84)
Total	100 (1566)	100 (1548)	100 (1550)	100 (1556)	100 (1543)	100 (1503)	100 (1534)	100 (1540)
Note:	Mainly kept in zoos or custom private residences due to large size and length of years lived. Easy to keep.	Non-venomous, dangerous snakes that constrict their prey, easy to keep.	Dangerous lizards able to cause morbidity (permanent injuries). Can be very small to very large. Easy to keep.	Venomous lizards, high conservation status, able to cause painful swelling. Easy to keep, inaccessible.	Mildly dangerous snakes, widely kept, very accessible, often easy to keep.	Highly dangerous snakes, easy to keep, accessibility is monitored.	Highly venomous, climbing snakes with an ambush feeding strategy, small in size but deadly and dangerous, accessibility is monitored.	Highly venomous ground snakes with an ambush feeding strategy, small in size but deadly and dangerous, accessibility is monitored

* Identified trends in the data.

active level of public outreach, respondents were also supportive of each other, with 26 per cent ($N = 427$) offering a free service to other people with interests in herpetology.

The last aspect of herpetological involvement to be discussed from the case study data is the types of knowledge within the network that interested respondents. These knowledge types were drawn from participant observation of the common or binding elements that Herpers shared with each other or needed to understand to be involved in their herpetological interest. Recording the use of these types of knowledge by survey respondents was intended to explore the shared knowledge field and priorities of the network. It is proposed that this is another common or binding element of exchange in a socially heterogeneous population, as is argued in the Community of Practice literature (Wenger, 1999). Respondents were asked to select the types of knowledge that they were interested in or use. They were able to select more than one type; consequently these categories are not mutually exclusive and the percentages provided will not total 100 per cent. See Table 8.3 for a detailed presentation of these results. The types of knowledge that respondents were interested in can be grouped into six styles: captive care knowledge, scientific knowledge, technical knowledge, commercial knowledge, legal knowledge and social knowledge. These categories are not mutually exclusive and have been created as a way to think about the general bodies of knowledge consumed, created and shared within this network.

In the respondent population, the types of knowledge that were of interest to a majority were animal behaviour (86.3 per cent, $N = 1373$), environmental conservation (76.6 per cent, $N = 1219$), captive breeding (73.9 per cent, $N = 1175$), animal handling (72.3 per cent, $N = 1150$) and scientific herpetological research (71.3 per cent, $N = 1135$). In general, an interest in legislative knowledge and commercial knowledge was limited to smaller cohorts (less than 63 per cent and less than 40 per cent respectively) and social knowledge in general was of interest to less than 52 per cent of the population. In terms of the creation, production and consumption of knowledge, 25 per cent ($N = 392$) of the respondent population publish herpetologically related articles. The median number of publications per respondent is 4 ($M = 14.44$, $SD = 30$, Trimmed Mean = 9.62, Median = 4, $IQR = 10$). A small percentage of the sample had published between 100–314 articles each, however the majority of respondents published under 40 articles (90.7 per cent).

8.2.3 Media Environment

From the analysis of the survey data on participant profiles, it is clear that participants were avid consumers of information on their reptile interests and used a variety of sources to get this information. The interview data extended an understanding of the media environment through which participants enacted and gained their knowledge about reptiles and amphibians. Notably, they often compiled their own repository of resources, such as books, journal articles, photographs and websites rather than expecting to be able to easily access the information in the physical space around them. As Jayden, a private reptile keeper, commented despite his area being a haven for reptiles, the public libraries did not have very good resources on reptiles. So not only does it take effort to meet other people with herpetological interests, it also takes an effort by the individual to gather information on the animals that they are interested in. These two drivers for self-directed pursuits often being intertwined.

Interview participants indicated that they gained information from mainstream news media that covered animals for sale, wildlife documentaries on television, and popular press articles that related to reptiles. Whilst reptile-related documentary hosts became points of attraction (key figures) in the herp world, popular press articles were often alienating for the community members. As Sven discusses, the popular press was not viewed as representing the point of view that people with interests in herpetology would hold and most participants had a distrust of journalists and what was reported in the mainstream media.

> When sometimes iguanas escape, from Oslo, someone finds an iguana on their terrace. They are frightened and they call the police and the newspapers write about green crocodiles on terraces trying to eat people, and of course, this creates a hysteria and it gives reptile society in Norway a bad reputation.

In light of personal and peer experiences such as this with the media, many Herpers were interested in alternative ways to gather up-to-date knowledge and easily digested herp stories that still contained the journalistic flair without the hysteria. Participants preferred options that allowed them to filter for information across media rather than to accept the mainstream perspective as their own. This approach indicates public perception to be an external boundary of the network, which will be discussed in Chapter 9 on boundaries.

Other reasons participants had for filtering information and selecting sources were personal preferences and concerns for information validity. These filtering preferences acted as a way for participants to discern what and who they may want to know amongst the vast amount of data available online. Many academics and professionals for example preferred to use email to make contact with people and avoided forums because they felt like they had no requirement for the information being exchanged and no desire to meet non-academics and anonymous others online. The few that did engage in forums did so for public education purposes, for opportunistic contacts and because they had been active in these spaces before becoming professionals or academics. One result of online population skew away from academics is that many participants

Table 8.3 Frequencies of types of knowledge that respondents are interested in

Knowledge field of interest	% (N)	Type of knowledge
Animal handling	*72.3 (1150)	Captive care knowledge
Common names of herps	*48.2 (767)	Captive care knowledge
Captive breeding	*73.9 (1175)	Captive care knowledge
Captive keeping	62.2 (989)	Captive care knowledge
Caging specifications	63 (1002)	Captive care knowledge
Veterinary care of herps	58.3 (927)	Captive care knowledge
Animal behaviour	*86.3 (1373)	Captive care knowledge
Environmental Conservation	*76.6 (1219)	Scientific knowledge
Latin or scientific animal names	*63.3 (1007)	Scientific knowledge
Current taxonomy	51.5 (819)	Scientific knowledge
Species identification keys	54.4 (866)	Scientific knowledge
Current work on herp by-products	19.2 (306)	Scientific knowledge
Scientific herpetological research	*71.3 (1135)	Scientific knowledge
Animal locality data	64 (1018)	Scientific knowledge
Animal photography	69.6 (1108)	Technical knowledge
Herpetological products on offer	39.2 (623)	Commercial knowledge
Trends in herp market demand	30.7 (488)	Commercial knowledge
Running a herp business	36.5 (580)	Commercial knowledge
Animal import/export procedures	33.7 (536)	Legal knowledge
Laws for captive keeping	62.2 (989)	Legal knowledge
Laws for buying/selling animals	54.2 (863)	Legal knowledge
Laws for collecting wild animals	51.7 (823)	Legal knowledge
Key people in herpetology	46.2 (735)	Social knowledge
History of herpetology	43.6 (693)	Social Knowledge
Political issues for Herpers	51.4 (817)	Social Knowledge
Injuries/deaths to Herpers by their herps	36 (572)	Social Knowledge

N = 1591

* Data points discussed in the text.

felt the lack of access to professional knowledge and expertise online in the spaces where they would usually go. This dynamic of use and non-use of forums is an example of how the distribution of the social composition of the community across its technical architecture is linked to the internal divisions of the community. This will be further explored in the chapter discussing the boundaries of the community (Chapter 9, Section 9.4.1).

Customised spaces on the Internet included the provision of information about animals from personal webpages, taxonomic databases that provided information on the relationships between animals, and the use of forums and instant messaging for questions and interacting with known and unknown others who were also interested in herpetology. Sven describes how he used customised Internet spaces such as forums to gather information on how to keep giant geckos.

> When my interest for lizards was awakened, I started reading. I discovered that reptiles needed lighting and heating and terrariums and how the terrariums should be built. There was nothing about this on the Internet in Norway, so I had to read through the English forums. So I went to kingsnake and I went to Gecko World and I went to other places on the net where I could find information and I read about the animals that I wanted to keep. Since there was no information about this in Norway I started building my own website and I started getting visitors and people started coming more to the net.

His experience of finding information on how to care for captive Herps is similar to the way many respondents used the online environment. For Sven, this led to the use of a consistent avatar online, which he invited me to know him as interchangeably with his given name. The consistency of his online identity allowed him to give and receive consistent information and interaction, whilst maintaining separation from his offline identity. The online environment allowed him the visibility and access that his physical environment did not. Whilst his local friends knew him through his avatar and his given name, he kept this separation as an added level of security to protect himself from online government surveillance, as keeping geckos in his own country was illegal. We will return to Sven and his active online engagement with other people with interests in herpetology in the section discussing support online (Chapter 10, Section 10.4).

Unlike Sven, Detlef developed a consistent persona across the online-offline context; however Detlef was that rare breed of forum user, the academic scientist. Regardless, his personal use of the forums was for a mix of public education, meeting people and having fun.

> I do use forums. Why do I do it? Its fun, you get to know people. […] Not many professional scientists frequent non-professional forums […] Clearly there's a large body of people on the forums where one doesn't have an awful lot of common ground with. […] Forums are an opportunity to try to bridge the gap I think. […] You get a bit of everything, right into wacko country.

He discusses how there can be a gap between the impression he gets of a person that he meets online and when he meets them in person.

> In a sense, in many people the Internet persona really is quite different from what they present themselves like in reality. […] There's a real contrast, more usually people are strident on the Internet and quiet in real life. Maybe on the Internet they can let off steam that they then let off privately. […] You meet people that you've corresponded [with] on forums. It's very interesting. Sometimes one is taken aback by what one sees because it doesn't match with the impression they project on the web. Like some people who write extremely carefully and you meet them and they turn out to be tattooed bikers, I've certainly had that. Not that I have anything against tattooed bikers, but it's not at all the image that you had in mind when you corresponded with that person on the Internet. It's quite revealing.

For Detlef there is often a contrast between people's online personalities and who they are in real life that is based upon his impression of who they are through what they say and the reactions that they demonstrate in this environment. Whilst this supports the literature on online identities, this point of view is not consistent across the respondent population. For example, Jeremy feels that that the people he meets online and then offline are fairly true to the impression that they have created over time. The main consistency in the experiences of participants in using forums over time being that participants appear to gain an impression of people through how they interact online and this is eventually resolved by that person's reputation in the network and when they are met in real life. However another common element is the diversity of people and the mix between people who are seeking information and interaction through acceptable netiquette and those whose approach is intentionally controversial or adversarial. Because forums appeared for the participants to be a mix of the known and unknown, the well-intentioned and the troll[2], some participants preferred to lurk rather than become visible and enter the crossfire. Darren discusses how he goes to the forums quite a bit, but that he doesn't contribute much visible content to them. In line with this more observant position, he discusses anonymity in online forums and describes how this does not remain as a cover for a person over time.

> I actually don't put a lot of input in the forums, I just sort of sit back and watch what everyone else is writing. It's the same thing, even on a lot of those forums

2 Herring et al. (2002, p. 372) describe a troll as a person who posts fruitless arguments that lure members into pointless and time-consuming discussion. The goal of a stereotypical troll is argued by Donath (1999) to be the drawing in of particularly naive or inexperienced readers such as 'newbies'. Herring et al. (2002) differentiate between trolling and flaming, in that the goal for flaming is to incite readers through insults, deliberate provocation or rebukes.

> there is so much bitching and backstabbing, 'this person' worrying about what 'this person' has got and done.
>
> Alexia: With most of the people on the forum, do you actually know who they are? Does it take long to find out?
>
> Most of them you don't know at first, but you'll normally work them out pretty quickly. If you've got a reasonable network, even if you don't know who they are, after just sort of watching them for a little while, you'll work out who they are anyway just by little tidbits that they put in, little statements that they make. If you don't know, you'll normally only have to ask one or two people and they'll say "Oh, that's such and such".

From the analysis of the interview data set, excerpts of which have been presented above, the use of Wellman's networked individual to describe agency within the Herper community is apt. In working through the depth and breadth of social experience that interview participants shared about their engagement with the online environment, it was clear that they were co-creating an informational and social environment for themselves that reflected what they needed from the community and what they wanted to contribute to it. In doing so, a mediated space has been developed that diversifies and influences the social composition of the community.

Within the analysis of the data collected by the survey, it is also possible to explore how participants' portfolio of participation provided insight into the similarity or difference of network influence in the virtual versus organisational and physical environments of the community space. The visualisation of website networks presented in (Chapter 7, Section 7.2.2) through co-link analysis is a commentary on the networked structure of the technology layer of the community. This visualisation assisted in identifying key mediating nodes that influence the online experience of the community. The following analysis, whilst not bivariate in nature, compares these results with other variables in the survey that indicate the levels of commercial involvement, organisational membership and scholarly engagement within the respondent population. This analysis will provide a comparison of the centrality of these influencers in the online environment with the social action (roles and participation portfolios) of the participant population. In the following analysis it is argued that differences between social action in these areas and the issue-network profile suggests themes of centrality, low representation, knowledge gatekeeping and knowledge legitimacy within the culture of the network. This analysis creates an interpretive link between the technological, social and mediating culture of the case study community.

In terms of commercial involvement, a small percentage of participants (3.7 per cent, *N*=59) earned their main income from selling herps and herp products, however 40.3 per cent, (*N*=642) privately bred and sold herps. In addition to these figures, we see that the knowledge interests for the sample included running a herp business 36.5 per cent (*N*=580), and herp market trends 30.7 per cent (*N*=488). This suggests the relevance of the commercial sector to over a third of the respondent population. One customer base for this sector is participants who keep a reptile collection. Most participants (84.1 per cent, *N*=1,335) currently keep a collection or have done so in the past (a further 57.4 per cent, *N*=136). Whilst it cannot be said that this a representative sample of the entire Herper network, these figures suggest that private reptile sales are characteristic and that there is a substantial interconnectivity between most participants with the commercial sector. In the community, private sales are often facilitated by selling animals through a personal website (maintained by 26 per cent of the sample, *N*=404) and forums, such as those on Kingsnake.com (1,145 in-links). These results suggest that selling reptiles online was a central action of the network.

Within the web of network influencers, organisational websites had fewer in-links but a greater general presence (represented by the orange nodes for .org in Chapter 7, Figure 7.1). These organisations do not form discrete clusters but occur within clusters that contain both .edu, .net and .com addresses. This suggests that voluntary organisations (conservation organisations and Herp societies) are embedded within the wider online network. Three-quarters of the population (76.6 per cent, *N*=1219) were interested in environmental conservation and over a third (37.7 per cent, *N*=601) where members of herpetological societies. This suggests that the centrality of organisations within the online issue network represents the interest in conservation of the participant population. However I would argue that because two-thirds of the population were not active members of these organisations, this raises the question of representative voice. As voluntary organisations are traditional sites for collective action and representation of community interests, these results suggest a disconnect between organisational visibility with collective representation within the community.

The third sector of influence in the online environment was the scholarly community. Within the survey population, 13.6 per cent (*N*=216) were professional academics and 11.3 per cent (*N*=180) were studying Herpetology at university. These figures contrast with the commercial role engagement and suggest a smaller participant cohort overall. Despite the smaller proportion of academic role involvement, 73.3 per cent (*N*=1135) and 63.3 per cent (*N*=1007) of the respondent population were interested in scientific herp research and the scientific names of animals respectively. Like the commercial sector, these suggest the interconnectivity of a small cohort with the wider network. The visualisation of the issue network shows that scientific databases (for taxonomy and scientific publications) are well connected with each other and .org sites rather than with .com sites. This dynamic speaks to the gatekeeping aspect of scholarly knowledge and the currency of this knowledge for voluntary organisations rather than the commercial sector.

8.3 Social Layer

This section provides a discussion of the social profile of the community through a discussion of its demographics, drawing on the quantitative results of the survey and occasionally extended by observations from the ethnography. These examples of data analysis presented make overt the methodology of the research and articulate what the methods deployed produced in terms of insight from the case study. The social composition of the population that this presents is then cross referenced with their ICT use to reveal how the demographic data also contribute to an understanding of the technological layer and the mediating culture of the community.

8.3.1 Demographics

The demographic profile of the community is drawn from the survey data, and augmented with excerpts from the interview data and knowledge gained from participant observation. The analysis for these data sets was conducted discretely for the research and examples of findings are included here to demonstrate the practice of triangulating these insights. The non-traditional format of presenting the findings that follows is taken to demonstrate how the case study methodology and associated findings come together to articulate the social ecology approach. The following discussion also provides insight into the particular biases of the respondent population for the survey and introduces some of the cultural and technical idiosyncrasies among those who get involved with the herper community. To do this, following is a discussion of the geographical context of the community to articulate the physical space of the community and suggest its eligibility to be referred to as an open social structure. The data on the age range of survey participants presented is interrogated with their ICT use to explore how the composition of the community is influenced through this dynamic. The occupational and educational profile of the survey respondents is presented to raise the discussion of who is likely to be active within the community and whether there are any particular skews to social composition across the technical architecture.

Geography

The survey sample for the case study consisted of respondents living in 47 countries, with many of them residing in the United States of America (68.5

per cent, *N* = 1,062) and Canada (3.2 per cent, *N* = 50). The second largest bloc were European countries, Germany (2.5 per cent, *N* = 38), Denmark (1.7 per cent, *N* = 27), the Netherlands (1.7 per cent, *N* = 27) and Italy (1 per cent, *N* = 16), then Australia (7.5 per cent, *N* = 117), the UK (6.8 per cent, *N* = 106), South Africa (1.5 per cent, *N* = 24) and India (0.8 per cent, *N* = 12). This mostly reflects the countries in which the ethnographic research was conducted and also the fact that the herpetological industry in general is extremely active in the USA, across Europe and in Australia. This data is also likely to be a result of the survey being conducted in English (excluding populations from non-English speaking countries such as Eastern European countries, China and South America). Another element for mapping the geography of the survey population, while retaining the individual anonymity of respondents, would be to map the geographic locations of the societies and organisations that survey respondents affiliated with through Google maps or open street maps. In addition to this, it is also possible to produce a map of the IP addresses locations for websites that participants used. This data however can be fairly inaccurate and does not reflect the potential global reach or use case of an individual website. As these mapping approaches were not undertaken for the case study population due to the 'scope creep' that this activities may bring to the methodology and researcher capacities, it is difficult to comment upon what their contribution to research insight may be. One likely outcome is that they would simply articulate the dispersed geography of the herper community in a visual format. Some insight on this however can be gained from the participant interviews and observations.

From the ethnographic data set, it is clear that the accessible social network within the community spans across the globe and is mediated by language, cultural and geographical boundaries. These boundaries are generally permeable to community members due to their pursuit of their interests through mediating hubs such as organisations and businesses and the capacity of some Herpers to act as translators and connectors across knowledge, cultural and language domains for others within their social networks and forum engagement. From the participant observation, it became clear that trade hubs, such as those Hong Kong and Belgium, actively redistributed animals around the globe and consumption hubs such as the USA and Europe for created demand for these animals. The pet market and therapeutics market that places value on these animals for what they look like, what they symbolise and what their body parts are reputed to do has long been catered to within South-east Asia and mainland China and globalised through population migrations, tourism and scientific research demands for organic materials for taxonomic and genetic investigations. These regions, with the addition of India, and the continents of South America, Africa and Australia, are also rich locations for the sighting and collection of reptiles and amphibians from the wild. This is a favoured pastime of Herpers who are interested in seeing and photographing these animals in their native habitat, scientists and smugglers. This geography forms part of the imaginary of the herper community and in part also reflects the early patterns of colonialism overlaid with the trade routes of commercial enterprise that began the early naturalistic societies from which the herper community originated. From the above discussion, it is clear that the geographic scale of the herper community is global. However that these global relations are mediated by the open social structure of the herper community as it is enacted through consumption and regulation cultures, social networks and the mobility and flow of Herpers and Herps across techno-spatial environment of the community.

Age

Within the interviews, many Herpers began their interest in reptiles and/ or amphibians when they were young. Often starting with an interest in dinosaurs they saw in books or on television or from chasing the lizards they found in their backyard or frogs fished from the local creek and taken home in a jar. But this was not always the case, with some starting their interest through the people they were exposed to in later life. This is supported within the survey dataset through a discussion of modes of introduction. In terms of socialisation into the network, the median mode of introduction to the network was by no-one, which was the case for over half of the respondents (53 per cent, $N = 822$, $M = 2.4$, $SD = 1.7$, Median = 1, $IQR = 3$). On the social side of things however, 40 per cent of the respondent population were introduced to their herpetological interests by other people. Three per cent (2.9 per cent, $N = 45$) were introduced by a partner or spouse, 16.6 per cent ($N = 257$) through another family member and 12.4 per cent ($N = 192$) and 8.3 per cent ($N = 128$) were introduced through friends or acquaintances respectively. A small subset were introduced through other ways (6.8 per cent, $N = 106$). See Table 8.4 below for these results.

Table 8.4 Frequencies of modes of introduction into the network

Mode of introduction	% (N)
Introduced by no-one	53 (822)
Introduced by a partner	2.9 (45)
Introduced by another family member	16.6 (257)
Introduced by a friend	12.4 (192)
Introduced in other ways	6.8 (106)
Total	100 (1550)

For the survey, given the consent process was limited to those who were 18 and above, this younger generation of Herpers is not represented in the sample. The average age of survey respondents was 34.45 years (*SD* = 12.48, Median = 32 years, *IQR* = 17, Skewness = .79, Kurtosis = .28). Upon inspection of the data, the implication of the large standard deviation is that there is a fairly even distribution of ages across the respondent population. The implications of a kurtosis value of greater than zero and skewness of greater than zero is that distribution is biased towards the lower values. Analysis of the frequency data suggested that a larger proportion of respondents were in the 21–30 age range. This may be linked to a greater Internet exposure among the younger generation to reptile- and amphibian-related activities online. Given that the average period of involvement in the network is nine years, it was an interesting exercise to find out whether older participants have been involved for longer periods than younger participants. A strong, significant positive correlation between age and years of involvement, $r(1509) = .637, p < .01$, supported the intuitive idea that those involved for 10 years or less are drawn from the 21–30 age cohort. This finding, when considered alongside the 21–30 somethings 'lump' in the age profile of survey respondents suggests a recent influx of younger newbies to the network.

Gender

When age was crossed with gender in the analysis of survey data, the older cohorts were more likely to be men, while the younger cohorts were more likely to be a slightly more even distribution between men and women. This suggested that the newbies to the network are more likely to have a greater gender diversity within the social composition. However the following discussion of gender, supported by the survey data, suggests that there are specific channels and spaces where gender is more likely to reveal how the social composition of the herper community is related to its mediating culture and ICT environment.

Initially, a univariate analysis of the gender profile of survey participants revealed a gender ratio of approximately 3 males to every female. Of the sample 72 per cent was male (72.4 per cent, $N = 1114$) and 28 per cent were female (27.6 per cent, $N = 425$). In the context of research showing the normalisation of the gender divide online (Ono & Zavodny, 2003) this is an unusually male-centric sample. However these figures are reminiscent of the male-centric population in a study of women in massive multiplayer online role-playing environments (MMORPGs) that also found a gender ratio of approximately 3 males (71 per cent) to 1 female (29 per cent) (Cole & Griffiths, 2007). This observation of culture-specific demographic suggests that the gender bias evident in the survey data is a product of the herper culture rather than an artefact of the online environment (Codoban, 2005). Within the survey respondents living situations, this was certainly the case. Most respondents, this being men, needed to negotiate their herpetological interests with others in their personal living spaces (83.2 per cent, N = 1287). For 43.1 per cent (N = 667) this was with a partner or spouse. For 32.6 per cent (N = 504) this was with other family members, and 13 per cent (N = 202) lived alone. However, the most telling influence of gendered relations and spaces within the survey data set was when bivariate analysis were conducted on the relationship between gender and mode of introduction to the network and gender with technology use and patterns of mediated engagement. In terms of mode of introduction, around half of the women (49 per cent, N = 206) in the sample, were introduced by other people such as partners, family members and friends in comparison to under half of the men (37 per cent, N = 401). A chi squared test for independence revealed a significant association between gender and channels of introduction, χ^2 (5, N = 1500) = 52.60, $p < .0001$, whereby women were more likely to be introduced by their partner than men.

8.3.2 Social Composition Stratified by ICT Use

In general, over half of the respondent population in the case study research was university educated and over three quarters of the respondent population was in skilled work. In terms of the occupation and educational profile, data was collected at a fairly generic level as inter-country comparisons of the education system and occupational equivalents are not well matched. This approach takes into account various systems like the Dutch system in which people can complete half of a university degree and still gain a qualification, which is not possible in Australia for example. The results are reported in Table 1. The median occupational level was student (Median = 5, *IQR* = 3) and the median level of education was university education (Median = 4, *IQR* = 2). For occupational levels, there is a kurtosis value of -1.34 and skewness value of -0.205 indicating a non-normal distribution. Upon inspection of the data, there were higher proportions of semi-skilled (21.4 per cent, N = 324) and semi-professional occupations (N = 24.3 per cent, N = 367). In the education levels the skewness (-0.39) and kurtosis (-1.12) indicate a non-normal distribution. Upon inspection of the data, it is clear that higher levels of education are well represented but also that just under a fifth of the sample (18.4 per ceant, N = 279) are educated up to the secondary school level. These results are presented in tabular format in Table 8.5.

This indicates the broad skill base in the respondent population. However the diversity of social composition reported in the demographics appeared to be mediated in the online spaces according to gender, levels of education and occupational skill levels when interrogated with a bivariate analysis of ICT use patterns reported in (Chapter 7, Section 7.2.1).

Table 8.5 Frequencies of occupation and education

Occupation	% (N)
Unskilled	2.2 (34)
Semi-skilled	21.4 (324)
Skilled-manual	13 (197)
Skilled-clerical	2.2 (33)
Semi-professional (managerial/technical)	24.3 (367)
Professional	16.5 (250)
Other	6.3 (96)
Total	100 (1512)

Education	% (N)
Up to secondary education	18.4 (279)
Trade/apprenticeship	11.1 (168)
1–2 years job qualification	18.6 (283)
University degree	29.9 (454)
Higher university degree	22 (334)
Total	100 (1518)

Using the t-test for independence, there was no statistically significant[3] difference between genders in the years of Internet use, however there was a small significant difference between males (M = 15.89, SD = 11.6) and females (M = 18.11, M = 12.96; t(1385) = -2.94, p = .003) in their time spent online[4] in the previous seven days. The magnitude of the differences in the means was very small (eta squared = .0006) A chi-square test for independence indicated a significant association between gender and Internet skill use, c^2 (3, N = 1526) = 18.65, p = .000, Cramer's V = .11, which suggested that women perceived themselves as more skilled on average than men. There was no significant association between gender and face-to-face contact, c^2 (6, N = 1389) = 6.70, p = .35, Cramer's V = .07, and contact through other channels over the Internet, c^2 (6, N = 1299) = 5.74, p = .45, Cramer's V = .07. There was a significant association between gender and email contact, c^2 (6, N = 1388) = 25.42, p = .000, Cramer's V = .135. Men were more likely to use email to contact more other

3 The word 'significant' here is being used in a strict statistical sense and refers to results with p values of less than .05.

4 For the response data to 'Time spent online in the previous seven days' outliers for 53 hours and above were trimmed in line with results from Tukey's Hinges test for outliers. This represented 5.2 per cent (N = 79) of the responses.

Herpers than women. On average, men used email to contact twice as many people (6–10) as women (3–5) in the seven-day period. These results, in which women spend more time online and have a higher level of perceived digital literacy than men but contact fewer people by email, are in contrast to research on gendered use of social networking sites which suggests that women are more likely than men to use the online environment for relationship maintenance (Muscanell & Guadagno, 2012). In the case of the survey respondents, men were more likely to contact other Herpers by email, despite women reporting higher levels of perceived digital skill and time spent online. When the social composition of the ICT environment was cross-sectioned by occupation and education, a similar effect was also observed. This data is not presented here however, the findings of the survey analysis suggested that professionals and academics were more likely to use in-person and email contact to maintain and develop their networks and were less likely to engage with other Herpers over other Internet-mediated channels, such as forums. Participants with basic educational background and those in low-skilled occupations tended to spend more time online and be more active in the digital spaces than others. These divides in the data suggest that the ICT environment does have a homogenising effect on the social composition of the network by affecting who is likely to engage there. So while the social diversity of the survey sample was clearly enhanced by the increased spatiality of its strong and weak social ties through online communication, it was also stratified by where these ties are likely to be actively communicating (email and/or other Internet channels) and who was likely to be doing the communicating.

8.4 Mediating Culture

From the interview data we are able to explore how the trends articulated in the preceding sections are experienced within the mediating culture of the herper community. The effect of media in the network from the interview data has ostensibly been to bring a diversity of people into common spaces where they were able to explore what it was that they shared without necessarily judging each other for their social status. Aashil, who was involved in the network at a time when advertising reptiles for sale was done through the local newspapers, describes the social diversity that existed then.

> There was one time … that I had a bunch of them [customers] coming at the same time to pick up animals, and there were these two guys, fresh out of the marines … Huge! Six foot five, full of muscle, shaved head, all-American boys. And then there was a couple that was like total stinky hippies, you know, patchouli-wearing hippies. There were five or six people down in the basement

> … all totally different aspects of life. People that would have been walking down the street and would probably spit on each other, and they were all like best of friends because they were all into the same things.

We continue, however, to come back to the Internet as a key facilitator for this diversity of people staying in contact with each other. As Alvin says of his experience of getting involved in his interests, it was this diversity that drew him into the networks, as well as being able to meet people virtually. This appeared to extend his opportunities for meeting people that he felt he had something in common with.

> One of my friends that I've met through the Internet I've known for 7 or 8 years now. We actually have never met in person but I know him. We email, we talk on the phone. Really in college, and what's happened on the Internet – just being exposed to a large variety of people – was how it really started.

This large diversity of people is also reflected by the discussions that I had with participants about whether there was a way of identifying of who 'a Herper' was. However a common element that did emerge was not necessarily about socio-economic status but more about social marginality. Marcie is thinking about the people in her local area and talking about how she has met other Herpers on a one-by-one basis, more randomly than anything else.

> You just kind of run into them. People always say reptile people are strange. Sometimes you can tell. Sometimes there is a stereotype and you can kind of guess, OK, he might be into reptiles. In [place] most young Herpers are typically young males, they typically have piercings and tattoos. Most have dyed black hair, spikey hair, face tags. I don't know … it's hard to say.
>
> Alexia: But you don't, Jason doesn't. He didn't.
>
> Exactly, so it's hard to say. That's why I meet people and they just don't believe what I do. They say you're too cute and innocent-looking, there's no way.

What we can see from this response, is that alternative presentations of the self are associated with the possibility of being a Herper and that public perception of the network is that these people are strange. This theme of social marginality because of an interest in reptiles and being thought a freak occurred throughout the discourses of the participants. This indicates that public perception and social marginality, rather than internal social homogeneity, are one indication of the external boundaries of the network. This idea will be further explored in the macro theme of boundaries (Chapter 9).

Even though there are no consistent herper stereotypes across the network, there are people to whom others look up to and identify with as an authentic Herper. These are generally people who have immersed themselves in their interests, engaged in different aspects of the network and connected with a wide range of people in face-to-face settings and online. They also have something to give in terms of knowledge, access and experience. Many animals have passed through their hands and often their stories of field adventures and knowledge of key figures is personal, and usually entertaining. These connected figures tend to have a sociable personality that enables them to be a central mediator across the different, and sometimes conflicting, domains of the network. They are a clear example of someone who has created their personal identity within the context of social diversity, online presence and across the internal boundaries of the network.

Regardless of the experience of social heterogeneity discussed above, as highlighted in the survey demographics, the influence of gender relations extended across the mediating culture of the network. Within the course of participant observation, head counts of herper spaces usually revealed a gender ratio of 3 males to every female; however the interview population was more biased towards men than the survey population. Of the 16 women interviewed, two were scientists, one was an amateur herpetologist, four were graduate biology students, two were employed as a reptile keepers and the remaining were hobbyists. This spread of involvement has no particular gender significance; however it does demonstrate that the common experiences shared by these women were drawn from different types of role involvement across the network. This observed gender imbalance was regularly experienced by interviewees, with women referring to the male-centric culture of the herper community, sometimes as a 'macho culture'. The interviews with women demonstrate that this gender imbalance and the associated subordination of perspectives in a relationship largely constrained the role options for women as girlfriends, wives, daughters and targeted some for sexual harassment. Those who engaged in the network outside of these constrained roles usually replicated the approach of the men in this environment. In the one case of an interview with a transgender women, she occupied a role comfortably that she had previously established as a man, and was respected as such within the community. For the most part however, participant observation and interviews demonstrated that participants were often able to connect through shared interests in reptiles and amphibians with people who had entirely different life biographies and socio-economic experiences, but this tolerance did not diffuse the macho culture and gender inequalities within the community.

This gendered subordination of roles in the context of perceived risk, danger and negative public perception is likely to have led to both the absence and low visibility of women in the community. Male participants who required a space for their herp collection, in the home and in their lives, often discussed the difficulty they had in finding girlfriends who were tolerant and supportive of their interests. Some women don't engage because they fear the animals. Other women in the network held the more traditional gendered position of being less socially visible because this network is, by and large, a man's world and they are not comfortable in it. Both Birgit and Jill discuss this absence and low visibility of females in the network. Birgit discusses the small number of women whom she knows are involved and makes the connection with their interests as often fostered by their male partners.

> I think compared to the number of boys, it's not many girls. And usually the ones who are interested, they're having reptile boyfriends. I don't know many people, except for Åshild, who have herself have found the interest. I think she is one of the very few which have found it herself, not through a boy. That's rather exceptional.

Jill describes her response to this lack of other women involved as driving her to connect with the few that she meets.

> I've gotta say that I absolutely reach out when I find another female working in the area, and I'm like, 'Aahhhh, we can be friends! Let's stick together'. I've always had a lot of male friends and so it doesn't bother me to have a lot of males around me, but sometimes the competitive environment that you get around a lot of men all the time can get a bit much for me.

This is in response to the competitive, male-dominated environment that she sees as characterising the herper community. This suggests how the social composition of the network is related to the mediating culture.

8.5 Conclusion

This chapter has provided a methodological discussion of community composition through drawing on the case study analysis and findings. In particular, it has revealed the role that the networked individual has upon the social composition of the network and how this can be articulated through qualitative and quantitative data. The social layer of the network particularly reveals both the diversity of participants in terms of age, geography and life experience in the case study research, but also the influence of gender, which was then taken up in the discussion of the mediating culture of the network presented in the qualitative analysis. In overview, the case study analysis suggested that participants now have the capacity to be more globally interconnected and maintain and share intimate connections through real-time and disembodied interactions. This has resulted in the choice-based disconnection of the network from its previous place-bound and group-bound social structures and the reattachment of people in more elongated networks. In the herper community, this mediated social process has integrated with, rather than replaced, the pre-existing social structures of networks anchored around organisations, key figures and mobile reputations. From the analysis, we already know that social diversity has not disrupted this pattern and that both in spite of and because of the more open social infrastructure; the small-world effect is still at play.

The key question for the research practitioner raised through this chapter is how a community that is characterised by social diversity maintains its boundaries and cohesion over time. This associated practical question by about the research methods that can be employed to reveal these patterns and social experience. A methodological discussion of articulating community boundaries and the expression of community cohesion within open social structures will be unpacked in Chapters 9 and 10 consecutively.

Chapter 9
Community Boundaries

9.1 Introduction

The aim of this chapter is to explore the methods that reveal community boundaries as defined by the research population, rather than as defined by the researcher. Section 9.2 considers the articulation of community boundaries within the qualitative data of the herper community case study through the structuring influences of place and legislation. Section 9.3 presents a discussion of boundaries from within the social layer of the case study data, focusing on quantitative and qualitative analysis of discursive boundaries and the influence of gender as a shaping characteristic within the community. Section 9.4 draws on the qualitative data to provide a real world example of how internal and external boundaries are expressed in the case study community.

Understanding the boundary construction behaviours of a community assists the researcher in building sensitised and nuanced insight. This is achieved by conducting research into social practices related to the development of the collective identity of the group and its mediating culture. When thinking about how community boundaries are conceptualised within the social sciences, we can turn to the literature exploring immigrant communities and other marginalised community experiences. Social boundaries are clearly expressed in the differentiation between wider society and a marginalised community. This is evident in the enactment of power differentials through social persecution and social stigma. Marotta (2008), drawing on the work of Georg Simmel on the social construction of boundaries, argues that:

> Humans are a boundary constructing species, but we are also able to defy the boundaries that we impose and which are imposed on us. Symbolic, psychological, social and cultural boundaries allow us to organize and order our world. (Marotta, 2008, p. 298)

In unpacking this idea that boundary construction is formative to social order (and disorder), Marotta suggests that these boundaries are socially ambivalent because they act to hinder and enable social practices. When viewing boundaries as a source of confinement, he argues that they can provide the grounds to suppress and exclude others. As a source of liberation, Marotta's perspective resonates with the body of literature that positions social boundaries as empowering communities through the construction of a collective identity. Marotta argues that identity construction through the construction of boundaries establishes the difference between 'self and other' (2008, p. 298). Through these ideas, we are introduced to the Janus-faced nature of social boundaries that become enacted through the polarisation of social practices around norms and values.

This understanding resonates with other boundary concepts that this chapter considers. The first section will consider the relationship between the geographic context of place and how this shapes and is shaped by open social systems. This speaks to the technological, infrastructural and place based layer of the community. The construction of internal and external group boundaries through demographic and discursive characteristics speaks to the social layer of the community and how this has influenced the patterns of social organisation. The emergent versus imposed parameters of community boundaries can be seen in how the mediating culture has produced a perception of the general public and the internal existence and action of opposition and contradiction that produce social form. These polarisations thread through the study of communities and can be thought of as the protoboundaries (Abbott, 1995) through which insight into digital communities emerges. From the consideration of the case study data and findings across the qualitative and quantitative spectrum presented in this chapter, we will begin to see that both internal and external community boundaries can be articulated as a way to define a clustering of people. When seen in overview, it is the network or webbing of boundary behaviours (Fuchs, 2005; Halpern, 2014; Jenkins, 2006; Lightfoot & Martinez, 1995; Mitra & Schwartz, 2001) that truly characterises the adaptive and open social structure of the community.

The investigation of the community construct through these parameters allows for a derived (rather than ascribed) definition of group boundaries. This understanding is informed, rather than determined, by existing knowledge and research practices that support the researcher in defining social boundaries (Butler & Wang, 2012; Lamont & Molnar, 2002; Star & Griesemer, 1989; Marotta, 2008; Williams, 2009). The main advantage to research practice of the derived definition of community boundaries is that it allows for the networked connectivity of places (Latham & Sassen, 2005; Neal, 2011; Sassen, 2000, 2001, 2008) and the greater social complexity that threads through this concept to be explored. This approach is resonant with the argument presented by John Law (2004) in his actor network theory (ANT) inspired (Law, 1992, 1999, 2002; Law & Urry, 2001) 'post-methods' thinking. He argues that there is a need for social scientists to become more flexible in their methodological approaches given the geographical complexities that arise through the elongation of social relationships from a proximity-base (offline or IRL) to the co-presence of mediated sociability (online) (2004, p. 3). From the social network analysis (SNA) conceptual perspective that this book is aligned with, Wellman and Leighton (1979) heralded the limits to community thinking that is spatially determined. They sought to steer research into communities beyond the 'lost', 'saved' or 'liberated' hypotheses by pointing out the conceptual limitations to community theory that did not accommodate for the technological disruption of place and de-territorialisation of social ties. While Law and Wellman represent different conceptual approaches into network thinking, they both take a relational perspective that sees a networked and fluid world through which global relations flow across flat and recursive structures. From this understanding, they argue that research approaches need to respond to this fluidity and interconnectivity. This challenge is taken up throughout this book and is relevant to the discussion of researching community boundaries; particularly in how they operate across the fluidity and interconnectivity of open social structures.

The definition of a community boundary that acknowledges networked places, mediated sociability and robustly holds social diversity tends to be both conceptually and methodologically complex, the technical reason for this being that open social structures tend to cluster rather than clump (Latham & Sassen, 2005). They bridge structural holes (Burt, 1992, 2000, 2004) through episodically active and spatially elongated social networks. When this is considered to be the case, gaps and silences constitute structural data. This idea has similarities with the notions of form that emerges from the 'assemblages' of STS and surveillance studies (Gerlitz & Lury, 2014; Haggerty & Ericson, 2000). However within these assemblages, the considerations of coherence, social cohesion, stability, activism and continuity that underpin the notion of community become untenable. The approach proposed in this book is to accept the spatial distribution and networked structure of digital community, and in doing so locate its 'social mass' through acknowledging the structuring influences and social architecture which organisations and institutions bring. I argue that it is through the interlacing of the flat, recursive structures of social networks with organisational structures, that, as theorists and research practitioners, we can accommodate for and harness the diffuse edges of a community. From this way of seeing, it is the boundary construction behaviours that emerge from within the community that are of analytical interest.

9.2 Technology, Place and the Built Environment

The derivation of group boundaries has several ways of being identified within sociological praxis. The place-based context of the group forms the geographic fabric across which physical and social exchange occurs. These exchanges are regulated through the meshwork of legislations that interlock local, regional, national and international governance systems. The legislative frameworks, and how they articulate from the local to the global, form an environmental niche within, and across, which the community flourishes and social action is shaped. The legislative frameworks however do not define a community boundary. What it defines is a social boundary that the community responds to, and often polarises over, through and across the weave of its social networks. The networks of public and private relationships contained within a community are also its mechanisms of social activism, self-regulation and illicit exchange. These channels and their imbrication with place articulate, at an intimate level, the local-global tensions that can be revealed by studying the geographic relationships and distribution of a community. The discussion of the herper community case study presented below provides an example of how legislation and place provide insight into community boundaries. This discussion demonstrates one way to articulate the internal intricacies and external boundaries of a community through a consideration of the regulatory structures it engages with.

9.2.1 Place, Legislation and Spatially Distributed Social Systems

The definition of place, and thus the territoriality, of the case study community is articulated through the distribution of social networks and institutions that present both local roots and global reach. The influence of geography upon community boundaries can be seen most clearly within the case study through the impact of legislature and its regulation upon the spaces of activity and exchange for the community both globally and at the local level. In the regulation and legislation of public, private and commercial engagement with reptiles and amphibians, there are both local laws governing their captive keeping and native habitats and there are international conventions that control the international trading of animals. National laws control the import and exporting of animals into and out of a country, the collection of animals from the wild, the keeping of animals in zoos and the captive market of retailing and keeping animals privately. These laws are managed through permit systems and are variably enforced across the network. The fact that participants knew that laws were different in different countries through what they saw on the Internet also influenced their levels of respect in their own minds for how these various laws were upheld. All participants who kept private collections or were responsible for public collections in zoos and museums did so by engaging in a permit system. In the hands of the Herpers, permit systems have a variety of loopholes that would usually open up a permit economy amongst scientists, museums and zoos at an international level and amongst private breeders and Herpers within a local legislative region. This indicates the porosity of the legal boundaries through 'user appropriation', as opposed to direct decisions to break laws. It was observed that people would trade permit paperwork in order to keep an approximate legal veneer over the collections that they had and to cover animals that were added to collections through other means, such as poaching or swapping.

This porosity and permeability of boundaries that comes from 'knowing how to get around the rules' is facilitated by the mosaic of laws across regions and countries and the networked mobility of people, animals and ideas. In this way, the legislative boundaries of countries become perforated by the networked interaction of the globalised economy. During participant observation, the researcher traced the story of a rare snake smuggled off an island between Trinidad and Tobago, through to the depressing grey council apartment complexes of Amsterdam. The act of smuggling the snake was highly illegal and contravened many wildlife protection acts. However the act of selling the snake in Amsterdam was legal. The financial incentive for this plan was lost, however, because the man who had brought the snake into Amsterdam was not connected to people who would be likely to pay a high price for a rare snake. Because of this he resorted to advertising it for 50 euro in the local online trading post before the snake died. Randomly, a young Herper in another part of the Netherlands found the advertisement online and decided that it was most likely a hoax, but a very good price for this rare snake. He decided to take the trek to the apartment in Amsterdam with an accompanying Herp mate, to help him identify the snake, and myself. The seller told an approximate story of the snake's history, minus a few salient details. The Herpers identified the snake, money changed hands and we walked out through the piss-stained corridors of the apartment complex, past police officers apprehending someone, and into the streets. All while holding a plastic kitchenware container fastened with duct tape that contained a venomous snake smuggled into this port city.

Those who just want to keep a reptile in a private collection at home struggle with this boundary when it is applied to the country they live in. Detlef discusses the way permeability within a jurisdiction comes at the site of the enforcing officers themselves. His example comes from the UK and involves the Dangerous Wild Animals Act, however many of the participants experienced this kind of local irregularity of regulation and enforcement of local captive keeping laws.

> The biggest problem with it being that there are no standards as to what you have to do. The whole thing is pretty much up to the subjective whims of whoever is in charge in your local government authority. […] It's an absolute lottery and there's no system that says if you fill conditions 'x' we will give you the permit for a fee of 'y'. At the moment it's relatively unregulated except for venomous and native species. You can keep what you want other than that.

Other than dangerous animals, the keeping of reptiles and amphibians appears to be relatively unregulated. This creates a contradictory system of regulation in which people are able to do what they want and are less likely to wish to have one segment of their captive collection under strict licensing whilst the rest is not. The impact of a legislative boundary that selectively criminalises people with interests in keeping captive collections of diverse reptiles has predictable effects upon those for whom abiding by the law is somewhat negotiable. In a discussion of who the stereotypical Herper would be in Norway, Sven notes the impact that prohibitive laws have on who is likely to be involved in the network.

> But perhaps there is more criminal herpetophiles in Norway, because if you are a normal person who loves reptiles and you have a job that requires that you have a clean criminal record, then you won't risk your job over a few geckos. So you will refrain from keeping them. If you follow this scale, you have people who care a lot for the law, people who respect a law, people who almost respect the law and keep geckos maybe, and people who don't respect the law. In a normal country where reptiles are legal you've got all of these types keeping reptiles and most of them are just normal people. But in Norway, you have cut off people that respect the law and only people who follow ethical rules for example over government rules, perhaps they will keep geckos, or people who pretty much don't care for the law.

Sven's articulation of how participants mentally oriented towards the legality of what they were doing and its social effects demonstrates that the boundary of who becomes involved in the network reflects the legal status of the activity.

9.3 Social Layer

Social boundaries can also be identified at the site of the individual, through the combination of whom they are willing to talk to about their interests and their demography. This can be seen as boundary construction articulated through the social layer. Discursive boundaries, conceptualised by Chamberlain (2005b) move beyond a discourse of the other in the social construction of boundaries. Discursive boundaries reveal the network through its conversational traces and knowledge exchange. A boundary in this context is less about inclusion and exclusion (ideas more connected to proximity through their notion of 'in' and 'out') and more about connection and disconnection (aligned with the notion of digital co-presence). The qualitative analysis presented from the case study reveals the prevalence of gender in influencing and dividing those who are active and visible in the network, versus those who lurk or choose not to engage. In this sense, we can see a gendered socio-demographic boundary emerging through hegemonic practices. This suggests how demographic attributes can be considered as an element of internal boundary construction and division within the community that also has the capacity to act an external boundary for the group.

9.3.1 Gender as a Boundary Construct

This section presents quantitative and qualitative analysis from the case study that considers community boundaries generated by patterns of social organisation. Within the herper community, the demographic composition is characterised by a higher proportion of male versus female members. This has created a social boundary for who is likely to participant and be visible within the community and reflects an endogenous male-centric culture with associated role inequalities.

Within the survey demographics and participant observation the gender ratio was one female to three males, this ratio being more biased towards men amongst older cohorts and more evenly distributed amongst younger cohorts. This gender ratio appears contradictory to the social diversity apparent in the mixing of people from all walks of life across the online and offline environments that we saw in the discussion of the case study in Chapter 8. The interview sample is clearly more biased towards men than the survey population and the gender ratio observed during participant observation. Of the 16 women interviewed out of the 80 interviewees, two were scientists, one was an amateur herpetologist, four were graduate biology students, two were employed as a reptile keepers and the remaining were hobbyists. This spread of involvement has no particular gender significance; however it does demonstrate that the common experiences shared by these women were drawn from different types of role involvement across the network. This observed gender imbalance was regularly experienced by interviewees, with women referring to the male-centric culture of the herper network as a 'macho culture'.

Male participants who required a space for their herp collection, in the home and in their lives, often discussed the difficulty they had in finding girlfriends who were tolerant and supportive of their interests. Some women don't engage because they fear the animals. Other women in the network held the more traditional gendered position of being less socially visible because this network is, by and large, a man's world and they are not comfortable in it. Both Birgit and Jill discuss this absence and low visibility of females in the network. Birgit discusses the small number of women whom she knows are involved and makes the connection with their interests as often fostered by their male partners.

> I think compared to the number of boys, it's not many girls. And usually the ones who are interested, they're having reptile boyfriends. I don't know many people, except for Åshild, who have herself have found the interest. I think she

> is one of the very few which have found it herself, not through a boy. That's rather exceptional.

Jill describes her response to this lack of other women involved as driving her to connect with the few that she meets. This is in response to the competitive, male-dominated environment that she sees as characterising the herpetological network in general and more specifically those networks that include an interest in snakes.

> I've gotta say that I absolutely reach out when I find another female working in the area, and I'm like, "Aahhhh, we can be friends! Let's stick together". I've always had a lot of male friends and so it doesn't bother me to have a lot of males around me, but sometimes the competitive environment that you get around a lot of men all the time can get a bit much for me.

During the interview she describes the culture of the herpetological network as being macho and based upon one-upmanship.

> It seems to me the more interested you are, the more macho you can get ... My overall impression is it's a pretty blokey sort of thing and it's quite competitive. There's a fair bit of one-upmanship in terms of "I've caught this, I've seen this, I've done this".

This style of competitive behaviour and one-upmanship was regularly witnessed by the researcher during participant observations, and was also referred to by male participants. Competition is an experience that spans the network from the hobbyist to the academic. For example a French researcher, Germaine, spoke of the competitive environment that he was exposed to.

> On the people level, it's very much the same, lots of competition, lots of politics. I don't like this side of things. It's not very enjoyable.

Similarly, Daniel, a researcher in the Netherlands trying to access the network for crocodile embryos, found that he had walked straight into a competitive environment that locked him out.

> There was a whole alligator community in Florida and Louisiana. I couldn't get into that because I emailed the wildlife people there. I emailed the scientists. The scientists didn't want anyone else muscling in. The wildlife people didn't want the paperwork of exporting stuff to me. So I was locked out of that network.

Often the kind of one-upmanship described by Germaine was present amongst people based purely on what animals they were interested in. As a breeder in the

US, Alvin, observed this during the period that he bred snakes for private sale on the market and was active on the forums.

> It's kind of weird … I did tree boas and tree pythons for a long time. There's some people that really hate tree python people and tree python people that hate tree boa people. "Tree pythons are better". "Tree boas are better". … They're almost identical, you know.

Darren saw this kind of competitive culture as linked to low levels of trust in others, which affected this participant's ability to get to know other Herpers.

> In the reptile game, [amongst private keepers] there is so much backstabbing going on. That everybody's got to know everybody else's business and nobody wants everyone else to know your business. Everyone's really, really untrusting of everybody else. Getting to know people is quite difficult.

In addition, this divisive, low-trust, competitive culture was seen by Louis to be the reason that there are low levels of activism across the network.

> The problem is always the same because human nature. All the human are protective and it's very hard to come all together and to make a big population of people who want to protect their hobby, because guys are stupid, because guys are competitive, because guys don't like each other. They are not in a big group. That's a big problem we got. We have no federation, we don't have the ability to be all together and go against the law …

These trends of low trust and low activism, which Louis has made the link for us to this gender-based competitive culture, will be further explored in the following chapter on trust in the network and activism and advocacy (Chapter 10, Sections 10.3 and 10.4). What this does indicate is this social inequality has ramifications not only upon how women experience their herpetological interests through the masculine lens, but also upon how the network as a whole functions.

The discussion above has demonstrated the competition and one-upmanship present in the network, but not how this pervades the culture of the network. From the participant observation, this can be indicated through the humour of the network and the presence of sexual harassment towards women both in the physical world and in the online environment. Not only is the culture referred to as macho and competitive by both women and men alike during interviews, but the humour of the culture is also correspondingly sexist and aggressive. In particular, this starts with the type of language used. During an interview with Jill, we discuss the enculturation into swearing as a form of communication.

Alexia: When I see my friends I say, 'I'm really sorry about my sense of humour, it's very masculine'.

Jill: I am incredibly crude, I have a foul mouth on me. It's shocking. [LAUGHS] It's bad, but there's nothing I can do about it. It's a working hazard, isn't it?

This can also be seen in the unnecessary swearing in some of the interview excerpts used throughout the analysis. The researcher also heard many jokes and allusions made by men about the phallic shape of reptiles and snakes. Other types of humour usually related to people getting hurt by animals. For example, many is the time that I have sat in a room listening to men laugh very hard whilst watching or hearing about another Herper being bitten by a non-venomous snake, lizard, goanna or crocodile. Pranks like this are usually how Herpers find out about each other's handling skills, when they give a newbie to the herp room the most aggressive animal to handle first up. Photographs of such moments are commonly shared amongst Herpers for a laugh. This type of humour is related to the aggressive aspects of the experience of working with animals. Women in this context learn to participate or get out of the way. Humour that relates to women is usually about gendered roles such as sex objects or mothers. For example, men referring to women using animal husbandry language, where a pregnant woman would be 'gravid' for example. One such allusion recorded during participant observation in France was during a lunch where the men joked about Elise eating like a python, without needing to be 'teased'.

Elise: I'm a good feeder …

Ladolfo: You don't even have to tease it.

Louis: Be careful. Too fat, they will not produce.

Teasing refers to the act of making a dead mouse look lifelike to a hungry snake by wiggling it in front of the animal to prompt it to bite the mouse. Snakes that are overweight do not get pregnant and is a natural concern for an animal breeder, which is the observation made by Louis. To the group of men assembled, the funny aspect of this exchange was the use of animal husbandry-related language to objectify a woman as getting too fat for child-bearing.

Informal discussions with female participants raised the experience of sexual harassment in fieldwork situations. During these discussions, women referred to conforming to gendered roles in fieldwork situations with older males, such as cooking and having to deal with sexual innuendo, being approached for sex and sexist comments. There is one recorded discussion relating to the experience of sexual harassment in the network. When asked an open question at the end of the interview, Jill begins with a qualifying statement saying that her experiences in the network have been mostly good but that she has experienced sexual harassment and implies that she was approached for sex in unwanted ways during fieldwork.

> I can only put that down to being the only female in a field situation for weeks on end, and you just absolutely … cop it bad. I've handled it badly in certain circumstances and better in others, but I find that when you're working in remote field sites and you're the only female, it can be really bad, it can be shocking. … It's more of an expectation. I mean I've had my arse slapped more times than I care to think about.

Sexual harassment is a serious aspect for women involved in the network and it is pervasive in the online environment. In the interviews, women appeared to engage much less than men with other Herpers in the online environment. Women interviewed who had partners with herpetological interests were often much less active in the online forums. Anika described herself as a lurker on the forums, watching and reading only, and Birgit doesn't have Internet access at home and got exposure to forum discussions through talking with her partner. These interviews gave the impression of a gendered invisibility of women in these environments, with a dependence upon men to be active online. Whilst this was not the case for all female participants, this gendered bias of Internet activity was clearly a strong component of the interviews. Given the smaller pool of women involved in the network, forums online also acted as an informal dating mecca for heterosexual males. Geerd describes a Dutch herpetological forum where the presence of new single females tended to attract an outpouring of sexualised male interest.

> We have some forums in the Netherlands, it's horrible. When a girl posts her picture, it's like in ten minutes 25 replies from all guys, 'Aw, nice looking'. And everyone's like, 'Oh, not again … Keep it low on the hormones, guys. Take it easy'.

This discussion of the participant observation and interview data demonstrated that participants were often able to connect through shared interests in reptiles and amphibians with people who had entirely different life biographies and socio-economic experiences, but this tolerance did not diffuse the macho culture. The gendered subordination of roles in the context of perceived risk, danger and negative public perception is likely to have led to both the absence and low visibility of women in the network. This suggests the limits to which one might think that demographic heterogeneity is likely to translate culturally as social equality within a community.

9.3.2 Discursive Boundaries: From a Metric Perspective

Another method through which community boundary construction (both internal and external) can be viewed is the generation of discursive boundaries. In his work on *Star Trek* fans, Chamberlain (2005a, 2005b, 2006) demonstrated that interest group boundaries were enacted at the person-to-person level. Chamberlain developed this concept by providing network maps of the relationships between people with whom participants discussed their *Star Trek* interests. This data was derived from interviews with participants and visualised through social network analysis techniques. From these visualisations he proposed a typology for everyday fans that he describes as Private *Star Trek* fans, Social *Star Trek* fans, and Discreet *Star Trek* fans (Chamberlain, 2005a). This boundary phenomenon is referred to in this book as the discursive boundaries of the networked individual. For the case study research, survey participants were provided with statements derived from these categories to indicate the discursive topology of their social networks. Respondents were asked to indicate their general social approach to talking about their herpetological interests. This ranged from being comfortable talking about it with anyone who expresses an interest to not talking about it to anyone else. Given the non-normal distribution of these variables, the median is reported. As depicted in Table 9.1, participants discussed their interests openly when relevant ($M = 3.9$, $SD = .724$, Median = 4, $IQR = 0$). This suggests that the micro boundaries or interpersonal boundaries of the network are fairly open and porous.

In addition to this, survey participants were asked to indicate the type of community experience that they participated in ranging from a closed group, to loose networks. On average, respondents participated in loose networks of Herpers who mostly knew or knew of each other ($M = 2.71$, $SD = 3$, Median = 3, $IQR = 2$). In terms of patterns of social organisation, the predominant formats experienced by respondents were several different groups (25.4 per cent, $N = 400$) or a loose network of people who mostly know or know of each other (33.9 per cent, $N = 534$). These results suggest that, for the sample, the herper network is experienced as an open social structure that is mediated by strong and weak social ties rather than traditional closed-group structures with distinct social boundaries. One interpretation of this finding is that the discursive boundaries of the networked individual are likely to have more influence on the boundary construction across the community. This interpretation suggests that there may be a relationship between a person's boundary construction of who they are likely to talk to about their herpetological interests (discursive boundaries) and the type of community experience that they have. This explores the notion that community experience is shaped by whom the respondent talks to rather than being a general and shared experience of a group. This is based upon the assumption that a social ecology, made up of a heterogeneous and spatially distributed population consists of different experiences of community.

Table 9.1 Frequencies of discursive boundaries of the respondent population

Discursive boundary	% (N)	
Don't really discuss herpetological interests with others	1.5 (23)	Discursively closed
Prefer to discuss herpetological interests only over the Internet	1.5 (23)	Internet only
Discuss herpetological interests with particular people	15.6 (246)	Select interactions
Discuss herpetological interests openly when it's relevant with anyone who expresses an interest	72.1 (1138)	Open interactions
Most of the people whom respondent talks with also have herpetological interests	6.2 (98)	Social immersion
Other discursive strategy	3.1 (50)	
Total	100 (1578)	

Table 9.2 Frequencies of styles of community experience

Style of group participation	% (N)	Network form
Participate in several different groups	25.4 (400)	Clique clusters, weak tie links.
Participate in a community that mostly knows and relies upon each other	15.8 (249)	Strong tie, cohesive cluster.
Participate in a loose network of Herpers who mostly know or know of each other	33.9 (534)	Hub and node connections of strong and weak ties.
Associate with Herpers met by chance, most probably don't know each other	14.9 (235)	Random network, not reciprocal.
Don't socialise with other Herpers	7.6 (120)	Social closure.
Other	2.3 (37)	
Total	100 (1575)	

Within the analysis very few Herpers did not talk about their interests with others or only talked about their herp interests online. Consequently these levels were collapsed into 'Other' in the variable describing the conversational approach that Herpers took to their interests (Discursive boundaries). Given that both variables are nominal variables, a chi-square test for independence was used. The small number of people who either didn't discuss their interests with other Herpers or did so only online meant that these categories were merged into a new category of 'limited discussion with other Herpers'. There was a significant association between discursive styles and type of community experience that participants had, c^2 (15, N = 1522) = 99.61, $p < .0001$. Participants who openly discussed their interests with others when relevant were more likely to experience the network as either a loose network of ties who knew or knew of each other (34.6 per cent, N = 392) or several different groups (26.9 per cent, N = 305). Participants who selectively discussed their interests with others were more likely to know loose networks of people, rather than the group engagement demonstrated by open communicators (see Table 9.3 below).

Table 9.3 Cross-tabulation of community experience and discursive boundaries

	Type of discursive boundary			
Community Experience	**Limited**	**Select**	**Open**	**Immersed**
Different groups	10.9% (5)	17.6% (43)	26.9% (305)	37.8% (37)
Known community	15.2% (7)	17.2% (42)	15.3% (173)	18.4% (18)
Loose network	17.4% (8)	34.4% (84)	34.6% (392)	30.6% (30)
Met by Chance	17.4% (8)	17.2% (42)	15% (170)	10.2% (10)
Don't socialise	39.1% (18)	11.5% (28)	6.3% (71)	0% (0)
Other	0% (0)	2% (5)	2% (23)	3.1% (3)
Total	100% (46)	100% (244)	100% (1134)	100% (98)

N = 1522

Those who mostly talked to other Herpers experienced the network through different groups (37.8 per cent, N = 37) or loose networks (30.6 per cent, N = 30) and were most likely, out of all the conversational styles, to experience the network as a community of people that they knew and relied on. These results suggest that people who were immersive or open communicators were most likely to experience the network through a traditional community format of group engagement, whilst those who were more selective in who they talked to about their interests were more likely to experience it through networks of known strong and weak social ties. These results are intuitive; however they are the first exploration of the association between the social approach of the networked individual and their type of community experience. This is a unique perspective provided by the application of the contextual approach of the social ecology concept to the experience of community.

From the quantitative analysis, we have seen that, in general, participants are happy to talk to most people who are interested in hearing about reptiles and amphibians and that participants experience the network through engagement in multiple groups and loose-tie networks. This makes the identification of social boundaries from the statistical data ambiguous, as there is no discrete form indicated by these responses.

9.3.3 Discursive Boundaries: From a Social Practice Perspective

As the quantitative discussion has highlighted, discursive boundaries are deeply tied to the notion of interaction. These are the boundaries constructed at the site of social engagement. The patterns of discussion become the social boundaries of a networked individual's experience of the community. In the herpetological network, where social networks are a basic pattern of the social organisation in the ecology, these discursive boundaries are an articulation of the boundary work done by the networked individual. We can see from the experiences of Adrien and Lucien how the line between the individual and the general public is negotiated discursively. Adrien, a successful pet shop owner in Paris, who deals regularly with the general public and public education, articulates where this external boundary lies for him.

> But you always have to have in mind that those people won't understand that you have a passion and [there's] no need to share it. Because if they don't have it, they will never have it. So there is no need to explain that it is interesting and you have an interest. They don't share it.

Not all people with interests in herpetology experience this boundary so distinctly and, as Lucien says, it comes down to who you are prepared to discuss your interests with and who is interested in hearing about them. For example, Lucien is willing to share his reptile interests with non-Herpers, but not if these interests are not relevant in a conversation.

> When I meet people, friends, I talk about a lot of things, because I know that they are not interested. I don't want to force them to talk about the animal. This is my hobby. People who are interested, no problem, we can talk about it. A lot of people have a passion and I like passionate people. It can be very annoying when you spend an evening with a guy talking about a passion and you don't care. A lot of people know me and unless they come home and they see, I don't talk about it.

On the other hand, some Herpers feel compelled to address the animal phobias that people have as a way to reduce the distance between a person with an interest in reptiles and amphibians and those without. Arild often takes new people out looking for animals, and shows them his collection as a way to address this social distance.

> If they're interested in it, then hey, maybe I can convert them into liking things that they are scared of. I take a lot of new people out and show them that there's nothing to be scared about. People who are terrified of snakes, I take them back to my place and let them play with my snakes. I think society is run by fear. I think it's horrible, it limits people so much.

Sometimes this technique works out well but sometimes it does not. Such stories are retold often and end with the animal biting someone and that person running out screaming. Anika takes a more passive approach to this social boundary bridging and has a range of photographs of snakes on her mobile phone to share how beautiful the animals are.

> Some people say, 'Oh, snakes are awful', and I say, 'Look, here's a cobra. They are nice, they're not dirty, they are beautiful'.

This demonstrates how mobile technologies become imbricated in the discursive boundaries of the network.

The discursive boundaries of the community are also articulated through the qualitative analysis of interview data in which some people identify as being more engaging, socially open and 'public-focused'. These participants are usually hubs within the network, are capable of translating knowledge between groups, and connect more empathetically with the 'general public'. They tend to be the sort of people that draw others into the interest network and connect people. Other participants don't talk to many people about their interests at all, do not engage online and don't generally like other Herpers. They tend to represent the more closed aspects of the network.

9.4 Mediating Culture

The derived definition of community boundaries through its mediating culture is a challenge proposed and conceptualised by Abbott (1995). He argues that:

> … we should start with boundaries and investigate how people create entities by linking those boundaries into units. We should not look for boundaries of things but for things of boundaries.
>
> (Abbott, 1995, p. 857)

Abbott (1995) refers to the 'things of boundaries' as the proto-boundaries of a community, its internal social divisions. He argues that these internal divisions give rise to the form of the group, the 'entities' that people create through 'linking boundaries into units'. Because of this, a community can be identified through internal divisions, tensions and polarisations. This differs from conventional approaches that look for similarities between community members, rather than their differences, to define group boundaries.

Drawing on the case study data, this section presents a discussion of proto-boundaries as they are socially enacted, the cultural differences within the herper community. In discussions with scholars in the herper network, they could articulate how the different involvement styles of the network work together. The discussion of these narratives will provide a sense of how form emerges from the interactions between these proto-boundaries. However, the study of the mediating culture of this community also provides more traditional examples of how the community constructs and engages with external boundaries between itself and 'wider society'. The external boundaries of this community can be most evidently seen through the articulation of 'public perception' from people outside of the community and who the 'general public' was from the point-of-view of people within the community.

9.4.1 Internal Boundaries

As this chapter has argued to this point, community boundaries are permeable and set within the context of networked individualism. To understand why a discussion of internal boundary construction is informative, we will need to understand how social form emerges within open social structures. Particularly when these structures are based upon the interlacing of organisational structures with lateral social networks and mediated sociability. Seemingly, these social networks have no actual edges due to their flat and recursive structures; however group behaviour may have dealt with this openness through its own forms of closure and clustering. With the increasing permeability of external group boundaries, it appears necessary to look at other boundary dynamics to identify groups of people.

A key idea to the identification of a social ecology, which is by default externally permeable through its open social structure, is the pivotal nature of internal group boundaries. Abbott's notion of protoboundaries as internal boundaries which define a group is drawn from the idea of interactional fields used by Chicago School scholars (Abbott, 1997). He describes interactional fields as community boundaries that consist of mutual constraints, such as geographic, social and economic constraints. In particular, he describes the motion of every group within such a community as dependent on that of the others. Because of this interdependency, these fields are a whole network of intertwined processes, rather than a single process (Abbott, 1997, pp. 1154–5). This idea speaks to understandings of community experience as occurring within social systems that are based upon network processes.

Abbott's description of interactional fields is reminiscent of the functionalist idea of an organic whole being the sum of interdependent parts that have specialised roles. In contrast to this, the conceptual frameworks used in the case study research did not rely on the interdependency of discrete or specialised parts within a social system. Each aspect of engagement within the community form is partial, as in the idea of portfolios of sociability, and each process is complex and overlapping. However, internal differences create tensions and ambiguity through which social relationships and processes may reconfigure and resolve. These internal boundaries articulate patterns of social cohesion in which differences and contradictory processes are given space to exist, creating a resilient and tolerant social structure. Through the social ecology concept, these are the processes argued to give rise to the form of the community.

This idea of internal boundaries giving rise to social form is in opposition to group cohesion created by closed external boundaries in which the 'other' is clearly defined. The proto-boundary concept proposed by Abbott sits neatly with the research design to turn a priori parameters of community into research questions. When this idea is placed in the context of networked individualism, we can draw from this that contemporary community boundaries (both internal and external) are enacted within person-to-person and role-to-role relations, in the partial sharing of knowledge and values and in the divisions that exist within the network.

The following discussion of proto-boundaries considers the social experience of internal boundary construction from the ethnographic perspective; however the survey data did provide some insights. Simple proto-boundary dynamics can be found within the survey data in the respondents' listing of the types of animals they were interested in and their types of herpetological involvement. This data provides a sense of who the person is in the network (their herpetological identity) and also who they are likely to socialise with through these interests. Exposure to the network has indicated that people tended to network with others who had common interests and that people who were interested in amphibians generally had little in common with people interested in reptiles. This was due largely to these animals being extremely different biologically and their associated pools of knowledge were correspondingly different. Other clear divisions exist between involvement styles, such as the hobbyist, the amateur and the professional herpetologist. These examples suggest how the identity project and interest profile of members becomes a part of the internal boundary generation of a community.

Subtle divisions within the community were both geographically and culturally tied through the consumption patterns in the pet markets of Europe and the USA. This section will discuss the qualitative data of the case study where participants share their experiences of and views about these divisions.

It will also focus upon how some participants occupy translator roles that connect across these divisions and act as cohesive elements across these internal boundaries. This way of viewing the herpetological network can give a sense of form to the social ecology, without being limited by functionalist discussions of organic wholes and the interrelations of parts. All aspects of this network operate both independently and in synergy. They differentiate and in doing so have a form of connection that is relevant. The stickiness of social cohesion in this type of social form is deeply tied to the social networks. This aspect will be discussed in Chapter 10 on the paradox of stability in change that can be observed in the retrospective narratives of the participants.

A pet shop employee and wholesale breeder, Darren, describes the division between breeders and academics as almost being based on a foreign language and different knowledge needs.

> From the private side of things, there's a really big gap between private keepers and academics. […] They‘re definitely different classes of people and it's not that they can't get along or don't get along, but if you listen to the academics, they like their big words. But if you get someone from the western suburbs of Melbourne, like me, and, although they're not dumb, it's a whole different language of things. You're talking about the same thing but they're using a different language that almost sounds like Japanese. […] But there is a gap between those two sides as well … because somebody like George and myself, we generally don't care about the relationship between this animal and that animal because it doesn't really apply to us, so we're not all that interested.

People such as Darren occupy translator roles within the network that make them well connected hubs. As was the case for most key figures interviewed, they were well connected mediators between the different aspects of herpetological involvement. It appears that the translator role is occupied by people who can speak the different languages and at different levels. When I asked Mark, a zoo employee and lifelong Herper, how he communicated with the different types of people involved in the network, he demonstrated the skill of speaking at different levels through his discussion of presenting talks at herp society meetings.

> I just change the level of intelligence that I'm … and I'm not saying that the kids with beardies are stupid. But there's no point in coming out with huge, great scientific names on exotic snake species that these guys have never seen or heard of in their life. […] I try to aim at the audience I've got. Usually you've got a mixed audience. You get a question from the kid up the front. 'I got my first bearded dragon … ' and you wait four minutes for the kid to ask the question. Usually it's a story about grandma and how he saw a snake at her property five

> years ago. But then you'll also sometimes get a vet that will turn around and pick up something I've said on parasites and want a bit more in-depth. Well, I can't give the vet the answer that I'd give the five-year-old kid. Because the vet's a vet and he'll understand it at a vet level, so I'll give it at the vet level.

Key to Mark's experience as a translator is his ability to pick his audience and modify the level that he is talking at, the technicality of the language he uses and the content he covers. This strategy also indicates that there are differentiated domains in the network that are separated by language, concepts and interests. The existence of translator roles is an indication of the presence of proto-boundaries in the network. Like Mark, Sam has also been involved in the network in many different ways over time. Initially he was a snake collector when he was a kid and ran a private business doing snake shows and public education. He was active online and his snake display business was a mobile job that brought him in contact with a range of key figures over time. Eventually one key figure suggested that he collect snakes in a remote region and this experience put him on track to become an academic. His perspective on how the herpetological network operates as a whole demonstrates both the connection and disconnection between different involvement styles.

> There are those who have an interest in the science as well as the fact that they keep their snakes as pets. […] On the fringe, they have friends that are just a 'one bearded dragon' kind of person. […] They'll deal with [Scientist] or [Scientist] in the newsgroups or by email or at conventions and meetings and stuff. They'll get involved in zoos, they might volunteer for work in the zoos and they probably do read some of the scientific literature. It's almost like a transition zone I suppose. You've got the professional at one end and you've got the real pet keeper at the other. Rather than all being in the one loop, they sort of graduate and there's overlapping as they go along. At either end they can be quite distinct.

Through this excerpt, we start to get an overall sense of the social form of the herpetological network and how the proto-boundaries and divisions give substance and space to the different ways that people can be involved and the diversity of values that people can hold whilst still being involved. These divisions however are geographically determined. In a discussion of the herper network in the UK, Detlef describes the geographical influence upon the ways people are involved and what kind of values they have for the animals. This geographic influence upon herpetological involvements was discussed as particularly strong between Herpers in the US and those in Europe. Detlef provides us with a microcosm of this kind of value boundary that shapes social dynamics within the network by geography.

> As far as I can see, what you don't have in the UK is the very serious semi-academic herpetoculturalist. If you go to Germany, you get large groups … I mean it's a small minority within the overall herpetocultural scene, but nonetheless you get a group of extremely serious herpetoculturalists who go out and do fieldwork, write books, catch things and do studies. You don't really get very much of that in the UK. There's far less of a transition between serious amateurs and professionals. The serious top end of the market is missing. Compared to the continent, we have more people who like their albino-heterozygosis-for-axanthic-heterozygosis-for-garlic-breath-for-fuckknowswhat. That's sort of fairly popular. In a lot of places in Europe there's perhaps less of an emphasis on all the mutants and colour varieties and all the rest. In the UK they're very fond of those, perhaps less on the diversity and more on the sort of odd varieties that people breed.

This articulation of proto-boundaries in the network is less about the amateur versus professional. It is more about aesthetic criteria versus biodiversity criteria for buying reptiles and amphibians in the captive market. Often these criteria appear to be linked historically to the consumption values of the region. In Europe for example, there is a long tradition of collectors and amateur naturalists, who were at the historical root of this network and set up its value system towards natural history and biodiversity. In new markets that came online at a time of genetic experimentation in breeding techniques, such as in the USA, these markets are far more aesthetically focused. The UK is clearly both a contradiction and articulation of this pattern of consumption and its social impacts. The cultural influence continues around these value systems and is also clearly linked to who supplies the pet market and how they do it. These patterns are manifested and perpetuated through the social networks of the suppliers, wholesalers and import–export trades, as was demonstrated by Adrien earlier when he talked about his global network of suppliers and breeders that supply his reptile pet shop business.

It is the intricacy of these proto-boundaries that creates the space for the full variety and diversity of involvement types and partial value-sharing of the network. This spatiality of social structure and geographic distribution links to patterns of cultural consumption, but the backbone of Internet mediation creates the truly flexible and resilient social ecology of the network. What we know from this analysis of boundaries is that there are definite social edges to this form, which can be contrastingly open and engaging or incredibly closed. These boundaries are made permeable by the actions of networked individuals in this competitive, macho, socially marginalised and heavily regulated environment. Daniel, whom we have met before in his mission to source crocodile embryos, talks about trying to enter into the network and encountering this space. His experience demonstrates the fundamental nature of social networks to this interest network.

> The community has a lot of nodes, and each person in that community is like a spider with sort of eight legs linking up to other nodes. But you have to hit the right node because there's a lot of empty space between the nodes, and you cannot ... you just don't make the right links if you don't know the right people. And it can take a lot of time to find the right contact.

Of this form, we can say that organisations and social networks play a large role, as do laws, key figures and the internal divisions or proto-boundaries of the network. These boundaries and technologies provide the pivotal space in which people with interests in herpetology can pursue these interests and meet others who share these interests. We know that the Internet is pivotal to the structure and social composition of the network. The resulting social architecture of the network, based on the Internet, is decentralised, permeable and pervasive. It facilitates an increased exposure to diversity, which is managed and resolved at the site of the individual and through their social networks and the spaces that they choose to engage in. Consequently this social architecture is more malleable, resilient and porous than traditional notions of closed or bounded groups has ever been.

9.4.2 External Boundaries

Other tensions exist in the interview data of the case study through the demonstration of the permeability of external boundaries creating an emphasis upon the delineation of internal boundaries in the course of group self-definition. External group boundaries however are articulated through discussions of public perception and discursive boundaries indicative of where the external boundaries of the network lay. These discussions allow us to explore the notion of 'social form' for the network from both an internal and external perspective.

In the field work for the research, I developed a sense of how public opinion played a part in positioning people with interests in herpetology as socially marginal, if not strange. Words used by participants to describe this public perception include: mad, loonies, crazy people, freaks, insane people, scumbags and unusual people. Daniel collaborates with herpetologists and students with herpetological interests and he describes these people as having an identifiable characteristic of difference.

> They have that same kind of quirky spark in their eye, you know, that they're on a mission that they realise most of the world doesn't get.

He contrasts this with the general public perception of reptiles and amphibians as vile. Helmut, an animal documentary producer in Germany, reinforces this idea by discussing reptile documentaries as receiving larger audience numbers because audiences are attracted to the fear and danger factors that have threaded through the narratives of participants so far. In Norway, social division between Herpers and the general public is extreme due to the illegal status of the hobby. Because of this extreme divide, I was curious as to how Herpers were perceived by other Norwegians who had no interest in reptiles. Were the laws reflective of public opinion, and were people so generally intolerant as to wish to repress a marginal interest group in their society? I had the opportunity to interview a small group of women at a garden party about what they thought. I had imagined that this group would be squeamish and intolerant and reflect the type of public opinion that had led to such repressive laws. Apart from an articulation of their fears, these women were surprisingly tolerant of the whole idea of people keeping reptiles and amphibians, but a little less tolerant of people keeping snakes. It appears that the social negotiation of these interests in Norway is less extreme than the legislation, providing those with herp interests the capacity to operate as I had seen them do. Public reactions in general seem to be very diverse. The idea of people keeping, trading and researching reptiles and amphibians is usually issue-driven. Take for example the public understandings of cane toads in Australia, or reactions to stories in the popular press. Fear and phobia, which is often attributed to an instinctual response to these animals, appears to be a normal response to reptiles and amphibians. This does tend to place people with a passion for these animals in a socially marginal position.

Many participants observed that there was a 'general public' who did not share their interests and values for reptiles and amphibians. Recall the experience of Alvin who did not sell his reptiles locally because he knew that his neighbours were not likely to be very accepting of this. In the section on the media environment, we saw that the popular press produced stories that created hysteria around the practice of keeping these animals as pets and that participants held a deep distrust of journalists because of this. Another reason for this is that the legal status of keeping reptiles and amphibians and working with them has varied over time in different countries, and this appears to have created a cultural imprint about what this says of the people who are interested in these animals. Lionel talks about this cultural artefact in Australia also, where keeping reptiles was illegal until recently.

> We have a cultural problem that arose from the fact that for decades, from 1974 until the 1990s, it was illegal to keep reptiles. People who kept reptiles were rigorously pursued. There's a whole generation of people who grew up equating keeping wildlife as bad for the environment. This is being exacerbated still because it's a newsworthy situation when people are busted with [illegal] reptiles and drugs, usually together.

This misfit between the legal situation, journalistic techniques and public perception of people who like reptiles is large enough to demonstrate the external social boundary of the network. Generally, this boundary is related to fear from both sides. For Herpers it is an experience of being socially marginalised for their interests and a fear of persecution by the press or the laws, or both. For the public, the pre-existing fear of reptiles and amphibians in general and the assumption that people who are interested in them are strange tends to alienate the general public from this interest group.

9.5 Conclusion

There is a tradition within community studies of defining group boundaries as a means through which to define the parameters of a community in order to explore its collective behaviours and identity formation. This chapter has explored research methods for providing a derived understanding of community boundaries. It started by looking at the relationship between place, through its mosaic of legislative boundaries, and open social structures. The next section considered how quantitative patterns of social organisation express internal group processes through the impacts of demographics and discursive boundaries. The final section presented a qualitative understanding of the relationship between the mediating culture of the community and the expression of internal and external group boundaries. Through this discussion, we have seen how the internal boundaries of the group express its structural characteristics and how the external boundaries are porously negotiated. This chapter has also provided an example from the case study community of how mixed-methods research can present a richer view of community boundary construction.

Chapter 10
Community Cohesion

10.1 Introduction

This chapter introduces the practice of how to translate a conceptual understanding of community cohesion into a mixed-methods approach that directs data collection, analysis and interpretation. Initially, section 10.2 will present a discussion of membership and participation in voluntary organisations from the herper community case study. These organisations are expressed through intersections with technology, place and the built environment. Section 10.3 will consider how the data collected within the case study illustrates its social layer, through configurations of social capital within the network. Notions of networked social capital used in this section draw on quantitative ways of indicating levels of social cohesion within a digital community, but not exclusively so. In this discussion, the qualitative data collected helps to unpack the presence and nature of trust. Levels of trust are commonly thought of as the social glue through which social capital is transmitted. Section 10.4 presents qualitative data collected that demonstrates how the mediating culture of a community articulates endogenous patterns of cohesion, through themes of social activism and continuity.

From the analysis of the case study data to this point, we now have a sense that the herpetological network is digitally mediated and yet is still experienced in a face-to-face format, with some differences as to who is likely to socialise where. To put this succinctly, the insight derived from this is that the herper community adopts multimodal forms of social interaction that blur the distinction between the online/offline world. Consequently, within this environment social cohesion is more likely to be identified within the configurations of space, organisation and interaction of the network, as argued by Latham and Sassen (2005) in their conceptualisation of digital formations. This is evident in the survey respondents' patterns of engagement indicating a socially heterogeneous network that has a coherent knowledge framework accompanied by experiential or embodied engagement for many of those involved. The loci where this engagement occurs can be witnessed in the survey respondents' communication hotspots (face-to-face, email and other Internet mediated communication) through which they mostly communicate openly with each other, with some preferring selective interaction. In addition to this, while the respondent population is actively involved in the network over time, they experience a mix of engagement with different groups and loose-tie networks of known people. This pattern of social organisation is likely to be acquired through a mix of engagement with place based societies and events and being active within the digital space of the community. Through the methodological discussion of these elements from the case study data, we can begin to see how the research insights were triangulated to illustrate social cohesion as a dynamic construct. From this point of view, community continuity and stability can be thought of as produced through resilient mechanisms of change rather than characterised by a resting state or static system with its elements in equilibrium or 'organic' balance.

10.2 The Stickiness of Technology, Place and the Built Environment

The space of the herpetological community, in a geographic sense, is found in the articulations of the private and public social practices through which it is constituted. Largely, the public spaces of the community respond to the locations of organisations in the built environment (for example, universities, museums and zoos), the pull and push of commercial enterprise through pet shops, wholesale businesses and wildlife tourism and the boundary definitions of legislative and knowledge jurisdictions identifying native habitats for animals and animal keeping and collecting practices. On the other hand, the private spaces of the community are articulated within social networks that laterally thread together public institutions with homes, backyards and garages and mediate access to the global flow of illicit practices. The intersections of public and private space are most visible within the voluntary organisations that act to group together those with common interests groups and provide geographic context to the exchange of access, information and support for community members.

One measure of social capital relate to levels of participation in voluntary organisations, as demonstrated in the work of Robert Putnam (2000; 1995). Membership and participation in voluntary organisations is a key indicator of social capital levels within a community that are geographically contextual. Through these intersections of social space, as articulated by respondents' engagement with technology, place and the built environment, we can begin to see how social space pools and eddies social interaction and has the potential to influence its underlying patterns of organisation.

10.2.1 Engagement in Voluntary Organisations

In the survey, participants were asked to report the voluntary organisations related to their herpetological interests that they were active members of, the regularity of the meetings and the estimated number of members of the organisation. Gathering this kind of data provides a sense of how active people are in voluntary organisations and the densities of membership within the population. Within the literature on civic participation, this data is seen as indicative of the social capital levels and thus the social wealth of a population (Katz, Rice, & Aspden, 2001). In total, 338 verifiable[1] herpetological societies were listed by respondents. Over half of the societies (58.9 per cent, N = 199) had a website in 2006 that remained active in 2012. In addition to having a web presence, this also indicates a sustained presence of these societies during the intervening period between data collection and analysis. In terms of active membership of voluntary organisations, just over a third (37.7 per cent, N = 601) of respondents participated in and attended society meetings[2], with an average of one active membership (54.8 per cent, N = 380). Twenty three per cent (N = 159) listed two active memberships, 12.1 per cent (N = 84) listed three, 6.9 per cent (N = 48) listed four and 3.3 per cent (N = 23) listed five active memberships. Membership sizes to these organisations were estimated by participants as ranging between 5 to several thousand members. Given that participants estimated membership numbers as a combination of absolute numbers, ranges of numbers (such as 3–5 or 50–100) and a general numeric idea (such as 'a lot' or 'thousands'), the average membership size was not calculated. Participants were also asked to estimate, with responses taking the same format as above, the number of members in the society they had listed that were likely to be members of other herpetological societies. The intention behind this was to calculate the hypernetwork or ecology of affiliation amongst organisations (McPherson, 1982, 1983, 2001; McPherson & Rotolo, 1995). In light of the nature of the data reported, this analysis was not conducted. However participant responses indicated, with numbers varying between a small sample to the entire membership, that at least some members in one organisation were likely to be members of other herpetological societies. This suggests the presence of organisational interconnectivity through membership affiliations.

During the process of validation of society names and existence through online searching, it was clear that these organisations consisted of small and large groups that spanned local and global scales and included societies that were small informal groups with interests in the local area to societies that were solely virtual. These patterns reflect the spatial distribution of participants'

1 Society names were cross-checked for spelling, alternative names and existence on the Internet. 220 societies listed were either not verifiable, did not refer to a specific society or event or were not herpetologically related societies.

2 Respondents considered 'society attendance' to include organised group attendance, exposition/swap meet attendance and attendances at conferences/symposiums.

social ties. Despite the engagement of only a third of the sample in herp societies, these organisations, in addition to some academic and commercial interests, represented the key mediators of herp engagement, connection and information provision online, as was depicted in the network map influential websites connecting the entire body of websites that participants used (1,123 verified websites). This suggests that while membership to these organisations does not represent the entire population of Herpers involved, these organisations influence the virtual exposure to the herp culture of this broader group.

10.2.2 The Geography of Membership and Participation

From the qualitative data collected it was apparent that because herpetological interests are specialised, participants were active in making place-based social connections according to their interests. The following discussion of the qualitative findings on membership and participation expands our understanding of the role that herpetological societies played in connecting people geographically, but also in how these community organisations were situated within other collective practices.

Alvin joined a herp society when he was eight years old with his brother. He contrasts this experience to the herp society where he's living now. In this discussion it is clear that herp societies are a good place to meet other Herpers, however not all herp societies are the same.

> I tried going to the herp society here. I tried going to the meetings. I think it really depends on your herp society. I know the one in Seattle was really large and there was a large diversity of people and there was a large diversity of interests. That was great, because you can find out about everything and you can also pick your own little group that you want to be part of. Here [place] is a lot smaller town and most of the people are older people that have a turtle or a couple of turtles or a couple of lizards. So they're not as diehard.

According to participants, being a member of a herpetological society has its perks. They have newsletters, field trips and guest presentations from key figures in the field. This is one way that people meet key figures and get to know 'who's who' in the network and be somebody in this network themselves (the identity aspect of collecting). There are keeping tips that people share and animals that people sell or swap. Randal's local herp society runs an annual count of the salamander populations in a frozen river in Canada. These are established conservation projects where participants can get recommendations and hands-on experience in the field with animal catching, photography, and have shared experiences over animals that they are passionate about. Membership of a herpetological society also holds other benefits. For Jeremy, the reason he was a member of a herp society when he first started out was because they were the only people who had permission to collect animals in the wild due to the permitting system in his region.

> The herp group had permits … where they could go out and a lot of stuff was brought back. In those days a lot of distributions and that were unknown and so they did that.

However many participants did not participate in herpetological societies or organisations as ways to meet people with a shared interest. For some, this was because they were socially isolated or living in locations that were not convenient for getting involved in societies and meeting other Herpers. For Lucy, her first experience of joining a herpetological society was affected by where she lived.

> I joined an amateur herpetologist group in my last few years of high school. … That didn't last for very long. Because we lived out of town on a property and never really saw any of them, and I just wasn't really involved. If you're not really involved, it's not very beneficial, so you just stop doing it. Immediately after that I left to go to university and that was even further away so I wasn't associated with that town anyway, so that was the end of that.

However, a large proportion of the respondent population did not want to join herpetological societies. These people were more likely to seek key figures and contacts directly based upon their profile and accessibility (both online and through contacts) within the network. Sam was not interested in joining herpetological societies to meet other people; he met people initially by getting in touch with key figures and through his workplace.

> I've really never had anything to do with herp societies. They've never interested me that much … The people I hung around with were [key figure] and [key figure]. Basically professional herpetologists who worked with venomous snakes. … I was keeper in charge of the reptile collection at the [Zoo] when I was 18. That was my first job out of school … That's, I suppose, when you start meeting lots of other characters.

This slow growth of contacts through networks is fairly characteristic of many respondents' experience. For example, an Australian private breeder and pet shop employee, Darren, discusses his slow entrance into the herpetological networks as unfolding through friends of friends.

> It was through that that one of my fellow friends met a guy that had a lot of snakes that was friends with [key figure], [key figure]. So I sort of was just lucky that I got

> into some of those guys through an associate of mine. He started keeping them and he met them from someone he knew and I sort of got into it …

Another way that participants met people who shared their interests was by attending herpetological expos. A Dutch cage builder who didn't use the Internet very much had been an active member of herpetological societies for 20 years and regularly attended expos to raise profile for his glass cage business and to meet other people with herpetological interests. He clearly had a large network of contacts that he had developed from his active attendance at society meetings and expos. Adriaan did not speak English and the interview was mediated by a bilingual Herper. When asked about whether he and his wife/business partner went to herp expos, the translator said that they had been doing it for 15 years.

> About 15 years, mostly in Germany, in the Netherlands and Belgium … . He goes there because they like to meet the people and also to compare the quality of his products to other products … if people can see in real time, they can see how the enclosures are made and they can call a week later.

Expos are also a drawcard not only for the animals and people, but also for exposure to new ideas and ways of doing things. These multiple reasons to go are very attractive to many people with an interest in the animals. A French breeder, Louis, was invited by his friend to attend a large expo in the United States held in Orlando.

> In '95 he says he's going to Orlando, so he says … do you want to come with me? And I just go there and it was unbelievable to see so many breeders and so many captive-bred animals and very nice displays and a different level of doing things.

From the way participants discuss the herpetological expos, they are where a wide variety of people mix together and often where people who know each other mainly online or by reputation get to see each other in person. Expos appear to be about visibility. Ignaas, a Dutch import-exporter who attends expos in the Netherlands, Germany and the United States, discusses what expos mean for his business.

> I think in the first time, you have to be present at expos. That they know you, that they see you on the market. You have to get a name on these expos … The only reason that I go to Daytona. It's not the financial reason, because it costs the flight and hotel and so on. It's expensive, but the Americans see that the guy who is selling the stuff is also in America and they can contact me personally.

This experience is similar for those who attend conferences. What is being exchanged is knowledge, however conference attendance appears to be mostly for networking.

Regardless of how people endeavour to meet other people with shared interests, the herpetological networks appear to be very interconnected socially and coherent through their geographic contexts. These findings extend the discussion of social capital and cohesion from focusing solely on participation in voluntary organisations to focusing on the myriad of ways that individuals navigate community structures and access points to make their own networks of choice. These findings suggest that the opportunity to do so is also a measure of the wealth of social capital (particularly in its affordances for serendipity and social mobility) within an open social structure. For the researcher, the insight here is to widen the scope of how community participation and engagement is conceptualised and to collect data on this based upon the social practices of the community.

10.3 Social Layer: Connective and Collective Behaviour

This section considers the collective behaviours of the community as they are measured through proxy indicators; such as the disposition amongst members for sociality, the levels of exchange amongst strong and weak tie networks and the levels of trust within the community. These discussions illustrate social capital levels from network perspectives, beginning with the predisposition of the actor, to their orientation towards trusting others (thought of as social glue), to their actual exchange practices. Social capital is a notion to describe the density of and capacity for social exchange in a population and across relational networks of social ties. As discussed in the literature review, it can be investigated through levels of general and group-specific trust, voluntary participation in organisations and resource exchange through social networks. This relates to the likelihood for exchange amongst group members (Delhey, Newton, & Welzel, 2011). As demonstrated in the work of Putnam (2000), social capital is also understood through levels of engagement in voluntary organisations. This relates to the respondent population as a whole. Here, the notion of reciprocity relates to the access to social resources through the networks of strong and weak social ties (Snijders, 1999). This reflects a relational sense of social capital (bridging and bonding capital) that merges with the ICT environment reviewed in the work of Keith Hampton in his 'Netville' study (Hampton & Wellman, 2003). These approaches are used to indicate the amount of cohesion and the social wealth of the group when looked at through levels of group trust, organisational engagement and social ties. What the data collected from the case study suggests for research methodology is that using only one approach to determining levels of social capital within a community is unlikely to illustrate actual levels of cohesive collective behaviours across an open social structure.

10.3.1 A Disposition towards Social Connection

Literature on social effects of Internet use, social networks and online sociability suggests the relevance of identifying a population's general orientation towards sociability, which includes personality traits, when discussing collective behaviour. Initially, data collected in the case study population was intended to illustrate how embedded the collective identity of the Herper was. Consequently, survey participants were asked to indicate whether they agreed or disagreed with the statements that their herpetological interests played an important part in how they saw themselves, that their reputation amongst other Herpers was important to them and that they had a responsibility to be involved with other Herpers. These factors, identity, reputation and responsibility, speak to the collective and cohesive elements within a community. The results are presented in Table 10.1 below and discussed in the following text.

Table 10.1 Frequencies of identity, reputation and responsibility to others

	Agree	Neither Agree nor Disagree	Disagree	Don't Know
	% (N)	% (N)	% (N)	% (N)
Identity	71.2 (1123)	19.3 (304)	8.1 (129)	1.4 (22)
Reputation	61.1 (974)	22.4 (354)	14.6 (230)	1.3 (21)
Responsibility	50.1 (790)	32.9 (518)	15 (237)	2 (31)

In terms of identity, on average participants agreed that their herpetological interests were important to how they saw themselves ($M = 1.4$, $SD = .69$, Median $= 1$, $IQR = 1$). Similarly, on average participants agreed that their reputation amongst other Herpers was important to them ($M = 1.56$, $SD = .79$, Median $= 1$, $IQR = 1$) and that they had a responsibility to be involved with other Herpers ($M = 1.56$, $SD = .8$, Median $= 1$, $IQR = 1$). This suggests that there is a concern for other Herpers in the respondent sample, which speaks to the capacity for group cohesion and group regulation.

Another factor that affects the connectivity of the individual within a group is their social personality. Without an orientation and pattern of behaviour that facilitates social connection, there is no network and there is no continuity in that network. The research literature on social networks suggests that a person's social personality affects their centrality, or connectedness, in their peer network (Kalish & Robins, 2006). This is supported by a proliferation of studies in this area in recent years (Amichai-Hamburger & Vinitzky, 2010; Brunet & Schmidt, 2007; Hardie & Ming Yi, 2007; Matessi et al., 2010; Mitchell et a., 2011; Orr et al., 2009; Pollet, Roberts, & Dunbar, 2011; Roberts et al., 2008; Swickert et al., 2002; Topi, Valacich, & Rao, 2002; Ward & Tracey, 2004).

Aspects of personality traits measured in the survey are four from the 'Big Five', extroversion, conscientiousness and agreeableness and openness to experience with participants indicating if they agreed, neither agreed nor disagreed, or disagreed. Upon investigation, these variables did not present a normal distribution and the median averages are discussed. Participants agreed that they were skilled in handling social situations ($M = 1.71$, $SD = .96$, Median $= 1$, $IQR = 1$), felt comfortable around other Herpers ($M = 1.32$, $SD = .63$, Median $= 1$, $IQR = 1$) and did not find it difficult to approach other Herpers ($M = 1.37$, $SD = .67$, Median $= 1$, $IQR = 1$). In terms of taking an agreeable approach to other Herpers, participants were likely to take time out for other Herpers ($M = 1.4$, $SD = .75$, Median $= 1$, $IQR = 1$) and were likely to feel concern for them ($M = 1.49$, $SD = .79$, Median $= 1$, $IQR = 1$). In terms of being conscientious, participants were likely to be prepared when it came to their herp interests ($M = 1.58$, $SD = .76$, Median $= 1$, $IQR = 1$) and to get down to work ($M = 1.41$, $SD = .79$, Median $= 1$, $IQR = 1$). They were also likely to have a vivid imagination when it came to their interests ($M = 1.71$, $SD = .86$, Median $= 1$, $IQR = 1$), but less likely to use it as a way to think up new approaches (45.4 per cent, $N = 718$ thought about their herp interests in this way).

As can been seen from the results presented, overall, the respondent population exhibits sociable personality traits, indicating a substantial proportion of the respondents have the capacity to be well connected. In particular, it is clear that respondents have a high level of comfort and extroversion around other Herpers (over 70 per cent of the respondent population felt this way). There is also a high level of altruism, which forms the basis of social capital and resource exchange, as indicated by a willingness to take time out for other Herpers (72.5 per cent, $N = 1139$) and to feel concern for other Herpers (62.4 per cent, $N = 979$). In terms of indications of conscientiousness, social skills, openness and intellect, respondents demonstrated lower general results for these questions (around 50 per cent).

From this understanding of the social layer from the point of view of the networked individual, there is a strong sense of self-focus evident. However this self-focus is balanced by a reasonable level of social predisposition for engagement with others. In this way we can argue that participation in the network is egocentric, but not self-obsessed (narcissistic). There appears to be a reasonable level of care for the opinions of others and a responsibility to engage or support others with herpetological interests. Conscientious following through on this engagement may be less of a characteristic of the population however, perhaps speaking to the macho, competitive and secretive nature of the mediating culture of this community.

10.2.3 Social Capital: Trust

General trust is argued to be the basis of reciprocity, social connectedness, peaceful collective action, inclusiveness and tolerance (Delhey et al., 2011). Here trust refers to in-group trust in other Herpers. The notion of particularised trust refers to close-knit groups that know each other (Delhey et al., 2011). Interpersonal trust was also investigated in order to understand if stereotypes played a role in the way Herpers trusted each other. Respondents were asked to indicate whether they agreed or disagreed with statements that most Herpers can be trusted, that you can't be too careful in dealing with Herpers and that there are types of Herpers whom they do not trust. The results for variables on trust are presented in Table 10.2 below.

Table 10.2 Frequencies of trust within the herper network

	Agree	Neither Agree nor Disagree	Disagree	Don't Know
	% (N)	**% (N)**	**% (N)**	**% (N)**
Trust in other Herpers	27.5 (435)	48.9 (772)	15.9 (251)	7.7 (121)
Can't be too careful	35.5 (557)	44.4 (698)	14.0 (220)	6.1 (96)
Types of Herpers who can't be trusted	81.1 (1279)	11.6 (183)	3.3 (52)	4.1 (64)

When asked whether most Herpers could be trusted, the median response was neither agree nor disagree ($M = 2.04$, $SD = .86$, Median = 2, $IQR = 1$), with almost double the number of people who agreed with this statement (27.5 per cent, $N = 435$) than disagreed (15.9 per cent, $N = 251$). When asked whether you can't be too careful around Herpers, respondents neither agreed nor disagreed with this ($M = 1.91$, $SD = .855$, Median = 2, $IQR = 1$), however more than double the number of people agreed with this statement (35.5 per cent, $N = 557$) than disagreed (14 per cent, $N = 220$). The median response for participants on both of these statements is neither agree nor disagree, but results suggest slightly stronger levels of caution (Miller & Mitamura, 2003) towards other Herpers than trust in them. When asked whether there are types of Herpers that you can't trust, on average respondents agreed with this ($M = 1.3$, $SD = .722$, Median = 1, $IQR = 0$), with most participants feeling this way (81.1 per cent, $N = 1279$). This indicates that there were high levels of distrust in particular types of Herpers within the network. This result far outweighs the dynamic between low levels of general trust and slightly stronger levels of caution towards other Herpers that are felt by participants and suggests that there are social aspects to this network that people are very distrusting of. This will be explored further in the qualitative analysis of trust presented below, in particular through discussions of the black market and illegal activities in the network. These results suggest the likelihood of lower levels of social capital, and consequently social cohesion, in participants' experience of the Herper network.

In the following discussion, it is the qualitative data that unpacks the complex nature of the relationship between trust and social exchange. It will explore the low-trust environment of the network and seek to understand the nature of social capital in this context. In this network, pockets of trust are clearly present, but overall there are dominant themes of secrecy, suspicion, competition and distrust. So how do Herpers support each other when they don't trust each other?

From the participant observation, generally participants demonstrated a high level of distrust in other Herpers, in the online environment and in the general public. Amongst Herpers, this is not surprising, but when this is related back to the literature, this is surprising. In the literature, trust is proposed to be a key cohesive agent in the creation of social capital, as a facilitator of social exchange and as a marker of a group. Trust in the qualitative data is discussed in terms of who participants trusted in their networks, distrust in the online environment and suspicion of the general public. In general, Herpers were observed to be cautious around strangers and displayed a deep distrust of journalists, police, customs officers and wildlife officers. There were several easily identifiable reasons for this in the narratives of the participants. Firstly, low levels of trust in the public were related to the negative public perception of Herpers' interest in reptiles and amphibians in the first place. The journalistic technique of controversy, fear and scandal to sell stories has also tended to vilify the public profile of herpetological interests and alienate Herpers. Alvin discusses the way he keeps his personal collection secret in his local environment, so much so that he does not sell locally and only sells animals online.

> Almost exclusively the only way I do it is Internet. One of the reasons I don't do it locally is because I'm kind of protective about it. I don't like people know I have rattlesnakes or snakes in general. Just because it can have that negative impression. I've known people who take their rattlesnakes out and let their neighbours see. I don't feel comfortable with that because most of the time the people I have talked to who live in my immediate area have an issue with snakes or reptiles.

This type of secrecy due to public perception is related to the external boundary of the network, as was discussed in the section on boundaries (Section 5.1.3). The regulations for keeping, catching, transporting and collecting reptiles and amphibians impacted on how participants pursue their herpetological interests and who they were likely to trust. If it is illegal to keep a reptile or amphibian in a country, such as in Norway, the pool of people whom a person doing this will trust is consequently smaller. This creates an environment of secrecy and anonymity. Birgit talks about buying a reptile in Norway in this climate.

> I actually don't know who it was. I was just buying it, like very no names, no nothing.
>
> Alexia: So how did you find that? Did someone through the park just say, 'If you want a snake, do this'?
>
> It was like, 'This one might know where you can get a snake', and then I was given a number. Then it was like, 'Meet me there and there and switch the money and you can get this ball python'.

However, it is not just the legal status and public perception of the animals that makes Herpers cautious. They are also suspicious of each other. This is articulated in participants' narratives through discussions about secrecy to protect personal collections and investments. Geerd keeps a private collection of venomous snakes in the Netherlands and does not share information about his collection with his acquaintances or online out of fear of having his collection stolen.

> I don't know anyone in the Netherlands personally that has been broken in or stolen. I'd rather not be the first one. I'm very careful. Also most people don't even know exactly what I'm keeping. I never post a list of all the snakes I have. I never post my address. I'm a bit careful. I'm allowed to keep them in the village where I live, there is no restriction, but not everyone needs to know.

His partner Anika reiterates this sentiment and shows how this is related to trust. When asked why she keeps other Herpers at a distance.

> Because he have a collection. We are always scared. I don't trust them.

This distrust of other Herpers that can be seen in these excerpts also includes distrust of known and anonymous others in the online environment. Geerd does not reveal his home address or collection details online because he does not want someone that he may not know to have access to this information.

This indicates the perception of participatory surveillance online amongst Herpers (Albrechtslund, 2008). This distrust of online surveillance is also found in the research literature on social networking sites. The literature proposes the metaphor of an electronic panopticon to describe surveillance of social spaces and users' data online (Acquisti & Gross, 2006; Campbell & Carlson, 2002; Fuchs, 2010; Tyma, 2007). For many Herpers, the threat of online surveillance is not just about increasing likelihood that other Herpers will steal their collections; it is also about authorities being present in these forums and keeping an eye on what people are saying and doing. This type of awareness and discussion of online surveillance as a threat was pervasive in the population and not without foundation.

Trust is deeply tied to the reputation of how a Herper deals with other Herpers. This is where the word-of-mouth culture is very important in the network. Trustworthiness is a crucial commodity for Louis. One reason for this in his opinion is because it takes a lot of knowledge to actually know what animals you are dealing with and people will take advantage of that ignorance. For example, identifying a snake, lizard or frog as male or female is not apparent unless you actually know what you are looking for because their sex organs are internal. When asked why he felt it was useful to have a good reputation, he replies:

> Because in reptiles, that's the only way to do a proper job. Really often some breeder are really secretive. If you have a good name, or if guys say, 'Oh, this guy is cool', you can go in his place and visit his snake room. If you don't have that you would never enter in the snake room for example. I think in reptile business there is a lot of motherfuckers, a lot of guys who fuck all the people. Sell bad animals, sell bullshit. They know they have two males and they sell this as a pair … Because you need a lot of knowledge for keeping and breeding reptiles. People play on that and use your ignorance to fuck you.

This secrecy is also related to the competitive environment and financial incentives of the network, but participants appear to feel that there are quite a few shady characters in the network. The prevalence of this attitude was seen in the survey responses indicating participants' extremely low trust levels in types of Herpers. Aside from the less controversial idea of keeping an amphibian in a tank at home when the law prohibits it, illegal activities include poaching animals from the wild and smuggling animals internationally. Poaching is rife in Australia and the US for example, where there is a rich biodiversity of reptiles and amphibians in the wild. Herpers distrust this aspect of the network for several reasons. One of them is that wild-caught animals tend to die if they have not been well medicated. The first-time buyer who cannot tell the difference between a wild-caught reptile and a captive-bred one will often experience the animal dying shortly after buying it. Secondly, it is illegal to collect animals from the wild without a permit. This system is in place to protect the biodiversity of animal life in the wild. Over-collection of animals in an area can lead to these animals being wiped out. This tends to be a very important reason for why Herpers will not share location data on animals in the wild with most people. They tend to feel a personal responsibility to conserve and protect these populations in their natural habitats. Because of the secrecy that accompanies this kind of knowledge, it is a valuable commodity across the network and only to be shared with a privileged few. In passing, Fabio mentioned that one of the advantages of his new girlfriend was that she knew the collection locations of animals that her previous partner collects from.

Because of these dynamics, people in positions of privilege such as academics, museum curators, veterinarians and government officials spoke of feeling like they had too much to lose to trust people. Cedrick is a museum curator and is extremely careful about who he associates with.

> If I was in a position where I worked in construction and I did this on the weekend, and I wanted to get a snake somewhere or I wanted to go to a national park and get a lizard and bring it home, the retributions are not as severe. Yes, you'll get in trouble. We know that for first people offenders they slap your finger and you're OK. In the position that I'm in here at the museum, I'm supposed to know better. If I go and in any way link with something illegal-related reptiles, whether it was where the reptile was captured or if I give information that leads to the capture of animals, it comes back to my livelihood. I'd probably be terminated here at the museum. And so for me the stakes are too big. I don't want to take the risk.

The result of this is that he is much less likely to trust other Herpers in general and is apprehensive of meeting friends of friends or people on the Internet that are not on a professional level with the same privileges to lose. To this end, he will orchestrate elaborate schedules of being present and absent when meeting up with friends who are visiting national parks and photographing animals in the wild in order to avoid this situation altogether. Some of the results of this lack of trust and dissociation with illegal activities discussed by participants were exclusion from shared knowledge and experience and the lack of medical care for people and animals on the other side of the law. This proto-boundary of trust and legality in prohibiting this kind of social sharing and support was a driving force for personal social networks to be a priority for many participants and the use of the Internet to gather information and meet people. These internal divisions within the network between open and underground activities were discussed in Section 5.1.3 on boundaries.

Poaching is what it is called within national boundaries, but when people illegally poach animals and ship them to another country, then it is smuggling.

Smuggling is perceived to have high financial incentive, with collectors in countries such as Germany and the Netherlands paying high prices for rare animals. Neto was interested in frogs in Costa Rica and set up a frog farm as a way to legally tap into the export market in poison dart frogs that he had been alerted to through the prosecution of a smuggler he read about in the popular press.

> There is a black market for poison dart frogs. These had caused the extinction of local populations in Costa Rica. People from different places in Europe go to Costa Rica and they capture lots of frogs and they take them back to Europe in the worst conditions in small plastic bottles. Most of them don't even make the trip. […]
>
> I heard in the news that they had arrested some smugglers. So I started researching a little bit and found out in magazines that people in Europe and other places pay astronomical amounts of money for things that most of the people in Costa Rica wouldn't even give a dime. I mean $500 ten to fifteen years ago for people in Costa Rica was an incredible amount of money. So that looked like an interesting possibility.

In this way, we can see that financial incentives keep the smuggling trade alive within the herpetological network. This environment impacts local Herpers personally when they see the populations wiped out in the wild, and also in terms of animal cruelty, since many animals die in the process of being illegally shipped as they cannot be transported in optimal conditions. Whether Herpers care about smuggling being illegal or not, they do tend to care about the effect that this has on the animals themselves. This has a substantial impact upon whom a Herper will trust in the network.

10.3.3 Social Capital: Information, Support, Access and Reciprocity

The literature on social networks argues that nets of strong and weak social ties, or bridging and bonding ties facilitates social capital in a network. Given the trust results, it is clear that these networks are likely to be important conduits of social capital. During the time of the online survey (2006) the notion of social capital in an integrated online/offline environment had no direct measures.[3] In terms of the presence of social capital within a community, it was considered necessary to adapt this notion to the kind of experiences that people with herpetological interests had. Tom Snijders and collaborators propose a resource

3 This has since been addressed by Williams (2006), who takes a comparative approach to measuring capital online and capital offline. Whilst these are useful measures, there is still room for discussion on how social capital can best be measured in this environment.

generator to measure levels of social capital in a network (Snijders, 1999; Van Der Gaag & Snijders, 2005). This tool is based upon network theory and proposes categories of information, access and support as key ways of identifying social resources. This reflects the social consequences of Internet use in the types of commodities that can be digitally mediated (see Katz & Rice, 2002; Wellman et al., 2001 for a discussion of this). Respondents were asked to indicate whether they received information, access or support from their networks of strong and weak ties and to indicate whether they reciprocated these things within the network. This will provide a discussion of the exchange of these social commodities and the role of strong and weak social ties in this process.

Social Ties (Strong and Weak)

Strong and weak ties are a basic principle of social network analysis that is used to indicate reciprocal webs of relations and the directional depth of social connection. They are argued to reflect the people who are close to a person that will provide them with deeper levels of support (such as close friends or family) versus the people who are not close to a person (such as an acquaintance) that is more likely to pass on new ideas and job contacts (see Granovetter, 1973 for the original discussion of this hypothesis). Participants were asked to list the number of people that they were close to in the network (strong ties) and the number of people that they were not close to (weak) who provided them with help, access and information. They were also asked to indicate how many Herpers they knew within a sense of geographic distance based upon time travelled and regional location. This indicates the geographic spread of a respondent's social networks. Overall it will depict how loosely or densely located people are amongst others with overlapping interests.

Given the tenuous position of social capital and cohesion in the network suggested by these results of low levels of organisational engagement and trust in other Herpers, a further measure of social capital, resource exchange, is explored. This assists understanding how notions of social capital fare when looked at through the exchange of social resources across strong and weak social ties rather than through group structures and perceptions of trust. This approach is synergistic with the concept of the networked individual being embedded in strong- and weak-tie networks. The notion of social capital through resource exchange within social networks is derived from the work of Van Der Gaag and Snijders. They focus on the social resource exchange in receiving and giving of help, access and information through strong and weak social ties. Van Der Gaag and Snijders (2005) found that 76 per cent ($N = 763$) of their respondent cohort had access to social resources, with most items being accessed by at least 50 per cent of the respondent population. Whilst this sample and results are not comparable with the current application, it is an indication of the level of social resource exchange that occurred in the development of this measure. Respondents were asked to indicate whether they knew people who were close (such as good friends and close family) and not close to them (such as other friends, acquaintances and contacts) that could assist them with help, access and information for their herpetological interests[4], and whether they did this for other Herpers. This was a simplified application of Van Der Gaag and Snijders' measure generated from insights gained during the ethnography. The common elements socially exchanged fell into three groups: information/knowledge exchange, practical help with herp collections, and access to herpetological resources which can be expensive, such as feeder mice, or have restricted access through gatekeeping, such as museum collections and herp jobs. This follows the advice of Van Der Gaag & Snijders (2005, p. 4) who argue that the measure cannot be comparable because the social resources exchanged need to be customised to the population under study to be relevant.

Participants were asked yes/no questions to indicate their strong-tie, weak-tie and reciprocal resource exchange relationships. At the end of this set of questions, they were asked to indicate the number of people whom they knew, that were close and not close, that could provide these things for them. Table 15 presents these results below. Seventy-five per cent (75.2 per cent, $N = 1121$) had strong-tie networks that could give them practical help with their herpetological interests and 63 per cent (63.2 per cent $N = 814$) had weak-tie networks that could give them this. Seventy-five per cent (74.6 per cent, $N = 1048$) gave practical help to people with herpetological interests. Clearly practical help was received more through strong-tie networks than by weak social ties; however these results suggest that practical help was actively exchanged across the network in the experience of the respondents. In terms of information, advice and knowledge sharing, respondents were slightly more active in sharing this kind of information than they were in sharing practical help. Seventy-seven per cent of respondents (77.2 per cent, $N = 1142$) had strong ties who could give them good advice or good information about their herpetological interests and 84 per cent (84.1 per cent, $N = 1108$) had weak ties who could do this for them. Eighty-nine per cent (88.6 per cent, $N = 1238$) did this for other people who had herpetological interests. Clearly, the respondent population were slightly more active in giving good information and advice than they were in receiving it from their strong and weak social ties. Notably, however, more weak social ties than strong ones were able to give what respondents believed was quality advice.

In terms of access to herpetological resources, these were the lowest levels of social exchange. This may be expected as fewer people take the role of providing access to scarce resources. Sixty-four per cent (63.6 per cent, $N = 939$)

4 In this question, close social ties were not limited to family relations as was the case for the Van Der Gaag study. This category was extended in light of the possibility that family relations cannot always be argued to be the strongest or closest ties in a person's life.

of respondents had strong ties who gave them better access to herpetological resources and 64 per cent (63.6 per cent, $N = 837$) had weak ties who gave them this. Sixty-four per cent (63.6 per cent, $N = 887$) of respondents gave better access to herpetological resources to others with these interests. Overall, the median number of strong ties that participants gained help, access and information from was 5 ($M = 8.54$, Trimmed Mean = 6.43, $SD = 14.2$, Median = 5, $IQR = 8$) and the median number of weak ties was 10 ($M = 40.32$, Trimmed Mean = 15.83, $SD = 295.89$, Median = 10, $IQR = 15$). These results suggest relatively strong numbers of social ties for a single portfolio of participation when compared with an average of 12 strong ties in total for Internet-active participants in a Swiss study ($N = 15{,}852$) examining the impact of the Internet on social ties (Franzen, 2000). Over 80 per cent (83 per cent, $N = 1{,}141$) of respondents had 10 or less strong ties and over 80 per cent (85.2 per cent, $N = 1, 054$) had 30 or less weak ties. The range of numbers of strong ties reported by participants was 0 to 200 (Skewness = 27.88, $SD = .07$, Kurtosis = 920.36, $SD = .13$) and the range for weak ties, 0 to 9,000 (Skewness = 24.80, $SD = .07$, Kurtosis = 722.54, $SD = .14$). A single individual felt that they had a very large network of weak ties, 9,000, with 3,000, 2,500 and 1,000 being extreme values for weak tie connections. These outliers have been retained for univariate reporting and discussion of online connections, however the extreme values were winsorised in the bivariate analysis instead of excluded, given the larger numbers of participant responses that this covered and the effect that exclusion versus substituting the highest Upper bound number had on the results of the tests (see Table 10.4 below for a comparison of these averages). It seems likely that this number of weak ties is accessible through many-to-many communication platforms such as forums and e-lists; however participants also reported being members of societies with membership numbers in this range.

A Return to the Discussion of Trust and Measures of Social Capital

In terms of the univariate findings presented in Section 10.2.3, the sample demonstrated distrust of and caution towards each other in general and had the highest level of distrust towards types of Herpers. Regardless of these lower trust levels, around a third of the respondents were engaged with herpetologically related voluntary organisations, and around 70 per cent of respondents exchanged social support and information actively amongst their strong and weak social ties. These findings reflect the previous bivariate analysis findings on the open discursive boundaries (being the facilitator of exchange) that also linked to the co-existence of styles of community experience as society- or group-based and based upon social networks. When not looked at through the lens of the discursive approach of participants, there was a strong bias in the population (70 per cent) to experiencing networks of strong and weak ties as the social form of their community experience. The higher importance of a social network base for community experience supports the appropriateness of measuring social resource exchange as a way to demonstrate the social capital of the population, rather than relying on respondent trust levels and active participation in voluntary organisations to indicate this.

The question that remains however is what relationship these low trust levels have with the different measures of social capital. We can see that overall it does not impede social connectivity and exchange across the respondent population, but we do not know what effect it does have upon established ways of understanding the cohesion and social wealth of a population.

Trust in other Herpers and Organisational Engagement

In terms of looking at the traditional notion of social capital and engagement in voluntary organisations, a chi-square test of association demonstrated that there was an association between organisational engagement and the likelihood of being more trusting of Herpers in general, c^2 (3, N = 1571) = 7.99, $p < .05$. Because this type of engagement is low in this sample, however, it clearly has less effect in supporting the general trust levels across the network.

Given that low trust levels are not an artefact of organisational participation in the network, the question remains as to why they are characteristic to the respondent perspective. In particular we do not know whether it is a phenomenon that is related to the prominent role of social networks and digital mediation in the network. From the research literature, we do know that the digital environment is a low trust environment and that there is emotional distance in weak-tie relationships. This leads to the supposition that their prominent role in this network may decrease the levels of trust in general.

Trust in Other Herpers and Resource Exchange through Strong and Weak Ties

Running a chi-square test of association on the trust variables and levels of support, access and information exchange across strong and weak social ties revealed no significant associations except between the trust statement that you can't be too careful and information exchange across weak ties, c^2 (2, N = 1180) = 8.43, p = .015. The association here indicated that those who either disagreed or were ambivalent (neither agreed nor disagreed) with this statement had slightly more weak ties that could provide them with good information or advice. As we have seen in the data the accumulation of weak ties is a stronger characteristic of participants who used Internet-mediated channels of communication. Therefore these results suggest that participants who were less cautious of other Herpers, and probably more likely to talk to people they didn't know online, had more opportunities to receive good advice or information. From this result, it seems likely that the low-trust online environment does not impede knowledge exchange between participants.

Table 10.3 Frequencies of resource exchange by strong ties, weak ties and reciprocity

	Strong ties			Total	Weak ties*			Total	Reciprocated*			Total
	Yes % (N)	No % (N)	DK % (N)	(N)	Yes % (N)	No % (N)	DK % (N)	(N)	Yes % (N)	No % (N)	DK % (N)	(N)
Practical help	75.2 (1121)	20.7 (309)	4.1 (61)	(1491)	63.2 (814)	28.4 (366)	8.4 (108)	(1288)	74.6 (1048)	20.5 (288)	4.9 (69)	(1405)
Information & Advice	77.2 (1142)	20.1 (297)	2.8 (41)	(1477)	84.1 (1108)	11.2 (148)	4.6 (61)	(1317)	88.6 (1238)	7.7 (107)	3.8 (53)	(1395)
Access	63.6 (837)	30.3 (447)	6.2 (91)	(1480)	63.6 (837)	28.2 (372)	8.2 (108)	(1317)	63.6 (887)	29.7 (414)	6.7 (94)	(1398)

Note: These are three separate variables and are presented together for comparative purposes.

Table 10.4 Mean average social ties from whom participants receive help, access and information

		Outliers Winsorised using Tukey's Hinges
	M (SD) Median (IQR) (N)	**M (SD) Median (IQR) (N)**
Strong Ties	8.54 (14.21) 5 (8) (1392)	7.02 (6.45) 5 (8) (1392)
Weak Ties	40.32 (295.89) 10 (15) (1237)	14.76 (13.84) 10 (15) (1237)

10.3.4 A Review of Social Capital to this Point

Social capital, when viewed through resources exchanged by strong and weak social ties, was a strong component of the respondent population's experience of the herpetological network. However, within the survey data, these figures contrast substantially with the low trust levels and the moderate levels of participation in voluntary organisations found in the respondent population. The results of low trust in types of Herpers and a cautious approach to others in the sample have even greater impact when considering research findings that particularised trust (trust in known others) is generally higher than trust in unknown others (general trust) (Sturgis & Smith, 2010; Uslaner & Conley, 2003). Strong and weak social tie resource exchange persisted however in the sample, with no association to trust levels. This suggests that a lack of trust did not impede the exchange of social resources. This result is supported in the discussion of levels of altruism and concern for other Herpers that respondents did report in Section 10.3.1. Organisational engagement did boost trust levels, which has been suggested in the research of Realo, Allik, and Greenfield (2008). It seems likely that these lower trust levels are influenced by the culture of the network and perhaps also by the lower levels of trust found in the online environment.

From the qualitative data it becomes apparent that trust in the herpetological network is affected by multiple factors. These factors include laws, public perception, the need for knowledge, the fear of losing positions of privilege and the very real effects that poaching and smuggling has on the animal populations in the wild and in transit. The analysis demonstrates some of the more universal values that Herpers hold towards conservation of biodiversity, humane treatment of animals, access to people's collections and wild spaces and their reputation amongst other Herpers. Despite these practices of secrecy and distrust, there are strong cohesive elements in the network that are about mentorship and online support. The community experience in this context is one of resource-rich social networks that connect closed and liminal spaces and are organised around key figures and group engagement.

From the perspective of the case study data, these points of observation produced insight into patterns of social organisation that mix organisational memberships with loose social networks of strong and weak ties. They speak to the importance of the co-presence of social networks with organisational engagement in this network and the equivocal position of trust within these patterns of social organisation. The coexistence of these forms of social organisation within the network was foreshadowed in the networked individualism and virtual community literature that emphasised the continued relevance of densely knit groups and group memberships online. This is opposed to much of the social capital literature that prioritises group behaviours as a form of social organisation and demonstrates the importance of the exploration of social capital within social networks to the research methodology.

10.4 Mediating Culture and Social Cohesion

When exploring the notion of cohesion, the literature on community focuses our attention upon the presence of supportive relationships, organisational presence and the capacity for collective action as other ways of identifying social cohesion. In the herpetological network, what is apparent from the experience of participants is that mentorship by key figures plays a large social role. Levels of activism are fairly low in the network, but they are present and the online networks play a very important role in mobilising people when legislature changes threaten Herpers' capacity to keep private collections in local areas. Herpers also appeared to gain a lot of support from their online interactions. What the case study data suggests for research methodology is that issues of cohesion need to include consideration of mentorship, activism and online support in the network.

10.4.1 Activism and Collective Action

In the case study analysis, collective action to protect group interests is relatively low. This reveals an interesting contradiction in the network. Most of the participants interviewed had a high value for supporting causes related to the social movement of conservation. This type of activism however is not about protecting the voice and space of people with interests in herpetology. Lionel was one of the few herpetologists interviewed who had driven an activist movement to change laws. His motivation for activism was related to the illegal status of keeping reptiles in Australia and he wanted to keep a collection and cultivate the hobby.

> So I started the reptile keepers association. I called in a few local guys. We started it and we basically hired a lawyer and we lobbied. It took us nearly ten years and we got the laws changed.

This direct activism however is unusual. As Louis says, usually the response of Herpers to changing laws is to go underground and use their alternative networks and climate of secrecy to continue on instead of taking action. In France, the laws changed around the captive keeping of dangerous animals.

> A few years ago they make a new law to make it harder to have dangerous animals. Now Adrien can't sell in his pet shop the retic' or Burmese, all the

> animal in Appendix 1. […] People still want these kind of things so they go in Germany, they go everywhere to get this. Now they go back to the illegality and to the hiding politic.

It seems that the liminal spaces of the network are so accommodating and accustomed to a persecuted or prosecuted status for keeping reptiles that they may well swallow up the impetus for Herpers to demonstrate a collective voice to protect their interests.

Where this collective voice is most visible is in the online environment. Participants who were active in the forums appeared to have a broad range of people that they could access. At no point was this more obvious than when a participant had turned to their online networks for help during tough times. Sven told us about how he had relied on the information and advice he found online to learn how to keep his Gecko collection. He had clearly developed a consistent identity online doing this over time and people knew his avatar. In the country where he lived, it was illegal to keep these animals and the day did come when the police turned up at his door and, alongside a stash of drugs, he had his gecko collection confiscated. As the wheels of the law began to turn, Sven turned to the people he knew over the Internet for help in rescuing his collection from euthanasia by the authorities.

> The reptile community at the Internet was already starting to grow, and at the point where I was taken, I knew about a lot of forums and stuff. I'd travelled with people here and there and I knew that [captive] reptiles were not illegal in other places. I was pissed off because they were taking my geckos. So I cried out for help from people all across the world and people spread my word. People came to help.
>
> Alexia: How did the people come to help?
>
> I came into contact with [key figure] who was the chairman of the British Federation of Herpetologists and he wrote letters to my government and put me in contact with [key figure], who is spokesman of the European forum for reptiles and amphibians, which is an umbrella organisation for the European herpetological organisations. He also wrote a letter to my government. I asked friends that I know to also write a letter to my government. This way we were able to put some pressure on the authority and they decided to place my animals in a reptile park instead of euthanising them.

From this example and previous excerpts discussing the support in the online environment, we can see that it is a particularly effective way of mobilising a collective voice that has real-world impact. During participant observation it was clear that Herpers would often give what support they could to others when they could see that it was something that they could assist with. This was more in the direct person-to-person kind of way. Participants articulated the point of view that animal activist groups such as PETA targeted the hobby of reptile and amphibian keeping when trying to change laws as this was an easy target. Regardless of the regular experience of having their capacity to be legally engaged curtailed, it appears that Herpers are more likely to continue on with their interests using alternative illegal channels that are well developed to cater to this.

The online environment however appears to be a space in which individuals can ask and receive help and support from the network and for people to collectively discuss shared reactions to polarising key figures in the community. The outcome of this collective discussion is when key figures who actively promoted themselves online, usually in a controversial way, became symbols that go viral as online memes. Such was the case of one Australian Herper who was highly visible online as a prolific forum poster using multiple identities and an online publisher. As Darren observed, it didn't matter what avatar this key figure used in the online forums, people could always tell that it was him. During participant observation, Internet-active Herpers from different countries independently raised a discussion about this person. They would discuss how he was illegally removing venom glands from snakes, using these devenomised snakes for public education displays and promoting this online. This was an incredibly controversial topic for venomous snake keepers, people interested in the human and ethical treatment of animals and those concerned with the general public profile of the herpetological interest network. Participants regularly offered their opinion (usually in disgust) of his actions and activities and discussed the petitions that they signed to have this person prosecuted by relevant wildlife authorities. My experience of this was notable in the repetition of the same passionate engagement of a participant with this topic, whether I was in Australia or in Germany. At the closure of data collection, this situation remained unresolved and the death threats, petitions and discussions of prosecution had not had any tangible effects on restraining the activities of the participant. However recent events have seen a YouTube video posted by this participant, and passed through the herpetological networks to relevant authorities, result in legal action being taken against him. In this case, the collective action behind this is a very slow process of years.

This form of collective action is unique to the Internet-mediated environment. The online buzz or white noise of many people discussing and offering their opinions and providing contacts, information and misinformation is what Manuel Castells (2003) referred to as the ephemerality of online communities and Andrew Keen (2007) disparagingly refers to as the cult of the amateur. What neither of these authors acknowledge is what the internet-active Herpers know; this online noise is a giant conversation of people figuring out what the issues are, who wants to talk about it, and who the contacts are. In the literature on social movements, this is referred to as a submerged network through which identity work and the cross-fertilisation of movement networks occurs during latency periods of inactivity in the life cycle of the social movement (Chesters & Welsh, 2005, p. 190). During participant observation it became apparent that those engaging in this conversation were laying down channels of action that took time to take effect. These channels were passive and whimsical, until there was something truly solid that could then be handed through them. At this point, the noise became a distinct signal and social voice that took advantage of the ubiquitous and decentralised architecture of the Internet. The high level of online interaction and visibility that related to this particular instance went on for a long time without tangible actions taking place. What this build-up achieved, however, was the articulation of the appropriate networks, due diligence, appropriate evidence and the right thing at the right time (serendipity) to create a tangible action.

10.4.2 Continuity

Another aspect of cohesion is continuity. This relates to the presence of ongoing support, ongoing institutional and organisational activities and ongoing participation in the network. This is in opposition to the more episodic nature of social movements that gather people together in a very similar way to the function of the herpetological network, but for short periods of time and through an issue focus. In the case study community, continuity is demonstrated through the historical accounts of participants of their entry into and engagement with their herpetological interests over time. Key to understanding the notion of stability in change as a feature of social cohesion is to understand where change occurs and how the community accommodates these changes over time. This is where a discussion of continuity also includes a discussion of discontinuities.

As we will see in the following sections, continuity is strengthened in the community by its capacity to facilitate the dispersion of participants through a variety of roles. It is also demonstrated in the online memory of the community whereby participants actively retrieve, repackage and host information provided by others who have intentionally disengaged. This can happen when a participant closes their herpetological business, for example, or herpetological societies fold.

In this section we will focus on two narratives of discontinuity that are not unusual in the experiences of participants. The first narrative is the story of Neto closing his frog farm business due to the illegal activities of his business partner.

> There were some problems. Apart from the floods, which were a distraction. I could have continued, but the biggest problem that I had was that I was working

> in a land that wasn't mine. So I had this agreement with somebody else. The relationship with this person was not going very well because he was tempted to do things in an unethical manner. To go out there and catch some frogs and use the farm as a cover. I wasn't willing to do that. That on top of other natural disasters made me decide not to continue. On top of that I had to decide what was the next thing for me. At that time I was offered a stable job at the university.

In this story, we see one or two of the reasons why a successful herp business will fold. This participant moved into academia and is no longer immersed in his herp interests as he had been. Regardless, he is able to draw on his past experiences in this business. While his work is not focused on amphibians, this interview was conducted at an academic conference that drew other Herpers. His past and present interests kept him engaging with Herpers and interested in this topics. This introduces the idea of dispersion through the network as a characteristic of the stability and continuity of the network over time. What this concept does show us is that change is inevitable but a network doesn't not 'lose' a person overall. In the education literature on student retention, this process of the retention of a person in a system, beyond that of a single institution or organisation, is referred to as systemic retention (Caison, 2004). This concept is used to demonstrate a focus on the retention of a student in the higher education system rather than at a particular university. In a parallel application, it allows us to think of the Herper who disconnects from an online forum, disengages from a herpetological society or closes a herpetological business as possibly being retained within the herper network through this process of systemic retention. This is an indication that the herper network contains within it enough diversity of people, roles and spaces to be resilient and tolerant of change and discontinuity. In the case of Neto, and that of many participants observed to go through disconnections and change, the consistent feature of identification with their herp interests and engagement with other projects that relate to these over time, speaks to this notion of systemic retention in the herper network.

However there are times when a person drops out of the network entirely. The second narrative is about another event in which a couple who were prolific in breeding, selling and sharing online information suddenly dropped off the herp radar, got rid of their collection and remove all of the information that they shared online. In the ensuing discussion, Ladolfo and Arild discuss how people in the network were able to retrieve and repost these resources despite the couple no longer participating nor condoning what they had previously shared freely.

> Ladolfo: They had a page with like hooks, tongs, safe ways of keeping the animals, shipping, bagging instructions. You know, husbandry. How to do it without dying, the beginners guide. […]

> Arild: Obviously something happened, they went from posting a lot. Depending on the topic you'd easily see five or ten a day on kingsnake and other places. They were very active. They were very well known, they'd been there a long time, they were well respected and they were nice people. If you sent them a private email, you'd get a response. One day their site is down. People were like, 'What the fuck?' They weren't posting, and a week later I think Harry posted once on kingsnake 'We're just concentrating on our music and we're not keeping venomous snakes anymore. See you later'. [...]
>
> I think last year he posted one time on kingsnake.com. He said something that he'd changed his views on keeping venomous by private people. I only saw one post. I checked back in a few days and I didn't see anything.
>
> Ladolfo: I even tried one of their old email addresses and they'd changed their email and everything.
>
> Arid: I still have printouts from their page because it had excellent information.
>
> Ladolfo: So Ralph managed to get from them venom 101. [...] Him and Jordan started a virtual herp society on just hot herps. And so they had the venom 101 stuff available for download for a while. I don't know if it still is, but they managed to get permission to repackage it and download it.

From this transcript excerpt, we can see that continuity can be an online process that is not about one person, but a collective online memory. This aligns with the process of collective recall found the internet literature exploring the hive mind (Pak-Hang, 2013) through terminology such as the 'wisdom of crowds' (Surowiecki, 2004) and 'smart mobs' (Rheingold, 2003). In these excerpts, like in many of the experiences of closures discussed by the participants, discontinuities do not equal conclusion and overall loss in the herpetological network; with aspects of the past digitally archived, socially retained and repackaged in the cut-copy-paste culture of the internet. Key to the findings from the case study data is the capacity for participants to disperse into different roles and involvements in the network over time and the active maintenance by participants of an online memory.

10.6 Conclusion

Through the discussion of social cohesion from the case study community, the Herpers teach us that the form of digital community is mobile, emergent and resilient in the face of change. Its memory is collective and digitally curated, with user-produced activities reminiscent of a hive mind that retains and translates knowledge. When social relationships implode, key figures lose reputation, societies fold and businesses close, laws change and online buzz has no apparent tangible outcomes, it is only a matter of time before these elements re-emerge in the mobile space of the network. As was described in the discussion of collective action through the 'white noise' of people 'figuring things out' online in Section 10.4.1, form can also be identified through its transient emergence and social expression rather than through a focus on the presence of overt hierarchical structures of order, organisational links and fixed spaces. This idea of how a social ecology can be thought of allows us to see social cohesion not in terms of an 'equilibrium' as proposed by Durkheim, or the 'status quo' as proposed by Pierre Bourdieu, but in terms of its dynamic nature of change, discontinuities, adaptability and persistence. The key to this resilience is the opportunism of the networked individual and their ever-morphing nets of strong and weak social ties. Continuity arises from the resilience of networked individualism, which is derived from the flexibility of strong and weak social ties and decentralised networks of information technology.

The case study findings suggest that this dynamic of change may be seen as producing stability, but not through the traditional concepts of system equilibrium and status quo. Networked individualism is the cog of differentiation and change in this network, with the individual actively adapting to a changing social environment through their changing allegiances and patterns of engagement in groups, online forums and across their social networks. This resilient mixing of networks of strong and weak social ties with organisational hubs and digital architectures is demonstrated by the interview population to facilitate lateral relations across the organisational hierarchies, new social ties and mobility through the physical places of the network. This mix of resilient and adaptive social engagement is what creates continuity and cohesion in this social system. While trust is usually proposed to be the grease to this process, the experience of participants suggested that this relationship is tenuous and potentially a poor indicator for levels of social capital. In terms of learning and directions that this chapter suggests for research methodology and practice, it would be to apply more than one measure or data collection approach to present complimentary insights into your key conceptual ideas.

Bibliography

Abbott, A. (1995). Things of Boundaries. [Article]. *Social Research*, 62(4), 857–82.

Abbott, A. (1997). Of time and space: The contemporary relevance of the Chicago School. *Social Forces*, 75, 1149.

Abbott, A. (1999). Department and Discipline: Chicago Sociology at One Hundred. Chicago: University of Chicago Press.

Ackland, R. (2013). Web Social Science : Concepts, Data and Tools for Social Scientists in the Digital Age. Los Angeles: SAGE Publications.

Ackland, R., O'Neil, M., and Pérez, C. E. (2014). *Tweeting the Frame: Frames and Fields in the Age of the Networked Individual.* Paper presented at the Social Media and Social Movements. http://linisevents.hse.ru/perez

Acquisti, A., and Gross, R. (2006). Imagined Communities: Awareness, Information Sharing, and Privacy on the Facebook Privacy Enhancing Technologies. In G. Danezis and P. Golle (Eds.), (Vol. 4258, pp. 36–58). Berlin/Heidelberg: Springer.

Albrechtslund, A. (2008). Online social networking as participatory surveillance. *First Monday*, 13(3). Retrieved from http://firstmonday.org/ article/view/2142/1949

Aldridge, J., and Décary-Hétu, D. (2014). Not an 'Ebay for Drugs': The Cryptomarket 'Silk Road' as a Paradigm Shifting Criminal Innovation. Retrieved from http://ssrn.com/abstract=2436643

Amichai-Hamburger, Y., and Vinitzky, G. (2010). Social network use and personality. *Computers in Human Behavior*, 26(6), 1289–95. doi: 10.1016/j.chb.2010.03.018

Anderies, J. M., Janssen, M. A., and Ostrom, E. (2004). A Framework to Analyze the Robustness of Social-ecological Systems from an Institutional Perspective. *Ecology and Society*, 9(1), 18.

Anderson, A. R., and Jack, S. L. (2002). The articulation of social capital in entrepreneurial networks: A glue or a lubricant? *Entrepreneurship and Regional Development*, 14(3), 193–210.

Anderson, B. (1991). *Imagined communities* (2nd ed.). London: Verso.

Angeletou, S. (2008). Semantic enrichment of folksonomy tagspaces. *The Semantic Web-ISWC 2008*, 889–94.

Bagozzi, R. P., and Dholakia, U. M. (2002). Intentional social action in virtual communities. *Journal of Interactive Marketing*, 16(2), 2–21.

Bakardjieva, M., and Smith, R. (2001). The Internet in Everyday Life. *New Media & Society*, 3(1), 67–83. doi: 10.1177/1461444801003001005

Barabasi, A. (2002). *Linked: The New Science of Networks.* Perseus Publishing.

Barabasi, A. L., and Albert, R. (1999). Emergence of scaling in random networks. *Science*, 286(5439), 509–12.

Bardzell, S., and Odom, W. (2008). The Experience of Embodied Space in Virtual Worlds An Ethnography of a Second Life Community. *Space and Culture*, 11(3), 239–59.

Bargh, J. A., and McKenna, K. Y. A. (2004). The Internet and Social Life. *Annual Review of Psychology*, 55(1), 573–90. doi: 10.1146/annurev.psych.55.090902.141922

Barratt, M. (2011). *Discussing illicit drugs in public internet forums: Is pseudonymity necessary or sufficient?* Paper presented at the Communities and Technologies 2011, Brisbane, QUT.

Barratt, M. J. (2011). *Beyond Internet as Tool: A Mixed-Methods Study of Online Drug Discussion.* (Doctor of Philosophy), Curtain University, Melbourne, Australia.

Barratt, M. J. (2012). Silk Road: eBay for drugs [letter to the editor]. [Letters to the Editor]. *Addiction*, 107, 683. doi: 10.1111/j.1360–0443.2011.03709.x

Barratt, M. J., and Lenton, S. (2010). Beyond recruitment? Participatory online research with people who use drugs. *International Journal of Internet Research Ethics*, 3(1), 69–86.

Barratt, M. J., Lenton, S., and Allen, M. (2013). Internet content regulation, public drug websites and the growth in hidden Internet services. *Drugs: Education, Prevention, and Policy*, 20(3), 195–201. doi: 10.3109/09687637.2012.745828

Barratt, M. J., Potter, G. R., Wouters, M., Wilkins, C., Werse, B., Perälä, . . . Blok, T. (2015). Lessons from conducting trans-national Internet-mediated participatory research with hidden populations of cannabis cultivators. *International Journal of Drug Policy*, 26(3), 238–49. doi: http://dx.doi.org/10.1016/j.drugpo.2014.12.004

Batty, M., Hudson-Smith, A., Milton, R., and Crooks, A. (2010). Map mashups, Web 2.0 and the GIS revolution. [Article]. *Annals of GIS*, 16(1), 1–13. doi: 10.1080/19475681003700831

Bauman, Z. (2001). Community : seeking safety in an insecure world. Cambridge: Polity Press.

Baym, N. K. (2010). *Personal connections in the digital age.* Cambridge: Polity Press.

Beck, U. (1992). *Risk Society: towards a new modernity* (M. Ritter, Trans.). London: Sage.

Beck, U., and Beck-Gernsheim, E. (1996). Individualization and precarious freedoms: Perspectives and controversies of a subject-oriented sociology. In P. Heelas, S. Lash and P. Morris (Eds.), *Detraditionalization: Critical reflections on authority and identity* (pp. 23–48). Cambridge, MA: Blackwell.

Beck, U., & Beck-Gernsheim, E. (2002). *Individualization: institutionalized individualism and its social and political consequences.* London: Thousand Oaks, Calif.: SAGE, 2002.

Beer, D. (2008a). The Iconic Interface and the Veneer of Simplicity: MP3 players and the reconfiguration of music collecting and reproduction practices in the digital age. *Information, Communication & Society*, 11(1), 71–88. doi: 10.1080/13691180701858919

Beer, D. (2008b). Social network(ing) sites ... revisiting the story so far: A response to danah boyd and Nicole Ellison. *Journal of Computer-Mediated Communication*, 13(2), 516–29. doi: 10.1111/j.1083–6101.2008.00408.x

Beer, D., and Burrows, R. (2007). Sociology and, of and in Web 2.0: Some Initial. *Sociological Research Online*, 12(5).

Beer, D., and Burrows, R. (2010). Consumption, Prosumption and Participatory Web Cultures. *Journal of Consumer Culture*, 10(1), 3–12. doi: 10.1177/1469540509354009

Bell, C., and Newby, H. (1972). Community studies: An introduction to the sociology of the local community. New York: Praeger Publishers.

Beneito-Montagut, R. (2011). Ethnography goes online: towards a user-centred methodology to research interpersonal communication on the internet. *Qualitative Research*, 11(6), 716–35. doi: 10.1177/1468794111413368

Benitez, J. L. (2006). Transnational dimensions of the digital divide among Salvadoran immigrants in the Washington DC metropolitan area. [Article]. *Global Networks*, 6(2), 181–99. doi: 10.1111/j.1471–0374.2006.00140.x

Benjamin, W. (1999). *Illuminations*. London: Pimlico.

Bente, G., Rüggenberg, S., Krämer, N. C., and Eschenburg, F. (2008). Avatar-Mediated Networking: Increasing Social Presence and Interpersonal Trust in Net-Based Collaborations. *Human Communication Research*, 34(2), 287–318. doi: 10.1111/j.1468–2958.2008.00322.x

Bergquist, M., and Ljungberg, J. (2001). The power of gifts: organizing social relationships in open source communities. *Information Systems Journal*, 11(4), 305–20. doi: 10.1046/j.1365–2575.2001.00111.x

Bird, S. E. (2011). Are We All Producers Now? *Cultural Studies*, 25(4–5), 502–16. doi: 10.1080/09502386.2011.600532

Blaikie, N. W. H. (1991). A critique of the use of triangulation in social research. *Quality & Quantity*, 25(2), 115–36. doi: 10.1007/bf00145701

Blumer, H. (1969). *Symbolic interactionism : perspective and method*. Englewood Cliffs, N.J.: Prentice-Hall.

Boase, J. (2008). Personal Networks and the Personal Communication System. [Article]. *Information, Communication & Society*, 11(4), 490–508. doi: 10.1080/13691180801999001

Boase, J., Horrigan, J., Wellman, B., and Raine, L. (2006). The Strength of Internet Ties *PEW INternet and American Life Project*. Pew Internet & American Life Project.

Boase, J., and Wellman, B. (2006). Personal Relationships: On and Off the Internet. In D. Perlman and A. Vangelisti (Eds.), *The Cambridge Handbook of Personal Relations*. Cambridge: Cambridge University Press.

Bodin, Ö., and Tengö, M. (2012). Disentangling intangible social–ecological systems. *Global Environmental Change*, 22(2), 430–39. doi: http://dx.doi.org/10.1016/j.gloenvcha.2012.01.005

Bolter, J. D., and Grusin, R. (2000). *Remediation: Understanding new media*. Camrbidge, Mass.: The MIT Press.

Borgida, E., Sullivan, J. L., Oxendine, A., Jackson, M. S., Riedel, E., and Gangl, A. (2002). Civic Culture Meets the Digital Divide: The Role of Community Electronic Networks. [Article]. *Journal of Social Issues*, 58(1), 125.

Bourdieu, P., and Wacquant, L. J. D. (1992). *An invitation to reflexive sociology*. Cambridge: Polity Press.

Bowker, G. C., & Star, S. L. (1999). *Sorting Things Out Classification and Its Consequences*. Cambridge, Mass.: The MIT Press.

boyd, d. (2006). Friends, friendsters, and myspace top 8: Writing community into being on social network sites. *First Monday*, 11(12), np.

boyd, d. (2007a). Social network sites: Public, private, or what. *Knowledge Tree*, 13, 1–7.

boyd, d. (2007b). Why Youth (Heart) Social Network Sites: The Role of Networked Publics in Teenage Social Life. In D. Buckingham (Ed.), *Youth, Identity and Digital Media* (pp. 119–42). Cambridge, MA: The MIT Press.

boyd, d. (2008). Facebook's Privacy Trainwreck. *Convergence: The International Journal of Research into New Media Technologies*, 14(1), 13–20. doi: 10.1177/1354856507084416

boyd, d., and Crawford, K. (2012). Critical Questions for Big Data; Provocations for a cultural, technological, and scholarly phenomenon. *Information, Communication & Society*, 15(5), 662–79. doi: 10.1080/1369118x.2012.678878

boyd, d. m., and Ellison, N. B. (2008). Social Network Sites: Definition, History, and Scholarship. *Journal of Computer-Mediated Communication*, 13(1), 210–30. doi: 10.1111/j.1083-6101.2007.00393.x

Brannen, J. (2007). Working qualitatively and quantitatively. In C. Seale, G. Gobo, J. F. Gubrium and D. Silverman (Eds.), *Qualitative research practice* (pp. 282–96). London: Sage.

Breslin, J. G., Passant, A., and Decker, S. (2009). *Social Semantic Web*. Berlin: Springer.

Broadfoot, K. J., Munshi, D., and Nelson-Marsh, N. (2010). COMMUNEcation: A rhizomatic tale of participatory technology, postcoloniality and professional community. *New Media and Society*, 12(5), 797–812. doi: 10.1177/1461444809348880

Brunet, P. M., and Schmidt, L. A. (2007). Is shyness context specific? Relation between shyness and online self-disclosure with and without a live webcam in young adults. *Journal of Research in Personality*, 41(4), 938–45. doi: 10.1016/j.jrp.2006.09.001

Bruns, A. (2007). Methodologies for mapping the political blogosphere: An exploration using the IssueCrawler research tool. *First Monday*, 12(5).

Bruns, A., Burgess, J., Highfield, T., Kirchhoff, L., and Nicolai, T. (2011). Mapping the Australian Networked Public Sphere. *Social Science Computer Review*, 29(3), 277–87. doi: 10.1177/0894439310382507

Buchanan, E. A., and Ess, C. (2009). Internet Research Ethics: The Field and Its Critical Issues *The Handbook of Information and Computer Ethics* (pp. 273–92). John Wiley & Sons, Inc.

Buckels, E. E., Trapnell, P. D., and Paulhus, D. L. (2014). Trolls just want to have fun. *Personality and Individual Differences*(0). doi: http://dx.doi.org/10.1016/j.paid.2014.01.016

Bulmer, M. (1984). The Chicago school of sociology: institutionalization, diversity, and the rise of sociological research. Chicago: University of Chicago Press.

Bunnell, T., Yea, S., Peake, L., Skelton, T., and Smith, M. (2012). Geographies of friendships. [Article]. *Progress in Human Geography*, 36(4), 490–507. doi: 10.1177/0309132511426606

Burrows, R., and Gane, N. (2006). Geodemographics, Software and Class. *Sociology*, 40(5), 793–812. doi: 10.1177/0038038506067507

Burrows, R., Nettleton, S., Pleace, N., Loader, B., and Muncer, S. (2000). Virtual Community Care: Social Policy and the Emergence of Computer Mediated Support. *Information, Communication & Society*, 3(1), 95–121. doi: 10.1080/136911800359446

Burt, R. S. (1992). *Structural Holes*. Cambridge, Mass.: Harvard University Press.

Burt, R. S. (1997a). The Contingent Value of Social Capital. *Administrative Science Quarterly*, 42(2), 339–65.

Burt, R. S. (1997b). A note on social capital and network content. *Social Networks*, 19(4), 355–73. doi: 10.1016/s0378–8733(97)00003–8

Burt, R. S. (2000). The network structure of social capital. *Research in Organizational Behavior*, 22, 345–423. doi: 10.1016/s0191–3085(00)22009–1

Burt, R. S. (2004). Structural holes and good ideas. *American Journal of Sociology*, 110(2), 349–99.

Butler, B. S., and Wang, X. (2012). The cross-purposes of cross-posting: Boundary reshaping behavior in online discussion communities. *Information Systems Research*, 23(3 Part 2), 993–1010. doi: 10.1287/isre.1110.0378

Caison, A. L. (2004). Determinants of Systemic Retention: Implications for Improving Retention Practice in Higher Education. *Journal of College Student Retention*, 6(4), 425–41.

Campbell, J. E., and Carlson, M. (2002). Panopticon.com: Online Surveillance and the Commodification of Privacy. *Journal of Broadcasting & Electronic Media*, 46(4), 586–606. doi: 10.1207/s15506878jobem4604_6

Carl, F. (2006). Resilience: The emergence of a perspective for social-ecological systems analyses. *Global Environmental Change, 16*(3), 253–67. doi: 10.1016/j.gloenvcha.2006.04.002

Carter, D. (2005). Living in virtual communities: an ethnography of human relationships in cyberspace. *Information, Communication & Society*, 8(2), 148–67. doi: 10.1080/13691180500146235

Castells, M. (1996). The Rise of the Network Society, The Information Age: Economy, Society and Culture (Vol. 1). Cambridge, Mass./Oxford: Blackwell.

Castells, M. (2001). *The internet galaxy* (Vol. 67). Oxford: Oxford University Press.

Castells, M. (2002). The Internet and the Network Society. In B. Wellman and C. Hathornthwaite (Eds.), *The Internet in Everyday Life.* Madden, MA: Blackwell.

Castells, M. (2010). *The rise of the network society.* Cambridge: Wiley-Blackwell.

Cham, K., and Johnson, J. (2007). Complexity Theory; a Science of Cultural Systems? *M/C – A Journal of Media and Culture*, 10(3), pp. 21–34.

Chamberlain, D. (2005a). Ordinary Cultural Consumption: Identity and Personal networks of everyday star trek fans. (Honours), Griffith University, Brisbane.

Chamberlain, D. (2005b, 6–8 December 2005). *Personal networks and the social world of ordinary Star Trek fans: Method and first results.* Paper presented at the TASA Conference, University of Tasmania.

Chamberlain, D. (2006, 4–7 December 2006). *Social Network building: combining qualitative interview with egonet analysis.* Paper presented at the TASA Conference, University of Western Australia and Murdoch University.

Chan, J., To, H.-P., and Chan, E. (2006). Reconsidering Social Cohesion: Developing a Definition and Analytical Framework for Empirical Research. *Social Indicators Research*, 75(2), 273–302. doi: 10.1007/s11205–005–2118–1

Chan, M. (2011). Shyness, sociability, and the role of media synchronicity in the use of computer-mediated communication for interpersonal communication. *Asian Journal of Social Psychology*, 14(1), 84–90. doi: 10.1111/j.1467–839X.2010.01335.x

Codoban, I. (2005). Internet usage and gender digital divide in a Romanian students' sample. *PsychNology Journal*, 3(2), 265–91.

Cohen, P. (1999). Shifting the main purposes of drug control: from suppression to regulation of use: Reduction of risks as the new focus for drug policy. *International Journal of Drug Policy*, 10(3), 223–34. doi: http://dx.doi.org/10.1016/S0955–3959(99)00014–6

Cole, H., & Griffiths, M. D. (2007). Social interactions in massively multiplayer online role-playing gamers. *CyberPsychology & Behavior: The Impact Of The Internet, Multimedia And Virtual Reality On Behavior And Society*, 10(4), 575–83.

Coleman, E. G., and Golub, A. (2008). Hacker practice: Moral genres and the cultural articulation of liberalism. *Anthropological Theory*, 8(3), 255–77. doi: 10.1177/1463499608093814

Coleman, G. (2012). Coding freedom: the ethics and aesthetics of hacking. Princeton, NJ: Princeton University Press.

Comunello, F. (Ed.). (2012). Networked sociability and individualism : technology for personal and professional relationships. Hershey, PA: Information Science Reference.

Crang, M., and Graham, S. (2007). Sentient Cities: Ambient intelligence and the politics of urban space. *Information, Communication & Society*, 10(6), 789–817. doi: 10.1080/13691180701750991

Crawford K. (2014). The Anxieties of Big Data *The New Inquiry* 30 May, http://thenewinquiry.com/essays/the-anxieties-of-big-data/

Crichton, S., and Kinash, S. (2003). Virtual ethnography: Interactive interviewing online as method. *Canadian Journal of Learning and Technology/La revue canadienne de l'apprentissage et de la technologie*, 29(2).

Cyr, D., Hassanein, K., Head, M., and Ivanov, A. (2007). The role of social presence in establishing loyalty in e-Service environments. *Interacting with Computers*, 19(1), 43–56.

Dayton-Johnson, J. (2003). Knitted warmth: the simple analytics of social cohesion. *Journal of Socio-Economics*, 32(6), 623–45. doi: 10.1016/j.socec.2003.10.002

Delhey, J., Newton, K., and Welzel, C. (2011). How General Is Trust in "Most People" Solving the Radius of Trust Problem. *American Sociological Review*, 76(5), 786–807. doi: 10.1177/0003122411420817

Denzin, N. K. (2010). Moments, Mixed Methods, and Paradigm Dialogs. *Qualitative Inquiry*, 16(6), 419–27. doi: 10.1177/1077800410364608

Denzin, N. K. (2012). Triangulation 2.0. *Journal of Mixed Methods Research*, 6(2), 80–88. doi: 10.1177/1558689812437186

Denzin, N. K., and Lincoln, V. S. (2005). Introduction: The discipline and practice of qualitative research. In N. K. Denzin and V. S. Lincoln (Eds.), *Handbook of qualitative research* (3rd ed., pp. 1–32). London: Sage.

DiMaggio, P., Hargittai, E., Neuman, W. R., and Robinson, J. P. (2001). Social Implications of the Internet. *Annual Review of Sociology*, 27, 307–36.

Dodge M. (2004) Flying through code/space: the real virtuality of air travel. *Environment and Planning A* 36(2) 195–211.

Dodge, M. & Kitchin, R. (2009). Software, objects, and home space, Environment and Planning A, 41(6),1344-65.

Domínguez, D., Beaulieu, A., Estalella, A., Gómez, E., Schnettler, B., and Read, R. (2007). *Virtual ethnography*. Paper presented at the Forum Qualitative Sozialforschung/Forum: Qualitative Social Research.

Donath, J., and boyd, d. (2004). Public Displays of Connection. *BT Technology Journal*, 22(4), 71–82. doi: 10.1023/B:BTTJ.0000047585.06264.cc

Dougiamas, M., and Taylor, P. C. (2003). *Moodle: Using learning communities to create an open source course management system*. Paper presented at the EdMedia 2003: World Conference on Education Multi-media, Hypermedia & Telecomunications, Denver, CO USA. http://www.aace.org/conf/edmedia

Duff, C. (2014). Assemblages of health: Deleuze's empiricism and the ethology of life. Dordrecht: Springer, 2014.

Durkheim, E. (1966). *The rules of sociological method.* New York: Free Press.

Dutta-Bergman, M. J. (2004). Interpersonal communication after 9/11 via telephone and internet: A theory of channel complementarity. *New Media & Society*, 6(5), 659–73. doi: 10.1177/1461444804047086

Dwyer, S. C., and Buckle, J. L. (2009). The Space Between: On Being an Insider-Outsider in Qualitative Research. [Article]. *International Journal of Qualitative Methods*, 8(1), 54–63.

Ege, G., and Koullapis, N. (2009). Social Nature of Time and Space in Online Games: Designing Fantastic Social Worlds. In D. Riha and A. Maj (Eds.), *The Real and the Virtual: Critical Issues in Cybercultures* (pp. 109–18). Oxford: Inter-Disciplinary Press.

Ellison, N. B., Steinfield, C., and Lampe, C. (2007). The Benefits of Facebook "Friends:" Social Capital and College Students' Use of Online Social Network Sites. *Journal of Computer-Mediated Communication*, 12(4), 1143–68. doi: 10.1111/j.1083–6101.2007.00367.x

Eun-Ok, I., Wonshik, C., Hyun-Ju, L., Yi, L., Guevara, E., and Kyung Suk, K. (2007). Patients' Attitudes Toward Internet Cancer Support Groups. [Article]. *Oncology Nursing Forum*, 34(3), 705–12. doi: 10.1188/07.onf.705–12

Eysenbach, G., Powell, J., Englesakis, M., Rizo, C., and Stern, A. (2004). Health related virtual communities and electronic support groups: Systematic review of the effects of online peer to peer interactions. *British Medical Journal*, 328(7449), 1166–70.

Fabrique, N., Romano, S., Vecchi, G., and Hasselt, V. (2007). *Understanding Stockholm Syndrome.* Washington DC: Law Enforcement Communication Unit, Training Division.

Featherstone, M., Lash, S., and Robertson, R. (Eds.). (1995). *Global modernities.* London/Thousand Oaks, CA: Sage Publications.

Feld, S. L. (1981). The Focused Organization of Social Ties. *American Journal of Sociology*, 86(5), 1015–35.

Feld, S. L. (1982). Social Structural Determinants of Similarity among Associates. *American Sociological Review*, 47(6), 797–801.

Feld, S. L. (1984). The Structured Use of Personal Associates. *Social Forces*, 62(3), 640–52.

Feld, S. L., and Carter, W. C. (1998). Foci of activity as changing contexts for friendship. In R. G. Adams and G. A. Allan (Eds.), *Placing friendship in context* (pp. 136–52). Cambridge/New York: Cambridge University Press.

Ferlander, S., and Timms, D. (2007). Social capital and community building through the Internet: A Swedish case study in a disadvantaged suburban area. [Article]. *Sociological Research Online*, 12(5).

Fielding, N. G. (2012). Triangulation and Mixed Methods Designs. *Journal of Mixed Methods Research*, 6(2), 124–36. doi: 10.1177/1558689812437101

Fisher, D. R., and Wright, L. M. (2001). On utopias and dystopias: Toward an understanding of the discourse surrounding the internet. *Journal of Computer-Mediated Communication*, 6(2).

Flick, U. (2007). *Designing qualitative research.* London: Sage.

Fligstein, N., and McAdam, D. (2011). Toward a General Theory of Strategic Action Fields. [Article]. *Sociological Theory*, 29(1), 1–26. doi: 10.1111/j.1467–9558.2010.01385.x

Fligstein, N., and McAdam, D. (2012). *A theory of fields*: New York: Oxford University Press.

Forrest, R., and Kearns, A. (2001). Social Cohesion, Social Capital and the Neighbourhood. *Urban Studies*, 38(12), 2125–43. doi: 10.1080/00420980120087081

Foth, M., and Hearn, G. (2007). Networked Individualism of Urban Residents: Discovering the communicative ecology in inner-city apartment buildings. *Information, Communication & Society*, 10(5), 749–72.

Fox, N., and Roberts, C. (1999). GPs in cyberspace: the sociology of a 'virtual community'. *The Sociological Review*, 47(4), 643–71. doi: 10.1111/1467–954x.00190

Fox, S., Raine, L., Horrigan, J., Lenhart, A., Spooner, T., Burke, M. (2000). The Online Healthcare Revolution: How the Web Helps Americans Take Better Care of Themselves *Pew Internet and American Life Project.* Washington, D.C.

Francisco, R. K. (2010). Splintering spheres of security: Peter Sloterdijk and the contemporary fortress city. *Environment and Planning D: Society and Space*, 28(2), 326–40.

Franzen, A. (2000). Does the Internet Make us Lonely. *European Sociological Review*, 16(4), 427–38.

Franzen, A. (2003). Social Capital and the New Communication Technologies *Machines That Become Us* (pp. 105–16).

Freeman, J. H., and Audia, P. G. (2006). Community ecology and the sociology of organizations. [Article]. *Annual Review of Sociology*, 32, 145–69. doi: 10.1146/annurev.soc.32.061604.123135

Frenkel-Faran, A. (2008). Book Review: Andrew Keen, The Cult of the Amateur: How Today's Internet Is Killing Our Culture and Assaulting Our Economy. London and Boston, MA: Currency/Doubleday, 2007. *New Media & Society*, 10(4), 674–77. doi: 10.1177/14614448080100040504

Friedkin, N. E. (2004). Social Cohesion. *Annual Review of Sociology*, 30(1), 409–25. doi: 10.1146/annurev.soc.30.012703.110625

Fuchs, C. (2005). The internet as a self-organizing socio-technological system. *Cybernetics and Human Knowing*, 11(3), 57–81.

Fuchs, C. (2006). The Self-Organization of Cyberprotest. In K. Morgan, C. A. Brebbia and J. M. Spector (Eds.), *The Internet Society II. Advances in Education, Comerce & Governance.* (pp. 275–95). Southampton/Boston: WIT Press.

Fuchs, C. (2008). Critical Theory in the Age of the Internet. *International Sociological Association, Barcelona, Spain.*

Fuchs, C. (2010). studiVZ: social networking in the surveillance society. *Ethics and Information Technology*, 12(2), 171–85.

Gans, H. J. (1962). The urban villagers: group and class in the life of Italian-Americans. New York: Free Press.

Gans, H. J. (2009). Working in Six Research Areas: A Multi-Field Sociological Career. *Annual Review of Sociology*, 35(1), 1–19. doi: 10.1146/annurev-soc-070308–115936

Garcia, A. C., Standlee, A. I., Bechkoff, J., and Yan Cui. (2009). Ethnographic Approaches to the Internet and Computer-Mediated Communication. *Journal of Contemporary Ethnography*, 38(1), 52–84. doi: 10.1177/0891241607310839

Garcia, D., Tessone, C., Mavrodiev, P., and Perony, N. The digital traces of bubbles: feedback cycles between socio-economic signals in the Bitcoin economy.

Garcia-Castro, A., Labarga, A., Garcia, L., Giraldo, O., Montana, C., and Bateman, J. A. (2010). Semantic Web and Social Web heading towards Living Documents in the Life Sciences. *Web Semantics: Science, Services and Agents on the World Wide Web*, 8(2), 155–62.

Gatson, S. N., and Zweerink, A. (2004). Ethnography Online: 'Natives' Practising and Inscribing Community. *Qualitative Research*, 4(2), 179–200. doi: 10.1177/1468794104044431

Gavrin, J. R. (2005). World Wide Web resources for cancer support groups. *Journal Of Pain & Palliative Care Pharmacotherapy*, 19(3), 69–73.

Gerlitz, C., and Lury, C. (2014). Social media and self-evaluating assemblages: on numbers, orderings and values. *Distinktion: Scandinavian Journal of Social Theory*, 15(2), 174–88. doi: 10.1080/1600910x.2014.920267

Giddens, A. (1984). The constitution of society: outline of the theory of structuration. Cambridge: Polity, 1984.

Giddens, A. (1984). The constitution of society: Outline of the theory of structuration.University of California Press.

Gille, Z., and Riain, S. Ó. (2002). Global Ethnography. *Annual Review of Sociology*, 28(1), 271–95. doi: 10.1146/annurev.soc.28.110601.140945

Goodings, L., Locke, A., and Brown, S. D. (2007). Social networking technology: place and identity in mediated communities. *Journal of Community & Applied Social Psychology*, 17(6), 463–76.

Goodsell, T. L., and Williamson, O. (2008). The case of the Brick Huggers: The practice of an online community. *City & Community*, 7(3), 251–71.

Granovetter, M. (1985). Economic Action and Social Structure: The Problem of Embeddedness. *American Journal of Sociology*, 91(3), 481. doi: doi:10.1086/228311

Granovetter, M. S. (1973). The Strength of Weak Ties. *The American Journal of Sociology*, 78(6), 1360–80.

Green, N. (2002). On the Move: Technology, Mobility, and the Mediation of Social Time and Space. *The Information Society*, 18(4), 281–92. doi: 10.1080/01972240290075129

Greenfield, A. (2006). Everyware: The dawning age of ubiquitous computing. San Francisco, CA: Peachpit Press.

Greschke, H. M. (2007). Logging into the Field – Methodological Reflections on Ethnographic Research in a Pluri-Local and Computer-Mediated Field. *Forum Qualitative Sozialforschung/Forum: Qualitative Social Research*, 8(3).

Guitton, M. J. (2012). The immersive impact of meta-media in a virtual world. *Computers in Human Behavior*, 28(2), 450–55. doi: http://dx.doi.org/10.1016/j.chb.2011.10.016

Haggerty, K. D., and Ericson, R. V. (2000). The surveillant assemblage. [Article]. *British Journal of Sociology*, 51(4), 605–22. doi: 10.1080/00071310020015280

Haklay, M., Singleton, A., and Parker, C. (2008). Web Mapping 2.0: The Neogeography of the GeoWeb. *Geography Compass*, 2(6), 2011–39. doi: 10.1111/j.1749-8198.2008.00167.x

Haklay, M., and Weber, P. (2008). OpenStreetMap: User-Generated Street Maps. *Pervasive Computing, IEEE*, 7(4), 12–18. doi: 10.1109/mprv.2008.80

Halpern, O. (2014). Cybernetic rationality. *Distinktion: Scandinavian Journal of Social Theory*, *15*(2), 223–38. doi: 10.1080/1600910x.2014.923320

Hammersley, M. (1990). What's Wrong with Ethnography? The Myth of Theoretical Description. *Sociology*, 24(4), 597–615. doi: 10.1177/0038038590024004003

Hammersley, M. (2008). Troubles with triangulation. In M. M. Bergman (Ed.), *Advances in mixed methods research. Theories and applications* (pp. 22–36). London: Sage.

Hampton, K. (2001). *Living the wired life in the wired suburb: Netville, glocalization, and civic society.* (PhD), University of Toronto, Toronto. Retrieved from http://ezproxy.deakin.edu.au/login?url=http://search.ebscohost.com/login.aspx?direct=true&db=edsref&AN=ABGEABIJ&site=eds-live Available from EBSCOhost edsref database.

Hampton, K., and Wellman, B. (2001). Long distance community in the network society – Contact and support beyond Netville. *American Behavioral Scientist*, 45(3), 476–95.

Hampton, K., and Wellman, B. (2003). Neighboring in Netville: How the INternet Supports Community and Social Capital in a Wired Suburb. *City and Community*, 2(3).

Hampton, K. N. (1998). The Wired Suburb: Glocalization On- and Offline. *American Sociological Association.*

Haraway, D. J. (2008). *When species meet / Donna J. Haraway.* Minneapolis: University of Minnesota Press.

Hardey, M. (2002). Life Beyond the Screen: Embodiment and Identity through the Internet. *The Sociological Review*, 50(4), 570–85.

Hardey, M. (2007). Going live: converging mobile technology and the sociability of the iGeneration. *M/C*, 10(1).

Hardie, E., and Ming Yi, T. (2007). Excessive Internet Use: The Role of Personality, Loneliness and Social Support Networks in Internet Addiction. [Article]. *Australian Journal of Emerging Technologies & Society*, 5(1), 34–47.

Hargittai, E. (2005). Survey Measures of Web-Oriented Digital Literacy. *Social Science Computer Review*, 23(3), 371–9. doi: 10.1177/0894439305275911

Hargittai, E. (2007). Whose Space? Differences Among Users and Non-Users of Social Network Sites. *Journal of Computer-Mediated Communication*, 13(1), 276–97. doi: 10.1111/j.1083–6101.2007.00396.x

Hargittai, E., and Centeno, M. (2001). Defining a Global Geography. *American Behavioral Scientist*, 44(10).

Hargittai, E., and Hinnant, A. (2006, 2006 2006 Annual Meeting, Montreal). *New Dimensions of the Digital Divide: Differences in Young Adults' Internet Uses.* Paper presented at the Annual Meeting of the American Sociological Association, Montreal.

Hawley, A. H. (1944). Ecology and Human Ecology. [Article]. *Social Forces*, 22(4), 398–405.

Hawley, A. H. (1950). *Human Ecology: A Theory of Community Structure.* New York: Ronald Press.

Haythornthwaite, C. (2002). Strong, Weak, and Latent Ties and the Impact of New Media. *The Information Society*, 18(5), 385–401. doi: 10.1080/01972240290108195

Haythornthwaite, C. (2005). Social networks and Internet connectivity effects. *Information, Communication & Society*, 8(2), 125–47. doi: 10.1080/13691180500146185

Herring, S., Job-Sluder, K., Scheckler, R., and Barab, S. (2002). Searching for Safety Online: Managing "Trolling" in a Feminist Forum. *The Information Society*, 18(5), 371–84. doi: 10.1080/01972240290108186

Heyer, C., and Brereton, M. (2006). *Socialising across channels: group multichannel communication.* Paper presented at the OZCHI 2006, Sydney, Australia.

Hine, C. (2000). *Virtual ethnography.* London: Sage Publications Limited.

Hine, C. (2008). Virtual ethnography: Modes, varieties, affordances *The SAGE handbook of online research methods* (pp. 257–70). Cambridge, Mass.: The MIT Press.

Hollinger, R. C. (1991). Hackers: computer heroes or electronic highwaymen? *SIGCAS Computers and Society*, 21(1), 6–17. doi: 10.1145/122246.122248

Houston, T. K., Cooper, L. A., and Ford, D. E. (2002). Internet support groups for depression: A 1-year prospective cohort study. *American Journal of Psychiatry*, 159(12), 2062–8. doi: 10.1176/appi.ajp.159.12.2062

Howard, S., Kjeldskov, J., Skov, M. B., Garnæs, K., and Grünberger, O. (2006). *Negotiating presence-in-absence: contact, content and context*. Proceedings of the SIGCHI Conference on Human Factors in Computing Systems, 909–912.

Høybye, M. T., Johansen, C., and Tjørnhøj-Thomsen, T. (2005). Online interaction. Effects of storytelling in an internet breast cancer support group. [Article]. *Psycho-Oncology*, 14(3), 211–20. doi: 10.1002/pon.837

Hsiu-Fen, L. (2008). Antecedents of Virtual Community Satisfaction and Loyalty: An Empirical Test of Competing Theories. [Article]. *CyberPsychology & Behavior*, 11(2), 138–44. doi: 10.1089/cpb.2007.0003

Im, E., Chee, W., Lim, H., Liu, Y., Guevara, E., and Kim, K. S. (2007). Patients' attitudes toward Internet cancer support groups. *Oncology Nursing Forum*, 34(3), 705–12. doi: 10.1188/07.onf.705–12

Indergaard, M. L., and McInerney, P. (1998). The Embedded Net: Making Silicon Alley, Remaking Cyberspace. *American Sociological Association.*

Isabella, S. (2007). Ethnography of Online Role-Playing Games: The Role of Virtual and Real Contest in the Construction of the Field. *Forum: Qualitative Social Research*, 8(3), 1.

Ivankova, N., and Kawamura, Y. (2010). Emerging trends in the utilization of integration designs in the social, behavioral and health sciences. In A. Tashakkori and C. Teddlie (Eds.), *The Sage handbook of mixed methods in social and behavioral research* (2nd ed., pp. 581–611). London: Safe.

Jacobson, D. (1999). Impression formation in cyberspace: Online expectations and offline experiences in text-based virtual communities. *Journal of Computer-Mediated Communication*, 5(1).

Jardine, N., Secord, J. A., and Spary, E. C. (Eds.). (1996). *Cultures of Natural History*. Cambridge, UK: Cambridge University Press.

Jenkins, H. (2006). Convergence culture: Where old and new media collide: NYU press.

Jensen, K. B. (2011). New media, old methods. Internet methodology and the online/offline divide. In M. Consalvo and C. Ess (Eds.), *The handbook of Internet studies* (pp. 43–57). Chichester, UK: Wiley-Blackwell.

Jepsen, A. L. (2006). Information Search in Virtual Communities: Is it Replacing Use of Off Line Communication? [Article]. *Journal of Marketing Communications*, 12(4), 247–61. doi: 10.1080/13527260600694308

John Levi Martin. (2003). What Is Field Theory? *American Journal of Sociology*, 109(1), 1–49. doi: 10.1086/375201

Johnston, J., and Laxer, G. (2003). Solidarity in the age of globalization: Lessons from the anti-MAI and Zapatista struggles. *Theory and Society*, 32(1), 39–91. doi: 10.1023/a:1023025130342

Jordan, T., and Taylor, P. (1998). A sociology of hackers. *The Sociological Review*, 46(4), 757–80. doi: 10.1111/1467–954x.00139

Josefsson, U. (2005). Coping with Illness Online: The Case of Patients' Online Communities. *The Information Society*, 21(2), 143–53.

Kalish, Y., and Robins, G. (2006). Psychological predispositions and network structure: The relationship between individual predispositions, structural holes and network closure. *Social Networks*, 28(1), 56–84. doi: 10.1016/j.socnet.2005.04.004

Kanuha, V. K. (2000). "Being" native versus "going native": conducting social work research as an insider. *Social Work*, 45(5), 439–47.

Katz, J. E., and Rice, R. E. (2002). Social consequences of Internet use: Access, involvement, and interaction: The MIT Press.

Katz, J. E., Rice, R. E., and Aspden, P. (2001). The Internet, 1995–2000 – Access, civic involvement, and social interaction. *American Behavioral Scientist*, 45(3), 405–19.

Keen, A. (2007). The cult of the amateur: how today's internet is killing our culture. New York: Doubleday.

Kelle, U. (2005). Sociological Explanations between Micro and Macro and the Integration of Qualitative and Quantitative Methods. *Historical Social Research*, 30(1), 95–117.

Kemp, J., and Livingstone, D. (2006). Putting a second life "metaverse" skin on learning management systems. Proceedings of the Second Life education workshop at the Second Life community convention, 13–18.

Kiessling, T., and Harvey, M. (2005). Strategic global human resource management research in the twenty-first century: an endorsement of the mixed-method research methodology. [Article]. *International Journal of Human Resource Management*, 16(1), 22–45. doi: 10.1080/0958519042000295939

Kitchin, R. & Dodge, M. (2011). *Code/space: Software and everyday life*. Cambridge, Mass.: The MIT Press.

Klaebe, H. G., Adkins, B. A., Foth, M., and Hearn, G. N. (2009). Embedding an ecology notion in the social production of urban space. In M. Foth (Ed.), Handbook of Research on Urban Informatics: The Practice and Promise of the Real-Time City (pp. 179–94). Hershey, PA: Information Science Reference, IGI Global.

Kleinberg, J. (2000a). Navigation in a small world. *Nature*, 406(6798), 845(841).

Kleinberg, J. (2000b). *The small-world phenomenon: an algorithm perspective*. Paper presented at the Proceedings of the thirty-second annual ACM symposium on Theory of computing, Portland, Oregon, United States.

Klemm, P., and Hardie, T. (2002). Depression in Internet and face-to-face cancer support groups: a pilot study. *Oncology Nursing Forum*, 29(4), 45–51.

Knox, H., Savage, M., and Harvey, P. (2006). Social networks and the study of relations: networks as method, metaphor and form. *Economy and Society*, 35(1), 113–40. doi: 10.1080/03085140500465899

Kobayashi, T. (2010). Bridging Social Capital in Online Communities: Heterogeneity and Social Tolerance of Online Game Players in Japan. [Article]. *Human Communication Research*, 36(4), 546–69. doi: 10.1111/j.1468–2958.2010.01388.x

Kobayashi, T., Ikeda, K. i., and Miyata, K. (2006). Social capital online: Collective use of the Internet and reciprocity as lubricants of democracy. [Article]. *Information, Communication & Society*, 9(5), 582–611. doi: 10.1080/13691180600965575

Kolb, D. G. (2008). Exploring the Metaphor of Connectivity: Attributes, Dimensions and Duality. *Organization Studies*, 29(1), 127–44. doi: 10.1177/0170840607084574

Kortuem, G., Kawsar, F., Sundramoorthy, V., adn Fitton, D. (2010). Smart Objects as Building Blocks for the Internet of Things. *IEEE Internet Computing*, 14(1), 44–51. doi: http://dx.doi.org/10.1109/MIC.2009.143

Krause, J., Croft, D., and James, R. (2007). Social network theory in the behavioural sciences: potential applications. *Behavioral Ecology and Sociobiology*, 62(1), 15–27. doi: 10.1007/s00265–007–0445–8

Kraut, R., Kiesler, S., Boneva, B., Cummings, J., Helgeson, V., and Crawford, A. (2002). Internet Paradox Revisited. *Journal of Social Issues*, 58(1), 49–74.

Kraut, R., Patterson, M., Lundmark, V., Kiesler, S., Mukophadhyay, T., and Scherlis, W. (1998). Internet paradox: A social technology that reduces social involvement and psychological well-being? *American Psychologist*, 53(9), 1017–31. doi: 10.1037/0003–066x.53.9.1017

Kuecklich, J. (2005). Precarious playbour: Modders and the digital games industry. *Fibreculture*, 5.

Labaree, R. V. (2002). The risk of "going observationalist" negotiating the hidden dilemmas of being an insider participant observer. *Qualitative Research*, 2(1), 97–122. doi: 10.1177/146879410200200l641

Lai-Yee, M. A. (2007). Cyberactivism : Internet Gratifications, Collective Identity and Political Participation. *Asian Communication Research*, 25.

Lamont, M., and Molnar, V. (2002). The Study of Boundaries in the Social Sciences. *Annual Review of Sociology*, 28, 167–95.

Land, C. (2012). Occupy Auckland. *Psychotherapy and Politics International*, 10(1), 79–82. doi: 10.1002/ppi.1256

Lange, P. G. (2007). Publicly Private and Privately Public: Social Networking on YouTube. *Journal of Computer-Mediated Communication*, 13(1), 361–80. doi: 10.1111/j.1083–6101.2007.00400.x

LaSala, M. C. (2003). When Interviewing "Family". *Journal of Gay & Lesbian Social Services*, 15(1–2), 15–30. doi: 10.1300/J041v15n01_02

Latham, R., and Sassen, S. (2005). Digital formations: IT and new architectures in the global realm. Princeton, NJ: Princeton University Press.

Latour, B. (2005). *Reassembling the social.* Oxford: Oxford University Press.

Law, J. (1992). Notes on the theory of the actor-network: Ordering, strategy, and heterogeneity. *Systems practice*, 5(4), 379–93. doi: 10.1007/bf01059830

Law, J. (1999). After ANT: complexity, naming and topology. *The Sociological Review*, 47(S1), 1–14. doi: 10.1111/j.1467–954X.1999.tb03479.x

Law, J. (2002). Objects and Spaces. *Theory, Culture & Society*, 19(5–6), 91–105. doi: 10.1177/026327602761899165

Law, J. (2004). After Method: Mess in Social Science Research Retrieved from http://deakin.eblib.com.au/patron/FullRecord.aspx?p=200755

Law, J., and Urry, J. (2001). Enacting the social. *Economy and Society*, 33(3), 390–410. doi: 10.1080/0308514042000225716

Lawrence, R. J. (2003). Human ecology and its applications. *Landscape and Urban Planning*, 65(1–2), 31–40. doi: 10.1016/s0169–2046(02)00235–9

Leigh Star, S., and Griesemer, J. (1989). Translations and Boundary Objects: Amateurs and Professionals in Berkeley's Museum of Vertebrate Zoology. *Social Studies of Science*, 19(3), 387–420.

Lemos, A. (2010). Post – Mass Media Functions, Locative Media, and Informational Territories: New Ways of Thinking About Territory, Place, and Mobility in Contemporary Society. *Space and Culture*, 13(4), 403–20. doi: 10.1177/1206331210374144

Leszczynski, A. (forthcoming). Spatial big data and anxieties of control. *Environment and Planning D: Society & Space.*

Lightfoot, K. G., and Martinez, A. (1995). Frontiers and Boundaries in Archaeological Perspective. *Annual Review of Anthropology*, 24(1), 471–92. doi: 10.1146/annurev.an.24.100195.002351

Lin, N. (1999). Building a network theory of social capital. *Connections*, 22(1), 28–51.

Lin, N. (2001). *Social Capital: A theory of social structure and action.* New York: Cambridge University Press.

Lupi, T., and Musterd, S. (2006). The Suburban 'Community Question'. *Urban Studies*, 43(4), 801–17.

Lupton, D. (2014). Quantified Sex: a critical analysis of sexual and reproductive self-tracking apps. *Culture, Health & Sexuality.*

MacDonald, D. W. (2011). Beyond the Group: The Implications of Roderick D. McKenzie's Human Ecology for Reconceptualizing Society and the Social. [Article]. *Nature & Culture*, 6(3), 263–84. doi: 10.3167/nc.2011.060304

Mahrt, M., and Scharkow, M. (2013). The Value of Big Data in Digital Media Research. *Journal of Broadcasting and Electronic Media*, 57(1), 20–33. doi: 10.1080/08838151.2012.761700

Mann, C., and Stewart, F. (2000). Internet communication and qualitative research: A handbook for researching online. London: Sage Publications Ltd.
Markham, A., and Buchanan, E. (2012). Ethical Decision-Making and Internet Research: Recommendations from the AoIR ethics working committee: AoIR.
Marotta, V. P. (2008). The hybrid self and the ambivalence of boundaries. *Social Identities*, 14(3), 295–312. doi: 10.1080/13504630802088052
Marshall, J. (2001). Cyber-space, or Cyber-topos: The Creation of Online Space. *Social Analysis: The International Journal of Social and Cultural Practice*, 45(1), 81–102. doi: 10.2307/23169992
Martin, J. (2013). Lost on the Silk Road: Online drug distribution and the 'cryptomarket'. *Criminology and Criminal Justice*. doi: 10.1177/1748895813505234
Martin, J. (2014). Drugs On the Dark Net: How Cryptomarkets Are Transforming the Global Trade in Illicit Drugs. Basingstoke: Palgrave Macmillan.
Matessi, G., Matos, R. J., Peake, T. M., McGregor, P. K., and Dabelsteen, T. (2010). Effects of social environment and personality on communication in male Siamese fighting fish in an artificial network. *Animal Behaviour*, 79(1), 43–9. doi: 10.1016/j.anbehav.2009.09.034
Matzat, U. (2010). Reducing Problems of Sociability in Online Communities: Integrating Online Communication With Offline Interaction. *American Behavioral Scientist*, 53(8), 1170–93.
Maxwell, J. A. (2010). Using numbers in qualitative research. *Qualitative Inquiry*, 16, 475–82.
McKenzie, R. (1967). The Ecological Approach to the Study of the Human Community. In R. E. Park and E. W. Burgess (Eds.), *The City* (pp. 63–79). Chicago/London: University of Chicago Press.
McNally, R. (2005). Sociomics! Using the IssueCrawler to map, monitor and engage with the global proteomics research network. *Proteomics*, 5(12), 3010–16. doi: 10.1002/pmic.200500163
McPherson, J. M. (1982). Hypernetwork sampling: Duality and differentiation among voluntary organizations. *Social Networks*, 3(4), 225–49. doi: 10.1016/0378–8733(82)90001–6
McPherson, J. M. (1983). An Ecology of Affiliation. *American Sociological Review*, 48(4), 519–32.
McPherson, J. M. (2001). Sampling strategies for the arts: A hypernetwork approach. *Poetics*, 28(4), 291–306. doi: 10.1016/s0304–422x(01)80005-x
McPherson, J. M., and Rotolo, T. (1995). Measuring the Composition of Voluntary Groups: A Multitrait-Multimethod Analysis. *Social Forces*, 73(3), 1097–1115.
McPherson, J. M., Smith-Lovin, L., and Cook, J. M. (2001). Birds of a Feather: Homophily in Social Networks. *Annual Review of Sociology*, 27(1), 415–44. doi: 10.1146/annurev.soc.27.1.415

Melrose, M. (2002). Labour pains: Some considerations on the difficulties of researching juvenile prostitution. *International Journal of Social Research Methodology*, 5(4), 333–51. doi: 10.1080/13645570110045963

Merton, R. K. (1948). Discussion. *American Sociological Review*, 13(2), 164–8.

Mesch, G., and Levanon, Y. (2006). *The Link between Online and Offline Community Activism*. Paper presented at the American Sociological Association Annual Meeting, Montreal. Conference Paper retrieved from http://ezproxy.deakin.edu.au/login?url=http://search.ebscohost.com/login.aspx?direct=true&db=sih&AN=26643659&site=eds-live

Mesch, G., and Talmud, I. (2007). Similarity and the Quality of Online and Offline Social Relationships Among Adolescents in Israel *Journal of Research on Adolescence*, 17(2), 455–65. doi: 10.1111/j.1532-7795.2007.00529.x

Mesch, G. S., and Talmud, I. (2010). Internet Connectivity, Community Participation, and Place Attachment: A Longitudinal Study. *American Behavioral Scientist*, 53(8), 1095–1110. doi: 10.1177/0002764209356243

Mika, P. (2004). *Social networks and the semantic web*. (PhD Thesis), Free University of Amsterdam, Amsterdam.

Miller, A. S., and Mitamura, T. (2003). Are surveys on trust trustworthy? *Social Psychology Quarterly*, 66(1), 62–70.

Miller, M. (2009). Selling Online 2.0: Migrating from eBay to Amazon, craigslist, and Your Own E-Commerce Website. *Library Journal*, 134(11), 82ff.

Mitchell, M. E., Lebow, J. R., Uribe, R., Grathouse, H., and Shoger, W. (2011). Internet use, happiness, social support and introversion: A more fine grained analysis of person variables and internet activity. *Computers in Human Behavior*, 27(5), 1857–61. doi: 10.1016/j.chb.2011.04.008

Mitra, A., and Schwartz, R. L. (2001). From Cyber Space to Cybernetic Space: Rethinking the Relationship between Real and Virtual Spaces. *Journal of Computer Mediated Communication*, 7(1).

Modell, S. (2009). In defence of triangulation: A critical realist approach to mixed methods research in management accounting. *Management Accounting Research*, 20(3), 208–21. doi: 10.1016/j.mar.2009.04.001

Moody, J., and White, D. R. (2003). Structural Cohesion and Embeddedness: A Hierarchical Concept of Social Groups. *American Sociological Review*, 68(1), 103–27.

Morkes, J., Kernal, H. K., and Nass, C. (1999). Effects of Humor in Task-Oriented Human-Computer Interaction and Computer-Mediated Communication: A Direct Test of SRCT Theory. *Human–Computer Interaction*, 14(4), 395–435. doi: 10.1207/s15327051hci1404_2

Murthy, D. (2008). Digital Ethnography: An Examination of the Use of New Technologies for Social Research. *Sociology*, 42(5), 837–55. doi: 10.1177/0038038508094565

Muscanell, N. L., and Guadagno, R. E. (2012). Make new friends or keep the old: Gender and personality differences in social networking use. *Computers in Human Behaviour*, 28(1), 107–12.

Mutz, D. C. (2009). Effects of Internet Commerce on Social Trust. [Article]. *Public Opinion Quarterly*, 73(3), 439–61. doi: 10.1093/poq/nfp042

Nafus, D. (2014). Stuck data, dead data, and disloyal data: the stops and starts in making numbers into social practices. *Distinktion: Scandinavian Journal of Social Theory*, 15(2), 208–22. doi: 10.1080/1600910x.2014.920266

Nardi, B., and O'Day, V. (1999). Information Ecologies: Using Technology with Heart. *First Monday*, 4(5).

Neal, Z. P. (2011). From Central Places to Network Bases: A Transition in the U.S. Urban Hierarchy, 1900–2000. *City & Community*, 10(1), 49–75. doi: 10.1111/j.1540–6040.2010.01340.x

Nie, N., and Erbring, L. (2002). Internet and Society: A Preliminary Report. *IT & Society*, 1(1).

Nie, N., Hillygus, D., and Erbring, L. (2002). Internet use, interpersonal relations, and sociability. *The Internet in everyday life*, 215–43.

Nie, N. H. (2001). Sociability, interpersonal relations, and the Internet: Reconciling conflicting findings. *American Behavioral Scientist*, 3, 420–35.

Nie, N. H., and Hillygus, D. S. (2002). The Impact of Internet Use on Sociability: Time-Diary Findings. *IT&Society*, 1(1), 1–20.

Ono, H., and Zavodny, M. (2003). Gender and the Internet*. *Social Science Quarterly*, 84(1), 111–21. doi: 10.1111/1540–6237.t01–1-8401007

Orr, E. S., Sisic, M., Ross, C., Simmering, M. G., Arseneault, J. M., and Orr, R. R. (2009). The Influence of Shyness on the Use of Facebook in an Undergraduate Sample. [Article]. *CyberPsychology & Behavior*, 12(3), 337–40. doi: 10.1089/cpb.2008.0214

Östlund, U., Kidd, L., Wengström, Y., and Rowa-Dewar, N. (2011). Combining qualitative and quantitative research within mixed method research designs: A methodological review. *International Journal of Nursing Studies*, 48(3), 369–83. doi: 10.1016/j.ijnurstu.2010.10.005

Paccagnella, L. (1997). Getting the seats of your pants dirty: Strategies for ethnographic research on virtual communities. *Journal of Computer-Mediated Communication*, 3(1).

Pak-Hang, W. (2013). From Culture 2.0 to a Network State of Mind: A Selective History of Web 2.0's Axiologies and a Lesson from It. [Article]. *TripleC (Cognition, Communication, Co-Operation): Open Access Journal for a Global Sustainable Information Society*, 11(1), 191–206.

Park, R. (1915). The City: Suggestions for the Investigation of Human Behaviour in the City Environment. *The American Journal of Sociology*, 20(5), 577–612.

Park, R., and Burgess, E. (1921). *Introduction to the Science of Sociology*. Chicago: University of Chicago Press.

Park, R., Burgess, E., and McKenzie, R. (1925). The City: suggestions for the Investifation of Human Behaviour in the Urban Environment. Chicago: University of Chicago Press.

Parker, S., Uprichard, E., and Burrows, R. (2007). Class Places and Place Classes: Geodemographics and the spatialization of class. *Information, Communication & Society*, 10(6), 902–21. doi: 10.1080/13691180701751122

Parks, M. R., and Floyd, K. (1996). Making friends in cyberspace. *Journal of Computer-Mediated Communication*, 1(4).

Parks, R. (2011). Social network sites as virtual communities. In Z. Papacharissi (Ed.), *A networked self. Identity, community, and culture on social network sites* (pp. 105–23). New York, NY: Routledge.

Parsons, T. (1951). *The social system*. Glencoe, Ill., Free Press.

Pasek, J., More, E., and Romer, D. (2009). Realizing the Social Internet? Online Social Networking Meets Offline Social Capital. *Journal of Information Technology & Politics*, 6(3&4), 197–215.

Pew. (2011). Media Ecology, from http://pewinternet.org/topics/New-media-ecology

Phelps, A., and Watt, A. I shop online – recreationally! Internet anonymity and Silk Road enabling drug use in Australia. *Digital Investigation*(0). doi: http://dx.doi.org/10.1016/j.diin.2014.08.001

Pike, K. L. (1967). Language in relation to a unified theory of the structure of human behavior. The Hague, The Netherlands: Mouton.

Pike, K. L. (1990). On the emics and etics of Pike and Harris. In R. G. Headland and M. McClelland (Eds.), *Emics and etics: The insider/outsider debate* (pp. 28–47). Newbury Park, CA: Sage.

Plano Clark, V. L. (2010). The adoption and practice of mixed methods: U.S. trends in federally funded health-related research. *Qualitative Inquiry*, 16, 428–40.

Platt, J. (1996). *A history of sociological research methods in America: 1920–1960.* Cambridge/New York: Cambridge University Press.

Plotkin, W. (1995). Rheingold: The Virtual Community: Homesteading on the Electronic Frontier. *Journal- American Planning Association*, 61(2), 284.

Plumwood, V. (1995). Human vulnerability and the experience of being prey. *Quadrant (Sydney)*, 39(3), 29–34.

Pollet, T. V., Roberts, S. G. B., and Dunbar, R. I. M. (2011). Extraverts Have Larger Social Network Layers. [10.1027/1614–0001/a000048]. *Journal of Individual Differences*, 32(3), 161–9.

Portes, A., and Vickstrom, E. (2011). Diversity, Social Capital, and Cohesion. *Annual Review of Sociology*, 37(1), 461–79. doi: 10.1146/annurev-soc-081309–150022

Poster, M. (1999). National Identities and Communications Technologies. [Article]. *Information Society*, 15(4), 235–40. doi: 10.1080/019722499128394

Postigo, H. (2007). Of Mods and Modders: Chasing Down the Values of Fan-Based Digital Game Modifications. *Games and Culture*, 2(4), 300–313.

Power, M. J., Neville, P., Devereux, E., Haynes, A., and Barnes, C. (2013). 'Why bother seeing the world for real?': Google Street View and the representation of a stigmatised neighbourhood. *New Media & Society*, 15(7), 1022–40. doi: 10.1177/1461444812465138

Preece, J., Nonnecke, B., and Andrews, D. (2004). The top five reasons for lurking: improving community experiences for everyone. *Computers in Human Behavior*, 20(2), 201–23. doi: 10.1016/j.chb.2003.10.015

Pronovost, S. (2009). Virtual Social Networking and Interoperability in the Canadian Forces Netcentric Environment. DTIC Document.

Putnam, R. (1993). *Making democracy work: civic traditions in modern Italy*. Princeton, NJ: Princeton University Press.

Putnam, R. (2000). Bowling alone: the collapse and revival of American community. New York: Simon & Schuster.

Putnam, R. D. (1995). Bowling Alone: America's Declining Social Capital. *Journal of Democracy*, 6(1), 65.

Quan-Haase, A., Wellman, B., Witte, J., and Hampton, K. (2002). Capitalizing on the Net: Social Contact, Civic Engagement, and Sense of Community. In B. Wellman and C. A. Haythornthwaite (Eds.), *The Internet in everyday life*. Oxford: Blackwell.

Rainie, L., and Wellman, B. (2012). *Networked: the new social operating system*. Cambridge, Mass.: The MIT Press.

Realo, A., Allik, J. r., and Greenfield, B. (2008). Radius of Trust. *Journal of Cross-Cultural Psychology*, 39(4), 447–62. doi: 10.1177/0022022108318096

Rheingold, H. (2000). *The virtual community : homesteading on the electronic frontier* (Rev. ed.). Cambridge, Mass.: The MIT Press.

Rheingold, H. (2003). Smart Mobs: Transforming Cultures and Communities in the Age of Instant Access: Cambridge, Mass.: Basic Books.

Rice, R. E., and Love, G. (1987). Electronic Emotion. *Communication Research*, 14(1), 85–108. doi: 10.1177/009365087014001005

Ritzer, G. (1996). The McDonaldization of society : an investigation into the changing character of contemporary social. Thousand Oaks, Calif.: Pine Forge Press, c1996. Rev. ed.

Ritzer, G., and Jurgenson, N. (2010). Production, Consumption, Prosumption. *Journal of Consumer Culture*, 10(1), 13–36. doi: 10.1177/1469540509354673

Roberts, S. G. B., Wilson, R., Fedurek, P., and Dunbar, R. I. M. (2008). Individual differences and personal social network size and structure. *Personality and Individual Differences*, 44(4), 954–64. doi: 10.1016/j.paid.2007.10.033

Robertson, R. (1995). Glocalization: Time-space and homogeneity-heterogeneity. In M. Featherstone, S. Lash and R. Robertson (Eds.), *Global modernities* (pp. 25–44). London: Thousand Oaks.

Rodríguez-Amat, J. R., and Brantner, C. (2014). Space and place matters: A tool for the analysis of geolocated and mapped protests. *New Media & Society*. doi: 10.1177/1461444814552098

Rogers, E. M., and Kincaid, D. L. (1981). *Communication networks: toward a new paradigm for research*. New York: Free Press.

Rogers, R. (2004). *Information Politics on the Web*. Cambridge, Mass./London: The MIT Press.

Rogers, R. (2009a). *The End of the Virtual: Digital Methods*. Amsterdam: Amsterdam University Press.

Rogers, R. (2009b). Mapping Public Web Space with the Issuecrawler. In C. Brossard and B. Reber (Eds.), *Digital Cognitive Technologies: Epistemology and Knowledge Society* (pp. 115–26). London: Wiley.

Rogers, R. (2010a). Internet Research: The Question of Method. *Journal of Information Technology & Politics*, 7(2/3), 241–60.

Rogers, R. (2010b). IssueCrawler Retrieved 17 May 2012, 2012, from issuecrawler.net

Rogers, R. (2012). Mapping and the Politics of Web Space. *Theory, Culture & Society*, 29(4–5), 193–219. doi: 10.1177/0263276412450926

Rothaermel, F. T., and Sugiyama, S. (2001). Virtual internet communities and commercial success: individual and community-level theory grounded in the atypical case of TimeZone.com. *Journal of Management*, 27(3), 297–312. doi: 10.1177/014920630102700305

Rybas, N. (2007). Developing Cyberethnographic Research Methods for Understanding Digitally Mediated Identities. *Forum: Qualitative Social Research*, 8(3), 1.

Sade-Beck, L. (2008). Internet ethnography: Online and offline. *International Journal of Qualitative Methods*, 3(2), 45–51.

Sampson, R. J. (2002). Transcending Tradition: New Directions in Community Research, Chicago Style. *Criminology*, 40(2), 213–30. doi: 10.1111/j.1745-9125.2002.tb00955.x

San Cornelio, G., and Ardevol, E. (2011). Practices of place-making through locative media artworks. [Article]. *Communications-European Journal of Communication Research*, 36(3), 313–33. doi: 10.1515/comm.2011.016

Santos, R., Rocha, B., Rezende, R., and Loureiro, A. (2007). Characterizing the YouTube video-sharing community. *Federal University of Minas Gerais (UFMG), Belo Horizonte, Brazil, Tech. Rep.*

Sassen, S. (2000). New frontiers facing urban sociology at the Millennium. *The British Journal of Sociology*, 51(1), 143–59. doi: 10.1111/j.1468-4446.2000.00143.x

Sassen, S. (2001). *The Global City: New York, London, Tokyo*. Princeton, NJ: Princeton University Press.

Sassen, S. (2002). Towards a Sociology of Information Technology. *Current Sociology*, 50(3), 365–88. doi: 10.1177/0011392102050003005

Sassen, S. (2008). Deciphering the Global: Its Spaces, Scales and Subjects. [Article]. *Social Thought & Research*, 29, 3–18.

Sassen, S. (Ed.). (2007). Deciphering the global: its scales, spaces and subjects. New York: Routledge.

Scardamalia, M. (2003). Crossing the digital Divide: Literacy as By-product of Knowledge Building. [Article]. *Journal of Distance Education*, 17(3), 78–80.

Scheper-Hughes, N. (2000). Ire in Ireland. *Ethnography*, 1(1), 117–40. doi: 10.1177/14661380022230660

Schroeder, R. (2010). Mobile phones and the inexorable advance of multimodal connectedness. [Article]. *New Media & Society*, 12(1), 75–90. doi: 10.1177/1461444809355114

Shanyang, Z. (2006). Do Internet Users Have More Social Ties? A Call for Differentiated Analyses of Internet Use. [Article]. *Journal of Computer-Mediated Communication*, 11(3), 844–62. doi: 10.1111/j.1083–6101.2006.00038.x

Sharp, J. (2000). The Internet. Changing the way cancer survivors receive support. *Cancer Practice*, 8(3), 145–7.

Shen, C., and Williams, D. (2011). Unpacking Time Online: Connecting Internet and Massively Multiplayer Online Game Use With Psychosocial Well-Being. *Communication Research*, 38(1), 123–49. doi: 10.1177/0093650210377196

Shin, J. (2008). Morality and Internet Behavior: A study of the Internet Troll and its relation with morality on the Internet. *Technology and Teacher Education Annual*, 19(5), 2834.

Siapera, E. (2006). Multiculturalism, progressive politics and British Islam online. [Article]. *International Journal of Media & Cultural Politics*, 2(3), 331–46. doi: 10.1386/macp.2.3.331_1

Sih, A., Hanser, S. F., and McHugh, K. A. (2009). Social network theory: New insights and issues for behavioral ecologists. *Behavioral Ecology and Sociobiology*, 63(7), 975–88. doi: 10.1007/s00265–009–0725–6; 10.1007/s00265–009–0729–2;

Simpson, J. (2002). Computer-mediated communication. [Article]. *ELT Journal: English Language Teachers Journal*, 56(4), 414.

Skågeby, J. (2011). Pre-produsage and the remediation of virtual products. *New Review of Hypermedia and Multimedia*, 17(1), 141–59. doi: 10.1080/13614568.2011.552642

Skinner, J. (2011). Social Media and Revolution: The Arab Spring and the Occupy Movement as Seen through Three Information Studies Paradigms.

Skoric, M. M., Chua, J. P. E., Liew, M. A., Keng Hui, W., and Pei, J. (2010). Online Shaming in the Asian Context: Community Empowerment or Civic Vigilantism? [Article]. *Surveillance & Society*, 8(2), 181–99.

Sloterdijk, P., and Hoban, W. (2011). *Bubbles*: Cambridge, Mass./London: Semiotext(e).

Snijders, T. (1999). Prologue to the Measurement of Social Capital. *The Tocqueville Review*, xx(1), 27–44.

Snow, D. (1980). The disengagement process: A neglected problem in participant observation research. *Qualitative Sociology*, 3(2), 100–122. doi: 10.1007/bf00987266

Spencer, H. (1876). *The principles of sociology*: London: Williams and Norgate, 1876.

Steinfield, C., Ellison, N. B., and Lampe, C. (2008). Social capital, self-esteem, and use of online social network sites: A longitudinal analysis. *Journal of Applied Developmental Psychology*, 29(6), 434–45.

Sturgis, P., and Smith, P. (2010). Assessing the validity of generalized trust questions: What kind of trust are we measuring? *International Journal of Public Opinion Research*, 22(1), 74–92. doi: 10.1093/ijpor/edq003

Subrahmanyam, K., Reich, S. M., Waechter, N., and Espinoza, G. (2008). Online and offline social networks: Use of social networking sites by emerging adults. *Journal of Applied Developmental Psychology*, 29(6), 420–33.

Surowiecki, J. (2004). *The wisdom of crowds*. London: Random House LLC.

Swickert, R. J., Hittner, J. B., Harris, J. L., and Herring, J. A. (2002). Relationships among Internet use, personality, and social support. *Computers in Human Behavior*, 18(4), 437–51. doi: 10.1016/s0747–5632(01)00054–1

Swyngedouw, E. (2004). Globalisation or "glocalisation"? Networks, territories and rescaling. *Cambridge Review of International Affairs*, 17(1), 25–48. doi: 10.1080/0955757042000203632

Thelwall, M. (2009). Introduction to Webometrics: Quantitative Web Research for the Social Science. San Rafael, CA: Morgan & Claypool.

Thrasher, F. M. (1927). The gang: A study of 1313 gangs in Chicago: Chicago: University of Chicago Press.

Tilly, C. (2004). *Social Movements, 1768–2004*. Boulder, CO: Paradigm Publishers.

Topi, H., Valacich, J. S., and Rao, M. T. (2002). The Effects of Personality and Media Differences on the Performance of Dyads Addressing a Cognitive Conflict Task. *Small Group Research*, 33(6), 667–701.

Touraine, A. (2003a). The Decline of the Social. [Article]. *Comparative Sociology*, 2(3), 463–74.

Touraine, A. (2003b). Sociology without Societies. *Current Sociology*, 51(2), 123–31.

Trappeniers, L., Godon, M., Claeys, L., Martinot, O., and Marilly, E. (2008). Cross-media experiences: Ambient community interactions in the city. [Article]. *Bell Labs Technical Journal*, 13(2), 5–11. doi: 10.1002/bltj.20296

Turkle, S. (1997a). Life on the Screen: identity in the age of the Internet. New York: Touchstone.

Turkle, S. (1997b). Multiple Subjectivity and Virtual Community at the End of the Freudian Century. *Sociological Inquiry*, 67(1), 72–84. doi: 10.1111/j.1475–682X.1997.tb00430.x

Turkle, S. (1999). Cyberspace and Identity. *Contemporary Sociology*, 28(6), 643–8. doi: 10.2307/2655534

Turkle, S. (2003). Technology and human vulnerability. A conversation with MIT's Sherry Turkle. *Harvard Business Review*, 81(9), 43.

Turkle, S. (2007a). Authenticity in the age of digital companions. Interaction Studies: Social Behaviour and Communication in Biological and Artificial Systems, 8(3), 501–17.

Turkle, S. (2007b). The secret power of things we hold dear. [Article]. *New Scientist*, 194(2607), 50.

Turkle, S. (2011). Alone together : why we expect more from technology and less from each other. New York: Basic Books.

Turnage, A. K. (2007). Email Flaming Behaviors and Organizational Conflict. *Journal of Computer-Mediated Communication*, 13(1), 43–59. doi: 10.1111/j.1083–6101.2007.00385.x

Tuters, M., and Varnelis, K. (2006). Beyond Locative Media: Giving Shape to the Internet of Things. *Leonardo*, 39(4), 357–63. doi: 10.2307/20206268

Tyma, A. (2007). Rules of Interchange: Privacy in Oline Social Communities – A rhetorical critique of MySpace.com. *Journal of the Communicaiton, Speech and Theatre*, 20, 31.

United Nations, and Rue, F. L. (2011). Report of the Special Rapporteur on the promotion and protection of the right to freedom of opinion and expression (G. Assembly, Trans.) *Promotion and protection of all human rights, civil, political, economic, social and cultural rights, including the right to development* (Vol. Human Rights Council, Seventeenth session, Agenda Item 3): United Nations.

Uprichard, E. (2012). Being stuck in (live) time: the sticky sociological imagination. *The Sociological Review*, 60, 124–38. doi: 0.1111/j.1467–954X.2012.002120.x

Urry, J. (2000). Mobile Sociology. *British Journal of Sociology*, 51(1), 185–203.

Uslaner, E. M., and Conley, R. S. (2003). Civic Engagement and Particularized Trust: the Ties that Bind People to their Ethnic Communitie. *American Politics Research*, 31(4), 331–60. doi: 10.1177/1532673x03031004001

Valenzuela, S., Park, N., and Kee, K. F. (2009). Is There Social Capital in a Social Network Site?: Facebook Use and College Students' Life Satisfaction, Trust, and Participation1. *Journal of Computer-Mediated Communication*, 14(4), 875–901. doi: 10.1111/j.1083–6101.2009.01474.x

Valkenburg, P. M., and Peter, J. (2009). Social Consequences of the Internet for Adolescents: A Decade of Research. [Article]. *Current Directions in Psychological Science (Wiley-Blackwell)*, 18(1), 1–5. doi: 10.1111/j.1467–8721.2009.01595.x

Van Der Gaag, M., and Snijders, T. (2005). The Resource Generator: social capital quantification with concrete items. *Social Networks*, 27(1), 1–29. doi: 10.1016/j.socnet.2004.10.001

van Dijk, J. (2006). The network society: social aspects of new media. London: Sage.

Vetere, F., Howard, S., and Gibbs, M. (2005). Phatic technologies: sustaining sociability through ubiquitous computing.

Walby, S. (2007). Complexity Theory, Systems Theory, and Multiple Intersecting Social Inequalities. *Philosophy of the Social Sciences*, 37(4), 449–70. doi: 10.1177/0048393107307663

Walther, J. B. (1995). Relational aspects of computer-mediated communication: experimental observations over time. *Organisation Science*, 6(2), 186–203.

Walther, J. B. (1996). Computer-mediated communication: Impersonal, interpersonal, and hyperpersonal interaction. *Communication Research*, 23(1), 3–43.

Walther, J. B. (1997). Group and interpersonal effects in international computer-mediated collaboration. *Human Communication Research*, 23(3), 342–69.

Walther, J. B., Anderson, J. F., and Park, D. W. (1994). Interpersonal Effects in Computer-Mediated Interaction – A Metaanalysis of Social and Antisocial Communication. *Communication Research*, 21(4), 460–87.

Walther, J. B., Loh, T., and Granka, L. (2005). Let me count the ways – The interchange of verbal and nonverbal cues in computer-mediated and face-to-face affinity. *Journal of Language and Social Psychology*, 24(1), 36–65. doi: 10.1177/0261927x04273036

Wang, F.-Y., Zeng, D., and Hendler, J. A. (2010). A study of the human flesh search engine: crowd-powered expansion of online knowledge. [Feature]. *Computer*, 43(8), 45–53.

Ward, C. C., and Tracey, T. J. G. (2004). Relation of Shyness with Aspects of Online Relationship Involvement. *Journal of Social and Personal Relationships*, 21(5), 611–23.

Wasserman, S., and Faust, K. (1992). *Social Network Analysis*. Cambridge: Cambridge University Press.

Watts, D. J. (2004). The "New" Science of Networks. *Annual Review of Sociology*, 30(1), 243–70. doi: 10.1146/annurev.soc.30.020404.104342

Wellman, B. (1979). The Community Question: The Intimate Networks of East Yorkers. *American Journal of Sociology*, 84(5), 1201–31.

Wellman, B. (2001a). Computer networks as social networks. [Editorial Material]. *Science*, 293(5537), 2031–4.

Wellman, B. (2001b). Physical place and cyberplace: The rise of personalized networking. *International Journal of Urban and Regional Research*, 25(2), 227–52.

Wellman, B. (2007). Social Network Analysis. In G. Ritzer (Ed.), Blackwell Encyclopedia of Sociology. Malden, MA: Blackwell Publishing. Retrieved from http://www.blackwellreference.com.

Wellman, B., Boase, J., and Chen, W. (2002). The networked nature of community: Online and offline. *IT & Society*, 1(1), 151–65.

Wellman, B., and Gulia, M. (1995). When Social Networks Meet Computer Networks: The Policy Implications of Virtual Communities. *American Sociological Association.*

Wellman, B., and Haythornthwaite, C. A. (Eds.). (2002). *The Internet in everyday life.* Oxford: Blackwell.

Wellman, B., Quan Haase, A., Boase, J., Chen, W., Hampton, K., Díaz, I., and Miyata, K. (2003). The Social Affordances of the Internet for Networked Individualism. *Journal of Computer-Mediated Communication*, 8(3), 0–0. doi: 10.1111/j.1083–6101.2003.tb00216.x

Wellman, B., Quan Haase, A., Witte, J., and Hampton, K. (2001). Does the Internet increase, decrease, or supplement social capital? Social networks, participation, and community commitment. *American Behavioral Scientist*, 3, 436–55.

Wenger, E. (1999). *Communities of practice: learning, meaning, and identity*: Cambridge: Cambridge University Press, 1999.

Whyte, W. F. (1943). Street Corner Society: The Social Structure of an Italian Slum. Chicago: University of Chicago Press.

Williams, D. (2006). On and Off the 'Net: Scales for Social Capital in an Online Era. *Journal of Computer-Mediated Communication*, 11(2), 593–628. doi: 10.1111/j.1083–6101.2006.00029.x

Williams, D. (2007). The impact of time online: social capital and cyberbalkanization. *CyberPsychology & Behavior: The Impact of The Internet, Multimedia And Virtual Reality On Behavior And Society*, 10(3), 398–406.

Williams, J. P. (2009). Community, Frame of Reference, and Boundary: Three Sociological Concepts and their Relevance for Virtual Worlds Research. [Article]. *Qualitative Sociology Review*, 5(2), 3–16.

Williams, J. P., and Copes, H. (2005). 'How Edge Are You?', Constructing Authentic Identities and Subcultural Boundaries in a Straightedge Internet Forum. *Symbolic Interaction*, 28(1), 67–89.

Williams, M. (2007). Policing and Cybersociety: The Maturation of Regulation within an Online Community. *Policing and Society*, 17(1), 59–82. doi: 10.1080/10439460601124858

Wilson, S. M., and Peterson, L. C. (2002). The Anthropology of Online Communities. *Annual Review of Anthropology*, 31(1), 449–67. doi: 10.1146/annurev.anthro.31.040402.085436

Wittel, A. (2001). Toward a Network Sociality. *Theory, Culture & Society*, 18(6), 51–76. doi: 10.1177/026327601018006003

Woodman, D. (2011). The Non-Unitary Habitus: Structural Individualisation and the Challenge of Conceptualising Class for the Contemporary World. Unpublished journal article. University of Melbourne. Melbourne.

Woolley, C. M. (2009). Meeting the Mixed Methods Challenge of Integration in a Sociological Study of Structure and Agency. *Journal of Mixed Methods Research*, 3(1), 7–25. doi: 10.1177/1558689808325774

Wright, K. B. (2005). Researching Internet-based populations: Advantages and disadvantages of online survey research, online questionnaire authoring software packages, and Web survey services. *Journal of Computer-Mediated Communication*, 10(3).

Xie, B. (2007). Using the Internet for Offline Relationship Formation. *Social Science Computer Review*, 25(3), 396–404.

Xie, B. (2008). The Mutual Shaping of Online and Offline Social Relationships. *Information Research: An International Electronic Journal*, 13(3), aper.

Yang, S. J. H. (2006). Context aware ubiquitous learning environments for peer-to-peer collaborative learning. *Educational Technology & Society*, 9(1), 188–201.

Yang, S. J. H., Chen, I. Y. L., and Shao, N. W. Y. (2004). Ontology enabled annotation and knowledge management for collaborative learning in virtual learning community. *Educational Technology & Society*, 7(4), 70–81.

Yee, N. (2006). The Demographics, Motivations and Derived Experiences of Users of Massively-Multiuser Online Graphical Environments. *PRESENCE: Teleoperators and Virtual Environments*, 15, 309–29.

Zontea, A. (2010). Advertising identities: virtual galleries as places of identity. *Journal of Comparative Research in Anthropology and Sociology*, 1(2).

Zuckerman, E. (2008). Meet the bridgebloggers. *Public Choice*, 134(1), 47–65. doi: 10.1007/s11127–007–9200-y

Index

For Product Safety Concerns and Information please contact our EU representative GPSR@taylorandfrancis.com Taylor & Francis Verlag GmbH, Kaufingerstraße 24, 80331 München, Germany

Batch number: 10725973

Printed by Printforce, the Netherlands